PRAISE FOR **THE FIVE**

'THE VICTIMS OF JACK THE RIPPER WERE NEVER "JUST PROSTITUTES"; THEY WERE DAUGHTERS, WIVES, MOTHERS, SISTERS AND LOVERS. THEY WERE WOMEN. THEY WERE HUMAN BEINGS.'

The Five

The Untold Lives of the Women Killed by Jack the Ripper

HALLIE RUBENHOLD

BLACK SWAN

TRANSWORLD PUBLISHERS
61–63 Uxbridge Road, London W5 5SA
www.penguin.co.uk

Transworld is part of the Penguin Random House group of companies
whose addresses can be found at global.penguinrandomhouse.com

First published in Great Britain in 2019 by Doubleday
an imprint of Transworld Publishers
Black Swan edition published 2020

Map by Liane Payne, based on an original map
published by J. Reynolds, 1851.

A CIP catalogue record for this book
is available from the British Library.

ISBN
9781784162344

Typeset in 11.28/13.87pt Dante MT Std by Jouve (UK), Milton Keynes.
Printed and bound in Great Britain by Clays Ltd, Elcograf S.p.A.

Penguin Random House is committed to a sustainable
future for our business, our readers and our planet. This book
is made from Forest Stewardship Council® certified paper.

For
Mary Ann 'Polly' Nichols, Annie Chapman, Elizabeth Stride,
Catherine Eddowes and Mary Jane Kelly.
And Sophie Christopher (6.9.90–3.6.19)

I write for those women who do not speak, for those who do not have a voice because they were so terrified, because we are taught to respect fear more than ourselves. We've been taught that silence would save us, but it won't.

Audre Lorde

Contents

Contents

The Five

The Untold Lives of the Women Killed
by Jack the Ripper

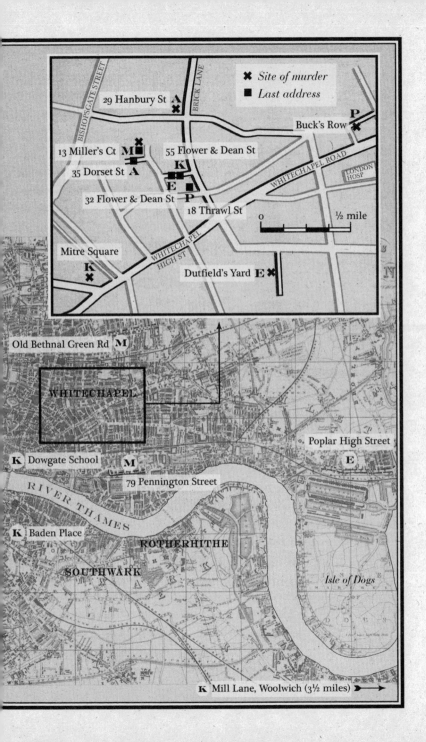

Introduction

A Tale of Two Cities

THERE ARE TWO VERSIONS of the events of 1887. One is very well known; the other is not.

The first version is the one printed in most history books. It is the one that those who lived through the age wished to recall, the version they recounted to their grandchildren with a wistful smile. It is the story of Queen Victoria and a summer of celebrations for her Golden Jubilee. She had been no more than a teenage girl when the nation's weighty crown had been placed upon her head. A half-century later she had become the embodiment of empire, and a suitably grand series of events had been planned to commemorate this. On 20 June, the precise day she had first mounted the throne, the royal heads of Europe, Indian princes, dignitaries and representatives from all corners of the empire – even the Hawaiian queen, Liliuokalani – converged upon London. West End shopkeepers adorned their windows in red, white and blue; royal standards and Union Jacks, festoons of flowers and coloured garlands could be seen hanging from every sombre stony edifice. At night, the embassies and clubs, hotels and institutions throughout St James's and Piccadilly threw the switches on the electric lights and turned on the gas jets illuminating the giant crowns and the letters V and R affixed to their buildings. Her Majesty's loyal subjects came to the centre of town from the suburbs and tenements; they punched their rail tickets from Kent and Surrey and pushed their way into the crowded streets, hoping to catch a glimpse of a royal coach or a princess in diamonds. They placed candles in the windows of their homes when the long summer twilight faded away, and toasted their monarch's health with beer and champagne and claret.

There was a service of thanksgiving at Westminster Abbey, a state banquet, a military review at Windsor and even a children's fete in Hyde Park for 2,500 boys and girls who were entertained by 20 Punch and Judy puppets, 8 marionette theatres, 86 peep shows, 9 troops of performing dogs, monkeys and ponies, as well as bands, toys and 'gas-inflated balloons', before being treated to a lunch of lemonade, cake, meat pies, buns and oranges. Throughout the summer there were Jubilee commemorative concerts, lectures, performances, regattas, picnics, dinners and even a yacht race. As the Jubilee corresponded with the traditional London 'season' there were also garden parties and balls. Ladies dressed themselves in the summer's fashion: lace-trimmed bustled gowns in black and white silk, and hues of apricot yellow, heliotrope and Gobelin blue. A magnificent ball was held at the Guildhall, where the Prince and Princess of Wales entertained their visiting regal relations, as well as the Prince of Persia, the Papal Envoy, the Prince of Siam and the Maharajah Holkar of Indore. All of high society danced beneath the banners and cascading arrangements of perfumed flowers. Tiaras and tie pins sparkled in the mirrors. Young debutantes were introduced to suitable sons. The whirl of Victorian life spun round and round to the dreamy melody of a sweeping waltz.

Then there is the other version.

This is the tale of 1887 which most choose to forget. To this day, only a scant number of history books recount it, surprisingly few people even know that it occurred, yet in that year this story filled more column inches than the descriptions of royal parades, banquets and fetes put together.

That Jubilee summer had been an exceptionally warm and rainless one. The clear blue skies that presided over the season's carefree picnics and al fresco parties had shrivelled the fruit harvest and dried out the fields. Water shortages and an absence of seasonal agricultural labouring jobs only served to exacerbate an already growing employment crisis. While the wealthy enjoyed the fine weather from beneath their parasols and from under the trees of their suburban villas, the homeless and poor made use of it by creating an open-air encampment in Trafalgar Square. Many had come into the centre of town looking for work at Covent Garden Market where Londoners bought their produce, but a drought meant fewer boxes of plums and pears to lift and haul. With no money for lodgings, they slept rough in the nearby square, where they were joined by an increasing population of unemployed and homeless workers who would rather turn to the street than face the deplorable and demeaning conditions in the workhouse. Much to the horror of observers, these campers could be seen making their morning ablutions and scrubbing their 'vermin infested' clothing in the fountains, directly beneath the nose of Lord Nelson, who peered down from high atop his column. When the autumn began to move in, so too did the socialists, the Salvation Army and various charitable organizations, handing out Bibles, admission tickets to lodging houses, coffee, tea, bread and soup. Tarpaulins were raised in makeshift bivouacs; impassioned daily speeches were made between the paws of the giant bronze lions. The excitement, sense of community and free refreshments swelled the number of outcast Londoners, which brought the police, which in turn brought the journalists, who roamed among the square's bedraggled population collecting the names and stories of these otherwise anonymous squatters.

'Mr Ashville' called himself 'a painter and glazier by trade'. He had been out of work for twelve months, thirty-three nights of which had been spent sleeping on the Embankment until the weather grew too cold and he moved to Trafalgar Square in the hope it might prove a bit warmer. Dejected and visibly worn by his experience, he attempted to remain positive about his prospects of one day finding employment.

A soldier's widow circled Trafalgar Square selling matches to support her young son, but she hadn't always lived like this. After failing to pay the final instalment on her hire-purchase sewing machine, she had lost her livelihood and then the single room she had called home. As she knew that going into the workhouse would mean that her child would be separated from her, roughing it in the square each night with him curled up under her shawl seemed a better option.[1]

An 'elderly couple' who had never before faced adversity found themselves sleeping together on one of the square's stone benches.[2] The husband of the pair had been employed as a musical director at a theatre but suffered an accident that rendered him unfit to work. With no savings, they soon fell behind on their rent and eventually were forced to make their bed under the stars. The thought of throwing themselves upon the mercy of their local workhouse was too shameful and frightening even to consider.

Hundreds came to Trafalgar Square to lay their heads against the paving stones, each with a similar tale to tell. It did not take long for political agitators to recognize that this con-gregation of the downtrodden was a ready-made army of the angry with nothing to lose. Londoners had long realized that Trafalgar Square sat on an axis between the east and west of the city, the dividing line between rich and poor: an artificial boundary which, like the invisible restraints that kept the disenfranchised voiceless, could be easily breeched. In 1887, the possibility of social revolution felt terrifyingly near for some, and yet not close enough for others. At Trafalgar Square, the daily speeches given by socialists and reformers such as William Morris, Annie Besant, Eleanor Marx and George Bernard Shaw led to mobilization as chanting, banner-waving processions of thousands spilled onto the streets and inevitably into violence. The Metropolitan Police and the Magistrates' Court at Bow Street worked overtime in an attempt to contain the protesters and clear the square of those they considered to be indigents and rabble-rousers, but, like the irrepressible tide, no sooner were they pushed out than they returned once more.

The fatal error came when, on 8 November, Sir Charles Warren, the Commissioner of Police, banned all meetings in Trafalgar Square. Those who had come to see this location in the heart of London as a rallying place for the common man and forum for political action took this as a deliberate act of war. A demonstration was planned for the 13th of the month. Its pretext was to demand the release of Irish MP William O'Brien from prison, but the grievances expressed by the protestors extended far beyond this particular cause célèbre. Over forty thousand men and women gathered to make their point. They were greeted by two thousand police, as well as the Queen's Life Guard and the Grenadier Guards. The clashes began almost immediately and the police fell on the protestors with their truncheons. Despite pleas for a peaceful demonstration, many of the participants had come equipped with lead pipes, knives, hammers and brick bats; forty of the protestors were arrested, more than two hundred were injured in the riot and at least two were killed. Unfortunately, Bloody Sunday, as it came to be known, did not signal the end of the conflicts. The tinkle of smashing glass and outbursts of public rage continued well into the start of the following year.

Through these two scenes moved two women whose lives and deaths would come to define the nineteenth century; one was Victoria, who gave her name to the era: 1837–1901. The other was a homeless woman called Mary Ann or 'Polly' Nichols, who was among those encamped at Trafalgar Square that year. Unlike the monarch, her identity would be largely forgotten, though the world would remember with great fascination and even relish the name of her killer: Jack the Ripper.

Roughly twelve months lie between the Queen's Golden Jubilee summer and Polly Nichols's murder on 31 August 1888. She was to become the first of the five 'canonical' victims of Jack the Ripper, or those whose deaths the police determined were committed by the same hand in the East End district of Whitechapel. Her murder was followed by the discovery of the body of Annie Chapman in a yard off Hanbury Street on 8 September. In the early morning hours of the 30th of that month, the Ripper managed to strike twice. In what became known as 'the double event', he claimed the lives of Elizabeth Stride, who was found in Dutfield's Yard, off Berner Street, and Catherine Eddowes, who was killed in Mitre Square. After a brief pause in his murdering spree, he committed his final atrocity on 9 November: a complete mutilation of the body of Mary Jane Kelly as she lay in her bed at 13 Miller's Court.

The brutality of the Whitechapel murders stunned London and most of the newspaper-reading world. All of the Ripper's victims had their throats cut. Four of the five were then eviscerated. With the exception of the final killing, all of these violent deaths occurred in the open, under cover of darkness. In each case, the murderer managed to abscond, having left not a trace of his or her or their identity. Given the densely populated district in which these killings occurred, the public, the press, even the police believed this to be remarkable. The Ripper always seemed one ghostly, ghoulish step ahead of the authorities, which bestowed upon the murders something extra terrifying and almost supernatural.

The Whitechapel-based H-Division of the Metropolitan Police did the best they could with their resources, but having never before faced a murder case of this scale and magnitude, they quickly found themselves overwhelmed. House-to-house inquiries were conducted throughout the area and a wide variety of forensic material was gathered and analysed. The police were besieged with statements and letters from those who claimed to be witnesses, those offering assistance, and others who just liked spinning tales. In all, more than two thousand people were interviewed and more than three hundred were investigated as possible suspects. Even with additional assistance from Scotland Yard and the City of London Police, none of this yielded anything useful. Genuine leads were certain to have been lost among the swirling wash of paper they were forced to process. In the meantime, as constables scribbled into their notebooks and followed potential malefactors down dark alleys, the Ripper continued to kill.

As the 'Autumn of Terror' wore on, Whitechapel filled up with journalists, each of them hovering over this seam of sensationalist gold with pencils sharpened. The inevitable insertion of the press between the ongoing police investigation and an East End population living in a state of heightened alert proved explosive. In the absence of any conclusive information offered by the police, the newspapers were keen to posit their own theories about the killer and his modus operandi. The papers were flying off the news stands and the hunt for more content and better angles became insatiable. Invariably, embellishment, invention and 'fake news' found its way onto the page. However, printing rumours and hot-headed opinion pieces disparaging the efforts of the police did little to quell the anxiety of those who lived in Whitechapel. By the middle of September, residents were described as 'panic-stricken'; most were too terrified to leave their homes at night. 'Hooting and shouting' crowds gathered outside the police station on Leman Street demanding the arrest of the killer, and a Whitechapel Vigilance Society was founded by local tradesmen eager to take matters into their own hands. All the while, the press speculated wildly about the identity of the culprit: he was a Whitechapel man; he was a wealthy 'swell' from the West End; he was a sailor, a Jew, a butcher, a surgeon, a foreigner, a lunatic, a gang of extortionists. The inhabitants of the neighbourhood began to attack anyone who fitted these descriptions: doctors with medical bags were set upon; men carrying parcels were reported to the police. Although sickened by events, many were also grotesquely intrigued by them. Just as crowds grew outside Leman Street Police Station, so they also gathered around the sites of the murders. Some stood staring at the places where the vicious deeds had been committed in the hope of finding answers, while others were simply entranced by the horror of the spectacle.

As the police had failed to apprehend and charge a suspect for any of the five murders, the itch to see justice meted out in the form of a trial would never be salved. Instead, the only thing that offered a few answers and a degree of closure was the series of coroner's inquests into the killings. These were held publicly in Whitechapel and in the City of London in the wake of each murder and covered extensively by the newspapers.

At a coroner's inquest, much like a criminal trial, witnesses were called before a jury to give their account of events with an objective of piecing together a clear and official picture of how the death was incurred. Most of the information that exists about the five victims has been drawn from witness statements given during the inquests; however, these present a problematic account of events. The mode of examination lacked thoroughness, there were few follow-up questions from the jury, and inconsistencies and vagaries in the testimonies were never challenged. Ultimately, the information disclosed in the course of the inquests only skims the surface of a far deeper and murkier well of potential answers.

If the Whitechapel murders served to expose anything, it was the unspeakably horrendous conditions in which the poor of that district lived. The encampment and riots at Trafalgar Square were merely a conspicuous manifestation of what had been chronically ailing in the East End and impoverished parts of London. It was a cough hacked in the face of the establishment. The emergence of Jack the Ripper was a louder and more violent one still.

For most of Victoria's reign journalists, social reformers and missionaries had been decrying the horrors of what they observed in the East End, but the situation began to grow more acute during the 1870s and 80s, as the effects of 'the Long Depression' bore down on the economy. What work there was for London's vast army of unskilled labourers – those who sewed and laundered the textiles, carried the bricks, assembled the goods, peddled in the streets and unloaded the ships – was poorly paid and insecure. Casual work on the docks might pay no more than 15 shillings a week; 'sandwich-board men' who carried advertisements around the streets might make 1s. 8d. per day. To worsen matters, rents had been steadily climbing. The destruction of large swathes of lower-income housing across the capital to make way for railway developments and broad new thoroughfares like Shaftesbury Avenue had the effect of decanting London's poor into fewer, more densely packed spaces.

Whitechapel was one of the most notorious of these, but was by no means the only sink of poverty in the capital. As social reformer Charles Booth's extensive study of London's impoverished areas in the 1890s revealed, pockets of destitution, crime and misery flourished throughout the metropolis, even within otherwise comfortable areas. However, Whitechapel's reputation trumped even that of Bermondsey, Lambeth, Southwark and St Pancras as being the most sordid. By the end of the nineteenth century, 78,000 souls were packed into this quarter of warehouses, lodging houses, factories, sweat shops, abattoirs, 'furnished rooms', pubs, cheap music halls and markets. Its overcrowded population was spiritually and culturally diverse as well as multilingual. For at least two centuries, Whitechapel had been a focus for immigrants from around Europe. In the late nineteenth century, a large number were Irish, desperate to escape the rural poverty of the mother country. By the 1880s they were joined by an exodus of Jews fleeing the pogroms of Eastern Europe. In an era highly suspicious of those of other nationalities, races and religions, integration, even within the slums, did not occur naturally. Nevertheless, irrespective of their antecedents, Booth's social investigators regarded these residents as fairly uniform in terms of their social class. With a number of middle-class exceptions, a significant percentage of the inhabitants of Whitechapel were identified as 'poor', 'very poor' or 'semi-criminal'.

The throbbing dark heart at the centre of the district was Spitalfields. Here, near to the fruit and vegetable market and the soaring white spire of Christ Church, were situated some of the worst streets and accommodation in the area, if not in all of London. Dorset Street, Thrawl Street, Flower and Dean Street, and the smaller thoroughfares contiguous to them, were feared even by the police. Lined primarily with cheap, vice-riddled lodging houses (or 'doss houses'), and decrepit dwellings whose damp, crumbling interiors had been divided into individual 'furnished rooms' for let, these streets and their desperate inhabitants became the embodiment of all that was rotten in England.

Those who strayed into this abyss from the safety of the middle-class Victorian world were struck dumb by what they encountered. The broken pavements, dim gaslights, the slicks of sewage, stagnant pools of disease-breeding water and rubbish-filled roadways foretold the physical horrors of what lay within the buildings. Vermin-infested rooms, eight by eight feet in size with broken windows, were inhabited by entire families. Health inspectors had found five children sharing a bed alongside a dead sibling awaiting burial. People slept on the floors, on heaps of rags and straw; some had pawned all of their clothes and owned barely a scrap to cover their nakedness. Alcoholism, malnutrition and disease were rife in this inner circle of hell, as was domestic violence – in fact, most forms of violence. Girls having barely reached puberty turned to prostitution to earn money. Boys just as easily slipped into thieving and pick-pocketing. It appeared to moral, middle-class England that in the face of this level of brutal, crippling want every good and righteous instinct that would normally govern human relations had been completely eroded.

Nowhere was this more apparent than in the common lodging houses, which offered shelter to those too poor to even afford a 'furnished room'. The lodging houses provided temporary homes for the homeless, who divided their nights between the reeking beds on offer here, the oppression of the workhouse casual wards, and sleeping on the street. They were the haunts of beggars, criminals, prostitutes, chronic alcoholics, the unemployed, the sick and old, the casual labourer and the pensioned soldier. Most residents could be described as several of these. In Whitechapel alone there were 233 common lodging houses, which accommodated an estimated 8,530 people without homes.[3] Naturally, those on Dorset Street, Thrawl Street and Flower and Dean Street bore the worst reputations. Four pence per night could buy someone a single, hard, flea-hopping bed in a stifling, stinking dormitory. Eight pence could buy an equally squalid double bed with a wooden partition around it. There were single-sex lodging houses and mixed lodging houses, though those that admitted both genders were acknowledged to be the most morally degenerate. All lodgers were entitled to make use of the communal kitchen, which was open all day and late into the night. Residents used this as a gathering place, cooking meagre meals and quaffing tea and beer with one another and anyone else who cared to drop in and visit. Social investigators and reformers who sat at these kitchen tables were appalled by the grotesque manners and the horrific language they heard, even from the children. However, it was the violent behaviour, degrading filth and overflowing toilets, in addition to the open displays of nakedness, free sexual intercourse, drunkenness and child neglect to which they truly objected. In the 'doss house', all that was offensive about the slum was concentrated under one roof.

The police and reformers were especially concerned about the link that existed between common lodging houses and prostitution. As few questions were asked of a 'dosser' so long as he or she could pay the 4 or 8 pence required for a bed, these places lent themselves to becoming hubs of immorality. Many women who regarded prostitution as their main source of income lived in or worked out of lodging houses, especially in the wake of the 1885 Criminal Law Amendment Act, which saw the enforced closure of many brothels. The result of this meant that a large number of prostitutes were forced to ply their trade in places separate from where they lived. A lodging house with 8-penny doubles was a convenient place to take a man who had been solicited on the street. Other prostitutes chose to sleep in a cheaper 4-penny single but see to their customers in dark corners outside, where quick sexual encounters, which frequently did not involve full intercourse, took place.

Lodging houses provided shelter for a wide variety of women facing an assortment of unfortunate circumstances. While some of them resorted to what has been called 'casual prostitution', to broadly assume that all did is categorically wrong. Inhabitants were inventive when it came to scraping together their 'doss money'. Most took on poorly paid casual labour cleaning, laundering and hawking goods, and supplemented by borrowing, begging, pawning and sometimes stealing what was needed. Pairing up with a male partner was also an essential part of defraying costs. Often these relationships were short-lived and formed out of necessity, though others endured for months or years without ever being sanctified in a church. Middle-class observers were regularly horrified by how easily and quickly poor men and women could embark upon and dissolve these partnerships. Whether or not they resulted in children also seemed to be of little consequence. Naturally, this code of morality diverged considerably from the accepted standard and threw another layer of confusion over what exactly it was that the female residents of these wicked lodging houses were doing in order to keep a roof over their heads.

During the Ripper's reign of terror, newspapers, eager to scandalize the nation with graphic details of slum life, regularly asserted that Whitechapel's lodging houses 'were brothels in all but name' and that the majority of women who inhabited them were, with very few exceptions, all prostitutes. In light of the terrible events, the public were willing to believe it. Hyperbole became enshrined as fact – despite the fact that the police themselves perceived the facts quite differently. A letter from the Commissioner of the Metropolitan Police, written at the height of the murder spree, told an altogether different story. After doing some rough calculations, Sir Charles Warren estimated that approximately 1,200 prostitutes inhabited Whitechapel's 233 common lodging houses. However, and more importantly, he qualified this statement by admitting, 'We have no means of ascertaining what women are prostitutes and who are not.'[4] In other words, the newspapers were in no position to make this determination when even the police found distinguishing a prostitute from among her sisters an impossibility.

Warren's figures present another intriguing prospect. If the lodging-house population was comprised of 8,530 people and one third, or 2,844, of those residents were female, and if it were to be accepted that 1,200 of these women could be identified as prostitutes, that would still indicate that the majority of them, or 1,644, were not engaged in any form of prostitution at all.[5] Much like the inhabitants of Whitechapel's common lodging houses, the victims of Jack the Ripper and their lives have become entangled in a web of assumptions, rumour and unfounded speculation. The spinning of these strands began over 130 years ago and, remarkably, has been left virtually undisturbed and unchallenged for all of this time. That which has continued to cling to and define the shape of Polly, Annie, Elizabeth, Kate and Mary Jane's stories is this: the values of the Victorian world. They are male, authoritarian and middle class. They were formed at a time when women had no voice and few rights, and the poor were considered lazy and degenerate: to have been both of these things was one of the worst possible combinations. For over 130 years we have embraced the dusty parcel we were handed. We have rarely ventured to peer inside it or attempted to remove the thick wrapping that has kept us from knowing these women or their true histories.

Jack the Ripper killed prostitutes, or so it has always been believed, but there is no hard evidence to suggest that three of his five victims were prostitutes at all. As soon as the bodies were discovered in dark yards or streets, the police *assumed* that they were prostitutes and that they had been killed by a maniac who had lured them to these places for sex. There is and never was any proof of this either. On the contrary, it was ascertained in the course of the coroners' inquests that Jack the Ripper never had sex with his victims. Additionally, in the case of each murder there were no signs of struggle and the killings appear to have taken place in complete silence. No one in the vicinity heard any screams. The autopsies concluded that all of the women were killed while in reclining positions. In at least three of the cases, the victims were known to sleep on the street and on the nights they were killed did not have money for a lodging house. In the final case, the victim was murdered while in her bed. However, the police were so committed to their theories about the killer's choice of victims that they failed to conclude the obvious: that the Ripper targeted women while they slept.

Unreliable source material has always been the obstacle to discovering the truth about these murders. Although a handful of police records exist, the coroners' inquests provide most of what is known about the actual crimes and the victims. Unfortunately, in three of the five cases, the official documentation from these inquests is missing. All that remains is a body of edited, embellished, misheard and reinterpreted newspaper reports from which a general picture of events can be teased. These documents have been approached with care on my part, and nothing contained within them has been taken as gospel. Similarly, I have also refrained from using unsubstantiated information provided by witnesses at the inquests who did not know the victims personally prior to their deaths.

My intention in writing this book is not to hunt and name the killer. I wish instead to retrace the footsteps of five women, to consider their experiences within the context of their era, and to follow their paths through both the gloom and the light. They are worth more to us than the empty human shells we have taken them for: they were children who cried for their mothers; they were young women who fell in love; they endured childbirth and the deaths of parents; they laughed and celebrated Christmas. They argued with their siblings, they wept, they dreamed, they hurt, they enjoyed small triumphs. The courses their lives took mirrored that of so many other women of the Victorian age, and yet were so singular in the way they ended. It is for them that I write this book. I do so in the hope that we may now hear their stories clearly and give back to them that which was so brutally taken away with their lives: their dignity.

Polly

26 August 1845 – 31 August 1888

I

The Blacksmith's Daughter

THE CYLINDERS TURNED. THE belts moved; gears clicked and whirred as type and ink pressed against paper. Floors rattled; lights burned at all hours. In some rooms, lengthy sheets of words hung from the ceilings on drying racks; in others, there stood towers of wooden boxes filled with tiny pieces of metal type. There were rooms where men bent and moulded leather, tooled gold leaf onto covers and stitched bindings. There were sheds in which copper plates were etched and lettering was forged. There were shops stacked high with books and newspapers and magazines, redolent with the delightful perfume of fresh paper and sharp ink. Fleet Street, and all the byways surrounding it, was a multi-chambered hive of printing. Every toiler was draped in canvas; filthy smocks and smeared aprons were the only fashion – the sootier, the blacker, the harder the worker. Printers' boys ran their errands arrayed head to toe in ink dust. Hardly a man in the publishing parish of St Bride's could have boasted of unstained fingers, nor would he have wished to. This was the home of the author, the printer, the newspaperman, the book-seller, and every profession dependent upon the written word.

Fleet Street and its densely populated tributaries flowed with human traffic. As one writer commented, it was possible to look back on it from Ludgate Hill, near St Paul's Cathedral, and see 'nothing but a dark, confused, quickly-moving mass of men, horses and vehicles' without 'a yard of the pavement to be seen – nothing but heads along the rows of houses, and in the road, too, an ocean of heads'.[1] Between this broad thoroughfare and that of High Holborn which paralleled it was a compact network of smaller alleys and passages lined with rotting wooden structures and damp brick buildings, which had been the homes and workshops of printers, thinkers and impoverished writers since the seventeenth century. No one was so far from their neighbour that they couldn't hear a sneeze, a wail or even a sigh. In the summer, with the windows thrown wide, the thumping and the churning of presses – steam-powered and those manned by hand – might be heard along nearly every street.

It was against the cacophony of this, in a cramped, old room, that Caroline Walker brought her second child, Mary Ann, into the world. She arrived on 26 August 1845, a day which the surrounding newspapers described as 'fine and dry'. The home into which she was born, a dilapidated 200-year-old house known as Dawes Court, on Gunpowder Alley, Shoe Lane, bore an address worthy of any of Charles Dickens's heroines. Indeed, the author of *Oliver Twist* had come to know these dingy courts and foetid alleys intimately in his youth while he worked as a shoe black, and later scribbled away in nearby rooms. Polly, as Caroline Walker's daughter came to be called, would spend her first years in the same lodgings as the fictional Fagin and his pick-pocketing boys.

The Walkers had never been a wealthy family; nor, given the limitations of her father's profession, were they ever likely to be. Edward Walker had trained as a blacksmith in Lambeth, on the opposite side of the Thames, until work along the

'Street of Ink' beckoned him across the river. He had turned his skills at first to making locks and then, quite probably, given his location, to the founding of type, or the creation of typeface.[2] Although blacksmithing was a skilled and respected trade, it paid only a passable living. A journeyman blacksmith at the start of his career might be paid between 3 and 5 shillings a day, a sum that was likely to rise to at leas t 6s. 6d. when he gained a permanent position, though the expansion of a man's family would stretch the extra pennies more thinly.[3]

Edward and Caroline and their collection of three children – Edward, born two years before Polly, and Frederick, four years after – were to make a humble but steady life on these wages. In the early decades of the Victorian era, this was not a simple task when illness or the sudden loss of work might have sent a family into rent arrears and then just as quickly into the workhouse. The average weekly expenditure for a medium-sized family like the Walkers was estimated at £1, 8s. 1d. The rent for one large room or two smaller rooms in central London was 4 shillings to 4s. 6d. a week. A further 20 shillings would be spent on food while 1s. 9d. was the least one might expect to pay for coal, wood, candles and soap.[4] A skilled labourer like Edward Walker would have also expected to put aside at least several pennies in savings, in addition to an estimated 1s. 3d. for their children's education.

While schooling would not become compulsory until 1876, more prosperous working-class parents often sent their boys – and sometimes their girls – to local charity or fee-paying schools. This was especially true among the families of those associated with the printing trade, where literacy was not only highly valued but considered essential. Some employers, such as Spottiswoode & Co., one of the era's largest publishers, went as far as to offer schooling on-site for boys under fifteen, and also ran a lending library for its staff in order to encourage literacy in the home. While Polly and her brother Edward might not have had access to such a resource, it is likely they attended either a National School or a British School. National Schools, like the City of London National School based on nearby Shoe Lane, were organized by the Anglican Church and offered part-time instruction for children who were still required to bring home an income. British Schools, which were favoured by those working families who considered themselves a cut above the poorest in the community, offered what was thought to be a slightly more rigorous learning experience, where older children taught younger pupils under the auspices of a schoolmaster or -mistress. As Edward Walker appears to have been a firm proponent of education, Polly, quite unusually for her gender and class, was permitted to remain in school until the age of fifteen. During this period, when it was conventional to teach reading but not writing to working-class girls, Polly acquired a mastery of both skills. Although the Walkers would have been able to afford little by way of luxuries, access to written material may have been the only advantage Polly was likely to have gained by growing up near the Street of Ink.

There were few other comforts to be enjoyed in the homes in which she passed her youth. The Walkers never lived far from either Shoe Lane or High Holborn. From Dawes Court they moved to Dean Street, Robinhood Court and Harp Alley. Space and privacy were almost unknown in the dwellings clustered within the slender medieval streets in the parishes of St Bride's and St Andrew's. An 1844 inquiry undertaken into the state of housing in populous London districts found that buildings situated in enclosed courts and narrow alleys, like the one in which the Walkers lived, were some of the 'worst conditioned . . . badly ventilated and filthy . . . in the entire neighbourhood'. Most families shared one room, the average size of which 'measured from 8 to 10 feet, by 8 feet, and from 6 to 8 feet from floor to ceiling'.[5] Into these compact rooms were pushed entire families. Dawes Court, which had once been a large timber-framed and plaster house, had been subdivided into three separate dwellings, before being apportioned once more into individually rented rooms, inhabited by no fewer than forty-five people. One bed may have sufficed for an entire household, with younger children on makeshift truckle beds stowed beneath. A table and a few chairs served as parlour, dining room and wardrobe. Every corner would have contained something of use, from brooms, pots and buckets to sacks of onions and coal. Social campaigners worried about such living conditions and the impact they had on the sense of morals and decency of the otherwise hard-working artisan class. Parents, children, siblings and extended family dressed, washed, engaged in sex and, if there were no 'adjacent conveniences', defecated in front of one another. As one family member prepared a meal, a sick child with a raging fever might be vomiting into a chamber pot beside them, while a parent or sibling stood by half-naked, changing their clothes. Husbands and wives made future children while lying beside present ones. Little about the human condition in its most basic form could be concealed.

Even at 4 shillings a week, the fabric of these buildings had little to recommend them. Tenants might expect damp and crumbling walls, soot-blackened ceilings with peeling plaster, rotting floorboards, broken or ill-fitting windows and gaps that allowed in the rain and wind. Blocked chimneys blew smoke back into the rooms and contributed to a host of respiratory illnesses. The internal corridors and stairwells were not much better; even, at times, positively hazardous. One such building was described as having 'a handrail broken away' and the stairs no better: 'a heavy boot has been clean through one of them already, and it would need very little . . . for the whole lot to give way and fall with a crash'.[6]

However, the pressing matters of access to clean water, sufficient drainage and fresh air frequently concerned inhabitants more than crowded living conditions in ramshackle buildings. The city's little courts suffered the worst, and inspectors regularly found only a single source of water used to service a number of households. Almost all of the butts in which supplies were stored were tainted in some way by 'a filthy accumulation on the surface'. In some cases, residents were made to rely on 'refuse water' for cooking and cleaning, which was gathered from stationary pools that stank in the summer. As many of these buildings did not have cesspools, the contents of emptied chamber pots 'ran into the courts or streets where they remained until a shower of rain washed them into the gutters'.[7] Unsurprisingly, deadly outbreaks of cholera, typhus and what medical inspectors described broadly as 'fever' were rife, especially in the warmer months.

As the capital's labouring classes knew too well, filthy, over-populated dwellings made a comfortable home for nothing but disease. Smoke-filled rooms as well as London's noxious yellow 'fogs' did nothing to improve the health of the over-worked and under-nourished. Polly was to learn this even before she had reached her seventh birthday. In the spring of 1852, her mother began to sicken. At first, Caroline would have displayed the symptoms of what appeared to have been flu, but the cough that she developed grew worse. As the tuberculosis that had settled in her lungs gradually began to consume them, her dreadful racking became blood-laced.

Feverish, thin and weary, Caroline continued to waste until 25 November.

In her death, she left behind a widower and three children, the youngest of whom, Frederick, had not yet passed his third birthday. At a time when working men were not expected to undertake the sole care of small children, it is a testament to Edward Walker's affection for his family that he persisted in doing so. Rather than leaving his sons and daughter with relations or even committing them to the care of the local workhouse, Walker was determined to give them a home. As he never remarried, it appears that Caroline's elder sister, Mary Webb, may have taken on the task of rearing the children and tending the hearth.[8]

At the time of Caroline's demise she could not have known that she had communicated her illness to Frederick, nor even of the danger that her constant proximity posed to her children. Little was understood about the pathology of tuberculosis until the end of the century. As the disease was spread via airborne particles over a period of regular exposure, it remained one of the Victorian era's greatest killers, especially within family groups. Women, who nursed ailing relations and neighbours, often introduced the infection unwittingly into their own households. Less than eighteen months after his mother's death, Frederick too began to sicken. Sensing that the boy would not live, Edward and Mary had him baptized on 14 March 1854. A month later, Frederick was laid to rest alongside his mother at St Andrew's Church in Holborn.

Even with the assistance of an aunt or other female relations, the loss of her mother would have made it necessary for Polly to grow up quickly. Whether or not she had wished to take on the role of the woman of the house, the responsibilities of this position would have fallen to her at a young age.

According to commentators of the era, the daughter of a bereaved husband was expected 'to be a comfort to her widowed father' and 'to keep his house and take care of his family'. In the absence of her mother, her first duty, even above her education, was to the home. This expectation would also have excluded her from seeking full-time employment, especially in domestic service, which would have required her to live elsewhere.[9] Certainly, by the age of nine, Polly would have acquired the basic skills necessary to keep house and cook meals for her father and brother. Much as convention dictated, it also appears that she remained beneath her father's roof throughout her teenage years, rather than taking work as a servant, as girls of her age and class regularly did. As Edward Walker's wages were able to cover the expenses of his reduced household, Polly's days were divided between her domestic duties and the luxury of prolonged schooling into her teenage years.

As a result of the family's misfortune, a uniquely strong bond appears to have been forged between Polly and her father which endured for most of her life. While Polly would have been expected to assume the physical burden of her mother's former role in the home, Victorian society also looked to the widower's daughter to provide her father with the emotional support he lacked. The era's literature regularly draws the daughters of bereaved men as paragons of selfless devotion: perfectly behaved, devoid of childish cares, resourceful, gentle and innocent. Charles Dickens's Florence Dombey, of *Dombey and Son*, a story written the year after Polly's birth, was one such irreproachable character. Having lost her mother, Florence strives successfully to win and secure her widowed father's love through her moral strength and self-sacrifice. In the case of Polly and Edward Walker, the devotion and moral strength appears to have been equally distributed between the two.

For most of her life, Polly rarely strayed far from her father, even in her choice of spouse. In 1861, nineteen-year-old William Nichols was living in a men's lodging house at 30–31 Bouverie Street, and working as a warehouseman, most likely in the printing trade. Nichols was the son of a herald painter, one who traditionally applied coats of arms to carriages and signs, but who increasingly in the nineteenth century had moved into printing stationery and bookplates. At some time prior to the spring of 1861, William had set out from his birthplace in Oxford to begin a career as a printer. Bouverie Street placed him directly at the heart of the scene. No fewer than seven magazines and newspapers had their offices between numbers 10 and 25, including the *Daily News*, once edited by Dickens, and *Punch* magazine, co-founded by social researcher Henry Mayhew. The London chronicled by both of these writers was the London of William Nichols and the Walkers. Mayhew, like Dickens, had known debt and poverty; he had experienced the precariousness of life along with much of the area's print fraternity. The world of 'Grub Street', as it had been called since the seventeenth century, was a close community of men from a variety of backgrounds who scribbled, read, produced and sold text, who drank together, borrowed money from one another and married into each other's families.

In this Dickensian-style story, the motherless blacksmith's daughter, who dutifully kept house for her father and elder brother, was introduced to William Nichols, a young man with a broad, sunny face and light hair. As Nichols was a contemporary of Polly's brother, who worked as an 'engineer', it is possible that Edward introduced him into the family. With two male shepherds to guard over the small, dark-haired, brown-eyed young woman, William would have been certain to have ingratiated himself into their close circle. Shortly before Christmas in 1863, a marriage proposal was made and accepted. The banns were read and on 16 January 1864, eighteen-year-old Polly and her beau were married at St Bride's, the printer's church. William proudly cited his profession as such on the register.

Polly and William's marriage would bring change for everyone in the family. Her father and brother, who had come to rely on her, would now have to welcome another man into their household with the full understanding that Polly's husband would soon be joined by a succession of children. The newly expanded Walker-Nichols clan moved to lodgings at 17 Kirby Street, situated in the down-at-heel area known as Saffron Hill, just north of High Holborn. As two households living as one, the Walker-Nicholses would have been seeking two, if not three separate rooms, so that the married couple might enjoy some degree of privacy. However, the building they inhabited on Kirby Street – which was divided into three floors, each occupied by one family – would not have been much of an improvement.

Much as would have been anticipated, three months after their nuptials, Polly was expecting the couple's first child. On 17 December 1864, the cries of William Edward Walker Nichols filled the rooms of 17 Kirby Street.[10] By the autumn of 1865, Mrs Nichols was pregnant once more and the need for larger accommodation would have begun to grow as obvious as her maternal belly.

By the 1860s a working-class family's budget would have been better spent living south of the Thames in Southwark, Bermondsey, Lambeth, Walworth and Camberwell than it would have near Fleet Street in the areas of Holborn and Clerkenwell. For 4 to 5 shillings a week, one might rent a small house with three to four rooms and possibly a yard at the back. However, this is not to imply the housing stock was superior to that found north of the river, nor would it have been a more economical choice unless equally well-paid work could be procured in the vicinity. By the summer of 1866, the Walker-Nichols household returned to Walworth, the part of the capital where Edward Walker had spent his youth. The family, who were now six in number, took a house at 131 Trafalgar Street, on what was described as 'a terrace of two-storey brick cottages'. Although the road and its dwellings were relatively recent constructions, having been built shortly after 1805, they had not weathered the passage of sixty years especially well. The insatiable demand for affordable housing meant that homes that had once been designed for the Georgian middle classes were now, in the Victorian era, divided up and occupied by multiple households. William and Polly's neighbours were carpenters, machinists, shopkeepers and warehousemen, whose large families lived in only marginally more space than those she would have known in Holborn. The Walker-Nicholses, with three male wage earners, were more fortunate in their ability to afford to inhabit all four rooms of their house. However, this situation was not to last.

In the Victorian working-class household, a family's level of comfort rose and fell like the tide with each birth or death. As the Nicholses' brood of children began to expand, so their means of supporting themselves would continue to be stretched. Infants arrived and departed at intervals. Their eldest child failed to live more than a year and nine months, but the family was soon joined by others. Edward John was the first child to be born at their home on Trafalgar Street on

4 July 1866. He was followed two years later by George Percy on 18 July and by Alice Esther in December 1870. For most of her life Polly had been fortunate in living under a roof supported by at least two male wage earners and few dependants, but this balance began to shift as the Walker-Nicholses' lives evolved. Shortly after the birth of her daughter, Polly's brother left home to begin a family of his own. The loss of Edward's financial contribution along with an extra mouth to feed would have tightened the household's purse strings and caused the Nicholses to begin to fret about their future prospects.

2

The Peabody Worthies

IN JANUARY 1862 THERE were few places worse than London in which to be an American. As the United States divided into Unionists and Confederates in the early months of the Civil War, so the small ex-pat community of Yankees and Southerners did the same in the drawing rooms of Mayfair. Earlier, in November 1861, a British ship, the *Trent*, became caught up in events when it was forcibly boarded by the Union navy in order to apprehend Southern envoys travelling to London. Parliament, the press, and soon the newspaper-reading public were up in arms at this flagrant act of American aggression. As Grosvenor Square-based Virginia businessmen broke off their friendships with New York investors and Londoners cursed the name of Abraham Lincoln, the American financier George Peabody sat in his Broad Street office, despairing. Shortly before the *Trent* affair, it had been Peabody's intention to make a generous philanthropic gift to his adoptive city's 'poor and needy . . . to promote their comfort and happiness'.[1] A variety of possibilities were discussed: a donation to charity schools or an investment in a scheme of municipal drinking fountains, but Peabody wished to address directly what he felt to be the most pressing concern among the working classes – housing.

Peabody himself had come from humble beginnings and had worked his way up from an apprenticeship at a Massachusetts dry goods store to owning an international import and export business. In 1838, he moved his headquarters to London and eventually expanded into banking. On his retirement in 1864, control of his merchant-banking firm, Peabody & Co., was assumed by his partner, J. S. Morgan, of the Morgan family of bankers. As Peabody neither married nor had legitimate children to inherit his considerable fortune, he wished to use it to effect good and alighted on the idea of creating a number of low-cost dwellings for London's labouring families. Preparations were made to announce his gift of £150,000 in the newspapers, when the *Trent* affair so soured relations between the US and the UK that Peabody feared his donation might be rebuffed.

In his founding letter, George Peabody made only a handful of stipulations as to who should benefit from his new model of social housing. In addition to being Londoners 'by birth or residence' he also requested 'that the individual should be poor, have moral character, and be a good member of society'. 'No one,' he further stated, 'should be excluded on the grounds of religious belief or political bias.' The Peabody Buildings would offer housing for all.

After an anxious several months, Peabody finally disclosed his intentions to the press on 26 March 1862 and work began on the first block of Peabody Buildings, to be situated on Commercial Street in Spitalfields. Ultimately, George Peabody's gift of £150,000 grew to £500,000, a sum worth roughly £45.5 million today. His generosity humbled the British public, helped to heal a rift in Anglo-American relations, and prompted a personal letter of gratitude from Queen Victoria. It also came to assist over thirty thousand Londoners out of the slums.

More than one hundred applications for the fifty-seven available apartments were received by the Peabody Trustees before the Commercial Street block was opened in 1864. Much as George Peabody had imagined, demand was intense. More sites were acquired and ground broken for further tenement blocks in Islington, Shadwell, Westminster and Chelsea. In 1874, work began on a site in Lambeth off Stamford Street, just adjacent to the large print works owned by William Clowes and Sons.

As Peabody's aim was to promote the health, happiness and moral well-being of the working classes, he intended that his tenements should offer accommodation superior to anything otherwise available to the labouring population. Unlike the mouldering ceilings and verminous interiors of most artisan housing, the Peabody buildings were built from brick, with boarded floors and cemented white walls. At Stamford Street, the four-storey blocks, consisting of one-, two-, three- and four-roomed gas-lit apartments, were arranged around a courtyard and boasted of modern conveniences. 'There are several cupboards, one in the kitchen having over it a meat safe, with doors of perforated zinc. In the passage outside is a coal-bin of neat and ingenious construction, capable of holding half a ton,' wrote the *Daily News* of Stamford Street's neighbouring development on Southwark Street. In the multi-roomed tenements, one room was 'fitted up for a kitchen . . . with a range in it, an oven, boiler, etc.'[2] Stamford Street even provided residents with picture rails, 'to avoid the necessity of driving nails into the walls'. With a central room designated for cooking, eating and living, family members could then enjoy a degree of privacy afforded by separate bedrooms, or might even choose to use an additional room as a parlour.[3] While middle-class journalists often remarked on the smallness of the rooms, which ranged from '14 or 15 feet

long by 11 to 12 feet wide', these dimensions offered a considerable improvement on the living space with which most of the
Peabody families had been made to contend in slum dwellings.

The maintenance of hygiene factored significantly into the
design of George Peabody's tenements, especially at Stamford
Street, where 'closets' (or indoor toilets) as well as 'water sinks'
were installed in the corridors, to be shared by two apartments.
The ground floor of each block also contained 'a spacious bath'
where gas-heated water was provided 'at the expense of the
trustees'. The tenants were able to enjoy access to this facility
'free of charge and as often as they please, there being no other
necessary preliminary than that of calling at the superintendent's office for the key'. As one journalist reported, the residents
'will have no excuse for not keeping themselves and their
clothes thoroughly clean', especially as an extensive laundry
room was provided in the attic floor of at least one block in
each development. At Stamford Street, this space included not
only 'tubs with water taps . . . and three large coppers for boil-
ing' but a tiled room with 'eight large light windows' designated
for clothes drying.[4] It was believed that Peabody's residents,
inspired by their well-scrubbed bodies and fresh-smelling
clothes, would wish to maintain their healthful surroundings,
not only by decorating their apartments with wallpaper and
whitewash but by keeping them tidy and free of filth. To this
end, Cubitt and Co., the architects of the Lambeth development, patented a waste-disposal system consisting of a shaft
which ran through the centre of each building into which
each tenement could dispose of their rubbish, to be captured
in a hopper below. Such a facility was necessary to preserve
standards of health, wrote *The Circle*, particularly 'when considering the very large number of persons who will all be
living upon the same premises'.

Wishing to secure the best possible outcome for their social experiment, the Peabody Trustees took pains to ensure that only the 'most deserving of the working poor', who displayed an appropriate moral character as well as the means to meet the weekly cost of their rent, were admitted as residents. The screening process was rigorous. All applicants who were householders required a letter of character from their employers in order to demonstrate that their jobs were not only relatively secure but that 'there was nothing in [their] conduct . . , to disqualify [them] from partaking in the benefits of the fund'.[5] This letter would then be followed by a visit to the applicant's home by the trustees. Anyone who was found to be a 'habitual drunkard' or who suffered an entanglement with the law was disqualified. Equally, those who were judged to have too comfortable an income or too large a family for the accommodations were also refused. Finally, before they gained admission, each of the household members needed to provide proof of inoculation against smallpox.

In 1876, the Nichols family were judged to be an ideal match for the Peabody Buildings on Stamford Street. When the trustees called upon them at their home on Trafalgar Street they would have found William, Polly and their three children washed and in their Sunday best, their rooms swept and tidy. There was no indication of low morals or alcoholism, and William's employer, the printing house of William Clowes and Sons, which lay just opposite the gates of the Stamford Street estate, endorsed him as an industrious family man. As one of the trustees' aims was to provide housing for residents local to their places of work, it is likely that William Clowes and Sons were responsible for drawing their employees' attention to the Peabody scheme. William Clowes and Sons were a formidable operation by the time William Nichols began drawing his 30-shillings-a-week salary from them. Their Duke Street premises contained six compositing rooms where type was assembled, and no less than twenty-five steam-driven printing machines, which Nichols assisted in operating. By the middle of the century, the company employed over six hundred members of staff and were engaged in printing some of the era's most memorable books, including many works of Dickens, who until his death in 1870 used to come to Duke Street to correct his proofs. Like its staff members, the company prided itself on its trustworthy and respectable reputation. Even its compositors insisted on wearing top hats and starched collars to work until the end of the nineteenth century.

After spending most of their lives in ramshackle dwellings, the prospect of making a home in the clean and modern rooms of Stamford Street must have thrilled Polly and her family. To have a proper stove on which to cook, a working indoor toilet and a place to dry laundry where it didn't gather soot or the scent of smoke would have seemed a luxury. The children would have a separate bedroom and the couple might even enjoy occasional privacy. Just as the Peabody trustees had envisioned for their tenants, William's home would be no more than a few minutes from his workplace, which would enable him to return for dinner with his family. Work, community and family, health, industry and moral well-being would all fit together as the era's social reformers intended.

On 31 July 1876, the Nicholses took up residence on the second floor of D block, at number 3. For the first time in her life, Polly would not be sharing a home with her father. Edward Walker had gone to live with his son and his young family on nearby Guildford Street. The new apartment with its four rooms and its abundant space would be theirs exclusively.

The 6s. 8d. the Nicholses paid in weekly rent would have

introduced them to an entirely unique living environment. Unlike privately operated slum dwellings, there were regulations about cleanliness and order, which were enforced by Stamford Street's superintendent and porters. Tenants were charged with keeping communal spaces clean; the corridors, steps and 'closets' were to be swept every day before ten o'clock and washed every Saturday. Children were allowed to play outside in the courtyard but were forbidden from making a ruckus on the stairs and passageways or misbehaving in the laundry. Residents could not sublet their apartments, or open a shop on the premises. Women were barred from 'taking in laundry' to make a few extra shillings from the tubs and basins in the attic floors. Should tenants break rules, they were threatened with 'being turned out'.[6] However, in many cases, it seems some of these regulations were very loosely applied. When a journalist from the *Telegraph* came to visit the Stamford Street buildings he reported children 'playing at hide and seek along the passages'. He remarked on their cheerfulness and that in spite of being 'poorly clad . . . most of them were clean and tidy and had their hair nicely arranged'. The superintendent remarked to the reporter that most new families to the buildings arrived with a set of bad habits acquired as a result of slum living. However, they soon learned that dirty windows and barefoot children incurred the disapproval of fellow Peabody residents. 'Poor people like to be as good as their neighbours,' he stated. Another visitor noticed 'flowers in the windows and bright, happy faces looking from them'. There were no 'quarrelling or fighting children . . . drunken women, or discouraged-looking men'.[7] Stamford Street's superintendent credited this to the buildings' distance from public houses; it kept women tending their homes. 'Most husbands', he said, were pleased to think that their wives would not be 'gossiping about from court to court' after a few glasses of beer, 'but minding the children and keeping the place clean'.[8]

But gossip they did, as well as occasionally flout the rules, and lead lives that were no more or less complicated than if they had inhabited lodgings on the opposite side of the buildings' gates. The Nicholses' neighbours in D block hailed from a number of different professions and circumstances. Among those who shared their building were railway porters, packers, policemen, widows, labourers, warehousemen, charwomen, carpenters and numerous employees of William Clowes and Sons. The three children of Cornealus Ring, who lived next door at number 2, would have run and tumbled with the Nicholses' own brood. Having lost his wife in childbirth, his sister looked after the family and his three-month-old infant. At number 9, William Hatches' family continued to grow. With six children they were at the outer limit of what the Peabody Buildings would allow, though his bachelor brother, Arthur, who lived next door at number 8, appears to have taken in the overflow. Polly and the other women would have kept a concerned eye on the building's widows: Anne Freeman at number 7, Emona Blower with her two children next door in 4, and Eliza Merritt on a pension of 65 pounds per year (perhaps unbeknownst to her neighbours) at number 1.[9]

This close community, who shared walls and water closets, who would have whispered over the mangles in the laundry rooms, bred no small amount of drama. The records of the Peabody Buildings tell tales of hopes and losses, of love or ruin, and the characters who made their homes beside the Nicholses. Walter Duthie was a Scottish railway porter, but his wife Jane had been born in Ambala, India. The Gaytons at number 10 aspired to a better life. While Henry Gayton worked as a picture packer, he also began a side business as an art dealer, before saving enough money to emigrate with his family to Australia. In 1877, Polly and her neighbours would have discussed poor John Sharpe, who had not only lost his wife but also his two children to illness. Sharpe had been made to leave number 6 and move to number 8, a single room. Devastated by his misfortune, he was unable to manage. By September, the superintendent was forced to turn out the grieving widower for his 'dirtiness'. There were small celebrations and love stories too. Jane Rowan, a widow with four children who worked as a laundress, was about to move to the buildings in Southwark before another resident, Patrick Madden, asked her to marry him.[10] Then there were the secrets, those acts that occurred behind closed doors or in snatched moments, which were never noted in the superintendent's record book.

Sarah Vidler was one of the Peabody's many widows who had been successful in securing her family a place at the Stamford Street buildings. On 19 April 1875, she and four of her five children – 11-year-old Sarah Louise, 14-year-old Jane and 16-year-old William, along with her married 21-year-old daughter, Rosetta Walls – moved into number 5, in D block. Rosetta's situation was not a happy one. The year before, on 4 January, she had married a ship's cook called Thomas Woolls (or Walls). The date of the wedding may have been in anticipation of her husband's next job aboard the *Russia*, a screw steamer that sailed from Glasgow on 2 February.[11] Undoubtedly, Woolls would have assured his new bride that their separation was to be only a temporary one, and for a time the couple would have lived for the short periods of weeks or months when he was in port. However, gradually, the absences were to grow longer and the pair drifted apart.

Rosetta's separation from her husband left her in a difficult position. While she was still legally bound to Woolls, she could not remarry. She remained a dependant in her mother's household, both of them working as charwomen, or day-servants, the most poorly paid and worst regarded of all service occupations. Rosetta took work where it was made available to her, so when her neighbour Polly Nichols required assistance around the time of the birth of a new son, in December 1878, this was an opportunity she was not in a position to refuse.

The summer before, the Nicholses had found it financially more expedient to exchange their four-room tenement for three rooms and moved into apartment number 6, directly next door to Sarah Vidler and her family. At the time, Polly was about four months pregnant with Henry Alfred, the child who would become her fifth.[12] At the end of 1876 she had given birth to Eliza Sarah, the circumstance that was likely to have prompted this new era of domestic belt-tightening.[13]

Three rooms, four children and another on the way would have introduced a new level of discomfort into the home environment, though the Vidler girls, who were old enough to assist with the Nicholses' smaller children, would have lent a hand when required. The two families appeared to have got on well together; Sarah's son William secured a position as a porter at William Clowes and Sons, while the two girls took on book-folding work, possibly on the recommendation of William Nichols. The internal adjoining doors of apartments 5 and 6, as well as the shared water-closet facilities, would have fostered a strong sense of intimacy between the two families, who would have been regularly in and out of each other's homes, with hardly an inch of space between each other's business.

It is impossible to know when the arguments began between Polly and William, or what precisely lay at the heart of their initial difficulties. The closer quarters, larger family and greater financial pressures may have played some role in them. However, as is the case with any domestic dispute, there are always two accounts to be considered. William later asserted that their disagreements were down to his wife's sudden affinity for drink. Whatever Polly's habits, they could not have been as unquenchable or uncontainable as her husband implied. If they were, it would have come to the attention of the superintendent and been noted in the family's records. Steps would have been taken to remove the Nicholses, as had been the case for other problem-drinking tenants. At the time of his daughter's coroner's inquest, Edward Walker offered another explanation; he claimed that his son-in-law had begun an affair with Rosetta Walls.

Walker would have heard these accusations from his daughter who, it seemed, had begun to make regular appearances at the house he shared with his son on Guildford Street in order to escape her toxic home environment. In the wake of the birth of her son on 4 December 1878, the couple's disagreements began to escalate; each of their shouted grievances shared through the wall with the Vidlers, scarcely a room away.

What rankled Polly, in the period following the birth of Henry, may have just been jealousy. She may have seen a warmth growing between her husband and the younger, curly-haired, blue-eyed woman next door. Rosetta was lonely for a husband and undoubtedly frustrated. With four children and a newborn to rear, Polly would have been exhausted. The situation may even have been exacerbated by post-natal depression. It is possible that her newly discovered affinity for the bottle was not simply William's invention either, but rather a means by which she was hoping to silence her doubts and feelings of estrangement from her husband.

It will never be known what Polly witnessed transpire between Rosetta and her husband, or indeed if she saw anything at all. Perhaps it was simply suspicion. Yet between the birth in December 1878 and the first few months of 1880, William Nichols claims that Polly stormed out of their home 'perhaps five or six times', and landed herself on her father's doorstep. According to Edward Walker, by then her husband 'had turned nasty'.

This level of disruption could not continue. Polly's father or her brother would have reminded her of her duty to her five children, one of whom was still a tiny infant. There was no room for her at Guildford Street. She would have to go back to her children, and she and William would have to work out their problems. But they couldn't. Polly would limp back to Stamford Street, and another round of angry confrontation would begin.

What must have dawned upon her one day was a simple fact: Rosetta Walls could not be removed from their lives. So long as they lived beside one another, so long as they continued to reside in the Peabody Buildings, Rosetta would be there. To Polly it must have seemed that William had made his choice, and now she must make hers.

On 29 March 1880, the day after Easter, Polly finally tired of arguing. Whether she had made plans to depart on that day or whether anger had suddenly pushed her to it, Polly Nichols decisively turned her back on her family home. She walked through the gates of the Peabody Buildings, never to return, leaving behind the life she had known and handing her children over to their father, the only person able to support them.

3

An Irregular Life

O N 31 JULY 1883, THE couple at 164 Neate Street with their five children attired themselves in their Sunday best. 'Mrs Nichols' (as she was called by her neighbours) fastened the little ones' difficult buttons and adjusted their uneven ribbons. She would have learned over the years which of the children sat still, and who had to be coaxed into good behaviour. She would have known which among them was most likely to cry and how to soothe them when they did. It was she who cooked their dinners and mended the holes in their clothes. It was she who had assumed the role of mother, and she would surely have felt some entitlement to lead them around the corner to the church on Coburg Road. As she did so, she proudly carried in her arms little Arthur, not quite three weeks old, wearing his white christening gown. He was the first child to be born to William and Rosetta Nichols, at the house they had taken almost exactly one year ago to the day. It is unlikely the neighbours or shopkeepers or even the clergyman who performed the rite of baptism guessed at their true circumstances. Instead, they stood before the font with their newborn between them and witnessed his acceptance into the Church of England. On that day too, four-year-old Henry Alfred, Polly's youngest, was also christened, his name entered beside those of his 'Christian parents', William and Rosetta, on the parish register.[1]

The comfortable domestic arrangement the couple enjoyed was not one that would have been open to them had they wished to remain at the Peabody Buildings. A decision had to be made as to their future together and what they were willing to risk in order to secure it. While living in adjoining flats was convenient, it was not an ideal situation for a man and a woman in love, who wished to share a home and a bed, despite being married to other people. If both the Nicholses and the Vidlers were aware of the affection that existed between the couple, then it would not be long before their neighbours discovered it and word found its way to the superintendent. 'Irregular unions', where couples cohabited or carried on relationships with those other than their spouses, were strictly forbidden under Peabody regulations. The Stamford Street ledgers document many examples where tenants were ejected when the truth of their circumstances was uncovered. In 1877, two of the Nicholses' neighbours, George Henry Hope and Fanny Hudson, were asked to leave after both had parted with their spouses. Arthur Scriven in K block lost his home because he had been 'living apart from his wife with another woman', while Mary Ann Thorne had been ejected for being 'a widow who gave birth to a child'. So long as William and Rosetta pursued their relationship, they gambled with both of their families' security. In the meantime, how William accounted for Polly's absence to the Peabody authorities, who were bound to have noticed it, is anyone's guess.

According to her own account of events, when Polly left 6 D block in March 1880 she went directly to Lambeth Union Workhouse on Renfrew Road.[2] However, it's far more likely that she would have gone first to the house where her father and brother lived. Someone who had never before passed through the gates of a workhouse would only have done so with extreme reticence and after all possible alternatives had been exhausted.

It is difficult to paint an accurate picture of the Victorian working-class experience without including the foreboding and ever-present shadow cast by the austere brick edifice of the workhouse. In 1834 the Poor Law Amendment Act sought to bring an end to what the government saw as the abuse of a system of charitable relief offered by local parishes. The poor were judged to be lazy and immoral paupers who refused to do honest work, bred bastards and enormous families while 'living off handouts'. Instead, the government wished to compel the indigent to lead moral, hard-working lives by reducing what was called 'outdoor relief', or charity that was paid to impoverished families while they inhabited their own lodgings. Rather than giving them the opportunity to drink away parish funds or indulge in illicit sexual behaviour which led to more illegitimate children, a new system of highly regulated 'indoor relief' was to be meted out inside the workhouse. The intention of this workhouse system was not only to regulate the lives of the poor by forcing them to earn their meagre sustenance, but to frighten them into leading upstanding, industrious existences outside its walls.

One of the workhouse's primary functions was to humiliate those who were forced to rely upon it. Regardless of their circumstances, the old, the infirm, the sick, the abandoned and the able-bodied were treated with equal disdain. If the head of a household lost his income, he and all of his dependants would have to join him under the workhouse roof. Upon entering, families were divided up by gender and made to live in separate wings. Very young children were allowed to remain with their mothers, but those over seven were placed into the workhouse school and isolated from their parents. All new inmates were stripped of their clothing and whatever personal belongings they possessed. They were then required to enter a communal bath and scrub themselves in water that had been used by every other person who had been admitted that day. Following this, much like prisoners, inmates were clothed in a functional uniform, which was never theirs exclusively. Their diet was a basic one of watered porridge, known as skilly, as well as small, poor-quality portions of bread, cheese, potatoes and occasionally meat. While minor improvements were made to the workhouse diet later in the century, in 1890 complaints about rat droppings in the skilly were still not uncommon.[3]

At the workhouse, no able-bodied person was to receive anything for free. Both men and women were assigned work appropriate to their genders. Men were generally tasked with jobs such as stone-breaking (the aggregate was then sold off for road making), pumping water, milling corn, chopping wood or oakum picking. This latter activity, which was often given to women, involved pulling apart old ships' rope with a spike and bare hands so that the fibres could be mixed with tar and used to caulk ships. Other tasks deemed suitable for female inmates included cleaning, working in the laundry and food preparation. The experience while inside was one of constant hunger, frequent illness and poor sleep in the dormitory pallet beds. Violence and brutal coercion by staff as well as fellow inmates was common. Poor sanitation, restricted access to water, exposure to vermin and contaminated food ensured that inmates suffered regularly from diarrhoea and infections that were known to spread rampantly.

The conditions inside the workhouse were well known

among those who gazed at its walls from the outside. The Poor Law Board of Guardians, who administered it, wanted it so. This way, self-respecting working-class families came to pride themselves on their resourcefulness in escaping the need for indoor relief, and looked down on those who hadn't. Within labouring communities, the social stigma of having spent time at the workhouse was so great that many would rather beg, sleep rough or enter into prostitution than place themselves at the mercy of the local parish union. Neighbours rarely forgot those who had been tarred by misfortune, and many families continued to suffer the humiliation that followed a stay within the workhouse walls long after they had departed.

For all of her life, Polly would have feared and reviled the workhouse. Both the Walkers and the Nicholses were hard-working families who would have held up their heads in the knowledge that they earned respectable livings. Life in the Peabody Buildings would have made them proud of their status and even more likely to look down their noses at those whose lack of industry or moral vice led them into the yard of Renfrew or Princes Road. However, in an era when divorce was an option only for those who could afford the exorbitant court fees, a working-class wife who wished to 'officially' separate from her husband first had to demonstrate her desperation and destitution. The only means by which this could be achieved was to enter the workhouse. For many wives, this ordeal was described as 'the most humiliating experience of their lives' and carried with it 'a permanent stigma'.[4]

In 1880, when Polly turned her back on her husband and walked out of her matrimonial home, she would have understood the consequences. It was an enormously bold step. While separation among the working classes was not uncommon, it spelled the end of a woman's respectable status among the 'morally-minded' of her community. Culpability did not matter; if a woman left her husband, she had failed. A decent wife was one who 'must be enduringly, incorruptibly good; instinctively, infallibly wise' and not simply for the sake of 'self-development, but for self-renunciation'. Her duty to her husband was 'to never fall from his side'.[5] Her duty as a mother was to never forsake or abandon her children. Leaving the familial home rendered her unfit, immoral, a specimen of broken womanhood. In parting with her husband, she was also committing herself to the embrace of poverty and further degradation. Traditional women's labour such as domestic service, laundry work, sewing or home-assembly piecework yielded a barely liveable wage, and unless she was to take refuge with another male family member, she would hardly be able to support herself.

To a small extent, the law recognized the situation in which separated working-class women found themselves, though it very reluctantly offered solutions. A wife needed to remain with her family, and the government, parish officials and the law did not wish to encourage or make it easy for women to leave their marriages. Even if Polly had been able to afford the costs of a divorce, in 1880 a wife could not cite adultery alone as a grounds for ending her union. While a man could divorce his wife for a sexual liaison outside the marital bed, a woman had to prove her husband was guilty of adultery in addition to another crime, such as incest, rape or cruelty. The Victorian double standard was enshrined in law, permitting a man to enjoy as many sexual dalliances as he wished, so long as he did not also rape the servants, have sex with his sister and beat his wife too severely. Had Polly possessed the means to bring a suit against William, and even if she had been successful in gathering evidence that he was having an affair with Rosetta, she still would not have had grounds for a divorce. However, by 1878, under the terms of the Matrimonial Causes Act, if William had been violently abusive to her and had been charged before a Magistrate with these crimes, the court would have upheld her right to secure a legal separation from him. Fortunately, and yet unfortunately, this was not the case either.

The reality was that most working-class women who wished to end their marriages had no choice other than to attempt to secure a type of unofficial separation with the assistance of the workhouse by claiming they had been deserted by their spouse. According to the Poor Law, a man could not simply turn his wife or children over to the workhouse and expect the ratepayer to foot the bill for their maintenance. Just as a woman had the duty to remain with her family, so the law viewed her upkeep as the responsibility of her husband; whether or not both spouses inhabited the same place was irrelevant. If an able-bodied man refused to pay for his wife's maintenance, the Poor Law Guardians would seek to recover the costs. They would bill him for the expenses, and if the delinquent husband did not discharge his obligation to them, they would make him suffer the indignity of being dragged before the Magistrate. The application of this rule was the working-class woman's only friend. However, the workhouses were wary of being made an instrument of domestic breakdown and the Guardians were taught to regard women who turned up at their gates claiming 'desertion' with scepticism. 'Continual quarrelling', claimed the 1876 *Handy Book for Guardians of the Poor*, 'the root of which is almost invariably drink on both sides' was 'most common among these cases of desertion'. The advice to Guardians was to make a thorough investigation into such a woman's circumstances before permitting her to become the object of sympathy.

Only after she left William would Polly have learned what was required in order to initiate their unofficial separation. It was then that she would have ventured into the workhouse with the objective of making her stay as brief as possible.

As part of the admission process, Polly would be made to undergo a verbal 'examination' by one of the Relieving Officers, an official who determined whether the applicant was worthy of receiving indoor or outdoor relief. This was likely to be an intimidating and censorious inquisition. Polly would stand before this man in her drab uniform and greying cotton cap and be asked to account for her present circumstances. There would be judgement and shame. He would start by asking for her complete name, her age, where she had been living, her marital status and about the number of children she had. She would then be requested to give particulars about who supported her, his occupation and wages. She would be asked if she had ever received outdoor relief or if she had ever been inside the workhouse. She would be asked if she had savings, or if she had ever been convicted of a crime. She would be asked about the legitimacy of her children. Finally, she would be asked if 'she has any relatives who are legally bound to support . . . her, and whether such relatives were able to support her'.[6] Here the details of her separation from her husband would be probed. The Relieving Officer in Polly's case was a man called Thomas Taverner, who scribbled down these details with the intention of requesting an interview with William Nichols.

Mr Taverner, who rode about town in his private coach, was noted for conducting business according to his own methods. William Nichols may have been summoned to the workhouse, or the Relieving Officer may have taken the liberty of paying him a visit. However it came about, whether in front of his fellow employees or neighbours or inside the gates of the workhouse, Nichols would have found this meeting to be a mortifying experience. When questioned, Polly's husband was certain to have asserted what he would always claim: that his marital breakdown was due to his wife's drinking. However, Thomas Taverner was not convinced by this story. Had William's account been entirely true, Taverner would not have ultimately made the decision to allow Polly to receive outdoor relief. As the Guardian's handbook suggests, 'Whenever it is found that a deserted wife is known to drink . . . out-door relief should not be given, but the workhouse alone offered.'[7] Instead Mr Taverner, on behalf of the Board of Guardians, decided that Polly Nichols should be awarded a weekly maintenance of 5 shillings. Her husband would pay over this sum to be collected by Polly in person from Thomas Taverner at the workhouse every week.[8]

Ideally, in such a situation it would be expected – or at least hoped – that a separated woman receiving a maintenance from her husband would be taken in by a relative. Unfortunately, whether through her own choice, or as a result of a family disagreement, Polly did not go to live with her father and brother but, rather, struck out on her own.

For a woman who had never before lived alone, who had always been surrounded by male protectors, this new mode of life would have come as a profound shock, both practically and emotionally. If rent for one room in a down-at-heel part of town cost 4 shillings a week, Polly would have virtually no money on which to subsist, unless she wished to take her chances at an insalubrious lodging house, where a bed might be had at 4 pence per day. She would have to find work. While this was not impossible, the employment she was likely to have found would have paid poorly in exchange for seventy to eighty hours a week of grinding, ceaseless, repetitive labour, like that offered in the capital's many large-scale laundries. Here, women who 'worked at the tub' might expect to receive 'from 2 to 3 shillings a day' while shirt and collar ironers, who slaved away in overheated conditions, were likely to earn 8 to 15 shillings a week.[9] Instead Polly might opt to take on 'slop work', earning 6 shillings a day for sewing together cheap clothing: trousers, coats, skirts and waistcoats. She would be paid by the completed piece and could expect to work from the earliest hours in the morning until late at night, with scarcely a break. Various types of home-assembly work were available to women; everything from 'fancy box' construction to artificial-flower making, all of which required extremely quick work and nimble hands. A woman might expect to work ten hours a day at this and earn as little as 2½d. per hour.[10] Factory work, which was no better than any of the other options, tended to favour younger female employees, and cleaning, or 'charring', was equally badly paid, poorly regarded and demoralizing.

Whichever choice she made, Polly faced a completely empty existence in a society where a woman without a family or a husband was viewed with deep suspicion, if not incomprehension. The sexes had their distinctly defined roles, and Polly, like every other female, would have been inculcated in the belief that a woman required a man to guide her, govern her and to bestow any meaning at all upon her life. As Tennyson explained in his poem *The Princess*:

> Man for the field and woman for the hearth:
> Man for the sword and for the needle she:
> Man with the head and woman with the heart:
> Man to command and woman to obey;
> All else confusion.

The 'confusion' occasioned by a woman of Polly's age, living apart from her husband and family, would have caused people to have concluded one thing alone: she was an aberration, a failure, and invariably, where the character of a woman was compromised, sexual immorality was also assumed. Regardless of whether or not she could support herself with laundry work or charring, the concept of a woman of childbearing age living and enjoying a single life was an absolute anathema to the Victorian era, regardless of one's class. Without a man, a woman had no credibility, no protection against the schemes and violence of other men, and no purpose in life. Without a woman, a man had no one to tend to his practical and sexual needs. It was therefore unthinkable that Polly, like her husband, would not attempt to enter into another relationship as soon as possible. However, what was permissible for William Nichols was not legally permissible for his wife.

With Polly no longer in their lives, William and Rosetta had grown weary of maintaining the pretence that they were not in love, and by early 1882 they found the opportunity to do something about their situation. At some point during the late winter or early spring of that year, Rosetta would have learned that her legal husband, Thomas Woolls, had emigrated to Australia on 8 February.[11] The possibility that Woolls might suddenly reappear and assert his matrimonial rights was now no longer a threat and freed the lovers to set up home together. They would have weighed their options carefully and calculated the expense. As an unmarried couple, they knew they could not remain in the Peabody Buildings, and finding suitable accommodation elsewhere would increase the pressure on William's finances. The 5 shillings he was paying to Polly was apt to make all the difference in his ability to afford a fresh start.

It's unlikely that before he set out with the explicit intention of terminating his wife's maintenance payments, William was well-versed enough in the law to know precisely what steps to take. After making enquiries, he would have learned that it was possible to cut Polly's support by demonstrating that she was living with another man. According to the Matrimonial Causes Act, 'no order for payment of money by the husband . . . shall be made in favour of a wife who shall be proved to have committed adultery, unless such adultery has been condoned'. Magistrates and officials recognized that couples like William and Rosetta might wish to cohabit with other partners (though immorally) following a separation; however, where the separated wife was concerned, this could only occur with the husband's consent.

It is possible that over the years William had become aware that Polly had attached herself to another man. The 1881 census notes a Mary Ann Nichols living with a George Crawshaw in a room at 61 Wellington Road, in Holloway, north London. Crawshaw is recorded as being a scavenger, and Mary Ann Nichols's occupation is cited as 'laundry work'. They both are noted as being married, though not to one another.[12] Although she was living across the river from Lambeth, she would have returned there weekly to collect her 5 shillings and been seen frequently by those who knew her. Gossip would have reached William's ears and now it was in his interest to learn the truth of the matter, a task which was easily enough accomplished with professional assistance.

Adverts placed by 'Confidential Inquiry Offices' and 'private investigation agents' featured regularly in London's newspapers. For a fee, which depended upon the complexity of the task, these businesses promised to 'discreetly investigate family matters requiring secrecy'. Procuring evidence for divorce cases was always listed prominently among their specializations, as was the service of having 'suspected persons watched'. In order to confirm his suspicions and wriggle free of his crippling financial obligation, William Nichols hired one such 'spy'. His agent evidently followed Polly through the streets and investigated her movements for long enough to determine that she was living with another man in a state of adultery. Having obtained the proof he required, William promptly refused to hand over Polly's weekly sum and began to make plans to leave D block with Rosetta.

When Polly went to collect her maintenance, Mr Taverner would have informed her that William was delinquent in paying it. Eventually, at the behest of Lambeth Union, Nichols was summoned to the Magistrates' Court in order to explain himself. He had his answer prepared well in advance. He produced the skilfully gathered evidence of his wife's 'adultery without consent'. According to Edward Walker, his daughter denied that she was living with another man, but the judge seemed convinced by the material.[13] It was ruled that William was now absolved of his financial responsibilities and, on 28 July 1882, he and his paramour packed their belongings, took his children by their hands, and bid goodbye to their lives at the Stamford Street Peabody Buildings. The superintendent duly noted in the ledger at the time of his departure that William Nichols had been a 'good tenant' but 'left in debt'. The words 'good tenant' were later struck through.[14]

In all probability, Polly's defence that she was not 'living in adultery' at the time the case came before the Magistrate was correct. Had she still been with George Crawshaw, or living under the protection of another partner, she would not have found herself completely destitute at the loss of her allowance. On 24 April 1882, Polly was left no choice but to enter Lambeth

Union Workhouse – this time for an indefinite stay. With the exception of a short period in the infirmary in January, she remained there for exactly eleven months, and discharged herself on 24 March 1883. It appears she attempted to find her feet, only to return for another stay from 21 May until 2 June.

Unlike a prison, in a workhouse, inmates were free to remove themselves from the care of the Union whenever they chose. However, without an offer of employment or any money at one's disposal, it could prove impossible to extract oneself from the cycle of poverty. Those who were discharged left with a final meal in their stomach and some bread. In theory, this was to tide them over until they were able to find work and earn enough for their shelter and sustenance. In reality, inmates frequently stepped from life in the workhouse directly into a life on the streets: begging, prostituting themselves or stealing in order to earn enough to pay for food and a night's lodgings. Many others ended up sleeping rough.

On this occasion, it was fortunate that when Polly left the workhouse her father and brother had a home for her. The house at 122 Guildford Street, not far from the Peabody Buildings, was already a tight squeeze for Edward, his wife, his five young children and his father. Whatever obstacles prevented Polly from living with her family in the past had now been surmounted. Edward Walker later made an emotional claim that he would have never turned his daughter out so long as he had a roof over his head, but life with his grown child would not always prove easy.

If Polly in the final throes of her marriage had acquired a taste for drink to dull the pain, then her thirst for this medicine had only grown more acute since her separation. As alcohol was largely prohibited in the workhouse, it is likely that her stay there prevented a dependency from taking root; however, after her discharge Polly was free to resume whatever habits she may have acquired earlier. Although Edward Walker never reveals what sort of work his daughter undertook while she lived with him, he does suggest that she spent a good amount of her time in the local public houses. With her brother's family continuing to grow, Polly may have wished to escape the confines of her increasingly awkward position there. Her internalized sense of shame, too, cannot be underestimated; she had lost her home, her husband and her dignity. More excruciating still, she had lost her children and the sight of her nieces and nephews surely served as a constant reminder of her worthlessness as a mother. Drink would have offered a way out.

The arguments began. Polly's drunkenness, even if not habitual, could not have contributed to a pleasant domestic environment in a small house. Although Walker insisted that his daughter 'did not stay out particularly late' and 'was not fast', nor had he 'heard of anything improper' happening among the group of 'young women and men' that 'she used to go with', Polly's behaviour at home eventually rendered life impossible.[15] After one such disagreement in 1884, Polly was said to have simply decided to leave. 'She thought she could better herself,' said her father, 'so I let her go.'[16]

When Polly left the protection of the paternal home, it is likely she did so to take up with a man she had met. In March 1884, Thomas Stuart Drew, a blacksmith who lived on neighbouring York Street, had been widowed. Now alone in his late thirties and with three daughters to care for, Drew found himself in a position identical to that faced by Edward Walker when he had lost his wife. His girls would have required a mother, and perhaps it was the similarity to the situation that Polly had known as a child that attracted her to the widower and his family. Whatever her father made of it, Drew appears to have offered Walker's daughter a settled home and an opportunity once more to feel of use in the roles of wife and mother. Although Polly and her father were no longer on speaking terms, when he saw her in June 1886, Edward Walker noted that she appeared respectable in both dress and demeanour.

The occasion on which they had met called for it. Earlier that month, at around midnight, Polly's brother and his wife had been sitting up in the kitchen chatting. Just as Mrs Walker left the room to go to bed she heard a sudden explosion from behind her. When she raced back to the kitchen she found her husband's hair ablaze; the paraffin lamp he had gone to extinguish had burst into a fiery ball. The couple's screams alerted their lodger, who attempted to help put out the flames, but by then Edward had suffered third-degree burns to the right side of his face and chest. They rushed him to nearby Guy's Hospital in a cab, at which point he slipped into a coma. By early evening, he had died.

For Polly, the shock of her only sibling's death was to be the first in a series of misfortunes to befall her that year. It is likely to be no coincidence that what had been a stable relationship with Thomas Drew soon began to falter. If Polly had come to manage her drinking in her new domestic arrangement, then Edward's unexpected demise may have driven her once more to the bottle. Come November, she and Drew were no more, and by the following month, he had taken another bride; a woman whom he could legitimately marry, and with whom he did not have to live in sin.

The consequences of separation in the nineteenth century were judged by many to be 'a living death', for while the law sanctioned a split between a married couple, it never permitted them to move their lives beyond that. Any future relationships would always be considered adulterous, while any children of those unions would be regarded as illegitimate. With divorce and remarriage an impossibility among the working classes, communities and families were often inclined to turn a blind eye to middle-aged couples who wished to cohabit, but as the social reformer Charles Booth remarks, even this level of toleration had its limitations. 'I do not know exactly how far upwards in the social scale this view of sexual morality extends,' he wrote, 'but I believe it to constitute one of the clearest lines of demarcation between upper and lower in the working class.'[17] For men like Thomas Drew and Edward Walker, proud skilled labourers who earned a respectable wage, this mode of living was ultimately beneath them.

Unfortunately, neither living with a husband nor living with a common-law spouse was an option for Polly in the autumn of 1886. Without the maintenance William had once paid her, without a home and without the means of sufficiently supporting herself, she had nowhere left to retreat but into the stony embrace of Lambeth Union Workhouse once more.

4

'Houseless Creature'

B Y OCTOBER 1887, AUTUMN had begun to sprinkle its chill over those who passed the night in Trafalgar Square. They curled up on the benches, while others slumbered on the flagstones, partially covered with yesterday's newspapers in a vain attempt to keep warm. Weary old men and women in ragged, battered bonnets propped themselves up against the wall below the National Gallery. Shoeless children rolled themselves into balls in the corners and slept like small dogs. W. T. Stead, the editor of the *Pall Mall Gazette*, walked through the scene of bodies in the square one night shaking his head and scribbling onto his pad: 'Four hundred sleepers, men and women, promiscuously side by side, I count in the shadows of the finest hotels in the world.'[1] Slumped at the base of one of the lions, or lying with her head against a bench, was Polly Nichols, cold and anonymous.

When morning came, the rough sleepers were joined by the steady trickle of the unemployed and 'friends of socialism'. Daily during that autumn they gathered in their thousands at the base of Nelson's Column. They came with their red flags and banners, singing songs and shouting slogans about working men's rights. Speakers mounted a makeshift dais and addressed the assembled to rousing cheers, jeers or hissing.

The poor weather, even the blinding sulphurous fogs that fell like a curtain over the spectacle, failed to discourage the audiences. They came, men and women, both the threadbare and the 'respectably dressed' in billycock hats and low-slung flat caps, and stood attentively with hunched shoulders and hands in their pockets, or balancing children on their hips. Among those who gathered in the square with Polly in the last weeks of October was the writer, textile designer and socialist William Morris, along with several of his associates from the Socialist League, including John Hunter Watts and Thomas Wardle. They came to observe and debate, and in the case of Watts take his place at the base of the column and pontificate.

The speeches and demonstrations drew as many spectators as it did do-gooders. Some came and helped with the distribution of bread and coffee to 'the homeless creatures' who had made Trafalgar Square their parlour. Others handed out Bibles or tickets to lodging houses, which were already filled to bursting. This congregation of the sympathetic who were there because of their interest in the plight of the poor and downtrodden also made for a rich harvest among beggars. The ranks of police, who were significantly outnumbered by the crowd, kept an anxious distance, patrolling, listening, watching and waiting for the scene to explode into violence. This it did, with regularity. From the end of October, the daily marches and processions grew more aggressive. The threats hollered through Trafalgar Square by several of the speakers kept the police on high alert. There were promises to set the city alight, to storm the Mansion House and to smash the windows of Regent Street. When setting out on their marches, the protestors seemed determined to outfox the police escort that followed them. On 19 October there were skirmishes as a crowd burst onto the Strand in an attempt to march towards the City of London. The police pushed them back into the yards around Charing Cross Station. Railings collapsed; demonstrators were injured and trampled. Rocks were hurled at the officers, who were also kicked and beaten. The following day there were marches to Bond Street. Terrified shopkeepers rushed to shutter their windows at the approach of 'King Mob'. On the 25th, the procession made it as far as Belgravia, where revolutionary songs were bellowed at the windows of high society.

Numerous attempts were made to clear the square of its 'troublemakers', especially in the wake of this series of violent events. The Commissioner of Police used the Vagrancy Act to take 'steps to arrest . . . all rogues and vagabonds throughout the Metropolis who are found wandering or sleeping in the open air at night during the cold weather'. Inspector Bullock was on duty during the night of the 24th when the clearance began. Trafalgar Square had been his beat and he came to know many of the faces of those who bedded down there. At around ten o'clock, a charity worker had turned up offering bread, coffee and lodging-house tickets to '170 outcasts' in the square. As the night was looking to be a particularly cold one, most of them went to the lodging houses listed on the tickets, 'but several returned saying they were full'.[2] Bullock offered to escort them to the casual ward of the workhouse at St Giles, 'but many of them said they could not think of going there'. The officer then made it clear that he would arrest them if they remained, and so sent thirty of them with two constables to the workhouse on Macklin Street. En route, eleven of them slipped away down the side streets of Covent Garden. Bullock was not at all surprised when the missing turned up again 'sitting and smoking in the Square, lounging about, and taking part in the scrambles for money thrown down by people passing on the terrace'.[3] It was then that he took ten of them, 'six women, two girls and two youths', which included Polly Nichols, into custody.

Polly, who had probably taken a few glasses that evening, did not go willingly into the cells. She swore, put up a fight and 'was very disorderly' at the police station. The following morning she was made to account for herself before Mr Bridges, the Magistrate. As the prisoners were marched into the courtroom, the journalist from the *Evening Standard* remarked that they 'presented a woeful aspect, being dirty and very ragged'. 'Nichols', according to a police statement, was 'the worst woman in the square'.[4] It was described how she and a group of other women had made a business of begging beneath the terrace that separated the National Gallery from Trafalgar Square. They waited for 'respectable people' to appear, at which point they would 'take off their shawls and shake themselves as if they were cold, in order to invite sympathy'.[5] As a ruse, this appears to have been successful, or at least profitable enough to buy Polly a drink and a bed at a lodging house, should she wish it. Begging had kept her safely out of the workhouse, although, as she explained to the judge, she had been reluctant to go to the casual ward 'because they were kept there in the morning, and so lost any work they had to go to.'[6] This was a doubtful excuse, and the Magistrate would have known it. As Polly Nichols had been tramping since May of that year, it's unlikely she had any regular work at all.

It would have been with a heavy and dejected heart the previous year that Polly, on 15 November 1886, had returned to Lambeth Workhouse. The security she had enjoyed with Thomas Drew had been pulled from under her feet, and she found herself once more in a position similar to that she had known after she parted with William Nichols. However, in this case her future was even less certain as she had lost the entitlement to receive a maintenance from her estranged husband. Into the admissions ledger beside her name had been written 'no home, calling: nil'. Following her brother's death and her rift with her father, the sense of isolation and shame must have been acute.

Fortunately for Polly, on this occasion her sojourn at the workhouse was not a lengthy one. Most workhouses operated schemes designed to prepare girls and young women for jobs in domestic service. Not only did this provide an opportunity for girls who might otherwise have ended up in a life of vice to acquire skills and a source of income, but it also helped to mitigate workhouse expenses; the fewer inmates, the lower the cost to the local ratepayer. Lambeth Workhouse appears to have extended this practice to include placing older women into service. The rationale would have been a similar one, in that it offered women who would otherwise be stuck in a workhouse cycle of poverty the chance to begin their lives anew. As most middle-aged women would have several decades of experience in cooking, cleaning, mending, and looking after children, their skills were easily transferable. They knew how to clean a grate, to scrub a floor, to nurse a sick infant and to prepare meals. There were plenty of employers willing to overlook the blemished background of a workhouse inmate in order to make use of their free or low-paid labour. To have been selected for such a scheme, Polly would have had to demonstrate a good character from the outset, proving herself worthy through her diligence, compliance and docility. As there was no alcohol to be had in the workhouse, this was unlikely to have proven too difficult. On 16 December, Polly was duly 'discharged to service', as the register reads, though to where is unknown.[7]

Regrettably, this placement was not to become a permanent one. Servants and masters were not always compatible and the unspecified circumstance that cost her the position by the following spring may not have been down to a failing on her part. Whatever the situation, it appears that in May 1887, Polly could not bear the prospect of yet another sojourn in the workhouse and instead decided to take her chances tramping. The life of a tramp or a vagrant was part iterant worker, part beggar, and sometimes, depending upon one's circumstances, part criminal or prostitute. Unfortunately, the Vagrancy Laws did not attempt to distinguish between any of these 'professional' identities; anyone who lived on the street was viewed similarly and simply categorized as a nuisance. However, a tramp's life and their means of supporting themselves varied markedly from person to person and was often determined by age, gender, whether they had an infirmity, or any number of other circumstances. A tramp took work where he or she could get it: selling various items on the street, taking labouring jobs such as loading and unloading goods at markets and at the docks, or doing odd bits of childcare or cleaning for working-class households. Life was lived hand-to-mouth and the quest for work, food and shelter was a constant one, which sent men and women 'tramping' from one end of town to the other, and back again. While some tramps argued that this lifestyle provided them with freedom from obligation, and that they enjoyed sleeping wherever they chose, the majority were pushed into this existence through want and a desire to avoid a lengthy and oppressive stay inside a workhouse. However, most were not averse to making use of the workhouse casual ward when it suited them.

The concept of the casual ward, or 'the spike' as it was frequently called, was devised in 1837 when the government required that Poor Law authorities provide temporary over-night shelter for anyone finding themselves destitute and in urgent need of accommodation.[8] Like the workhouse, the casual ward, which often formed a wing of the workhouse, was not designed for comfort. The objective was always to dis-courage vagrancy, whilst offering the most basic assistance. Vagrants would be given a nauseating meal of skilly and bread and could spend the night in one of the single-sex dormitories, in exchange for several hours of work the following day. By the end of the century, anyone who entered a casual ward was made to spend two nights on the grubby beds for a full day's labour in between, picking oakum, undertaking cleaning jobs or breaking stones. If the superintendent believed an inmate wasn't working hard enough for their keep, they could be detained. Both the casual ward and the workhouse were known havens for bullies.

The spike was no less miserable than the workhouse proper; a stay there was made bearable only by its brevity. Neverthe-less, demand for accommodation was constant. In the late afternoon, a queue outside the casual-ward door would begin to form. Admission usually began between five and six o'clock, and there was no guarantee that beds would be available for all comers, especially in the winter. Not unlike entry into the workhouse, inmates at the casual ward, having secured a place, were fed their skilly and then required to strip off their filthy street clothes. These were not washed, but 'stoved' at a high temperature to kill any lice or fleas. In exchange for their attire, the inmates were given nightshirts into which they changed after bathing in the blackened waters of the communal tubs. The American author Jack London, who passed a night in the spike while writing his exposé *People of the Abyss*, was horrified to observe that twenty-two inmates washed in the same water before using 'towels wet from the bodies of other men'. London noticed that one of these men had a back covered in 'a mass of blood', the result of 'vermin attacks'.

It was a combination of these vermin attacks, the discomfort of the straw-filled mattresses in their narrow berths and the air of menace within the dormitories that made a decent night's sleep difficult to come by. Social investigator Ellen Stanley, who passed a night in a women's dormitory, claimed her stay was spent 'in a state of constant misery the whole night through'. She remarked that she was 'covered with vermin' and '. . . could neither sit nor lie'. In order to 'get a breath of fresh air' in the close, unventilated room, she was forced to move 'as near the door as I could get' in the hope that some breeze might 'come in through the narrow opening.'⁹ Although the inmates were locked in at seven o'clock and expected to get some rest, Stanley describes the general agitation that prevailed. Discomfort and disturbance punctuated the entire night: women were sick from the food, others came in drunk, children cried, fights broke out. Some just sat up chatting and 'singing lewd songs' by the light of the single gas jet. Whether or not they had managed to catch some slumber, they were roused at 6 a.m. to begin their work. There was more skilly and stale bread, and then a final hellish night before release at nine the next morning.

One of the problems with spending the night at the casual ward was that it often hampered opportunities to find work the following day. Most labouring jobs began before 9 a.m. and those truly in pursuit of work might have a long walk to a potential place of employment. If there was no work to be had and no money to be found for food or shelter on that day either, a vagrant would be forced to begin the entire cycle once more and join the queue at another casual ward. As the law prohibited vagabonds from returning to the same spike within a thirty-day period, most tramped in a circuit between neighbouring facilities, often using a series of different names in order to evade the regulations. A tramp's existence was spent in an almost perpetual state of hunger, exhaustion and discomfort: cold, soaked in rain, itching from bites, sore-footed from miles of walking in worn-through shoes, to say nothing of the psychological torment endured. Life was led entirely hand to mouth and hour by hour in search of an opportunity to earn or beg a few coins. If they could secure a day or even a few hours of employment unloading cargo, carrying an advertising board, or minding the children of sweat-shop labourers, they might earn enough money for a night or so in a cheap lodging house. This was, of course, if the funds were not drunk away in a fit of despair. In the middle of the nineteenth century it was estimated that 'seventy thousand persons in London . . . rise every morning without the slightest knowledge as to where they shall lay their heads at night'.[10] Whether they passed an evening in a casual ward, a lodging house or, as was just as frequently the case, beneath the stars, these tramps were what we today would recognize as London's homeless population, and Polly was among their number.

In piecing together the narratives of those who fell victim to Jack the Ripper, it is remarkable that both the police and the press appear to have ignored the fact that a significant number of outcast women who slept in lodging houses also slept rough on a regular basis. A lodging-house bed, like a casual-ward bed, was used in rotation with nights spent curled up in doorways. Such an existence was an inevitable part of tramping. But as William Booth, the founder of the Salvation Army, asserts, this omission may not have been intentional; the

well-to-do classes simply did not fully appreciate what precisely it meant to be homeless. 'To very many, even of those
who live in London, it may be news that there are so many
hundreds who sleep out of doors every night,' he writes in *In
Darkest England and the Way Out*, one of the era's most influential explorations of poverty.

> There are comparatively few people stirring after midnight,
> and when we are snugly tucked into our own beds we are apt
> to forget the multitude outside in the rain and the storm who
> are shivering the long hours through on the hard stone seats
> in the open or under the arches of a railway. These homeless,
> hungry people are, however, there, but being broken-spirited
> folk for the most part they seldom make their voices audible in
> the ears of their neighbours.[11]

Rough sleepers may have felt invisible to 'respectable society', but they filled London in their numbers. In 1887 the
estimate of those sleeping in Trafalgar Square varied between
'more than two hundred' and 'six hundred' each night. William Booth recorded 270 on the Thames Embankment and 98
in Covent Garden Market during one night in 1890.[12] At least
as many were believed to shelter in Hyde Park. However,
these locations were only the most conspicuous haunts. Each
of the capital's neighbourhoods were riddled with others. The
area around Spitalfields Church was another favourite, in addition to those 'little nooks and corners of resort in many
sheltered yards, vans, etc., all over London'.[13]

While the experience of homelessness in Victorian London
was one of wretched misery for all who were forced to endure
it, women like Polly who found themselves without shelter
might also expect to become victims of sexual violence. As

women who lived without male protection or a roof over their heads were considered outcasts, and outcasts were regarded as defective women, so it followed that outcasts were also morally corrupt and sexually impure. It was generally accepted without question by all levels of society that such women would do anything for food and a bed. Because they were desperate they were there to be used. In some cases, their permission needn't even be solicited.

Mary Higgs, who went undercover as a female tramp, was horrified to find that in her ragged dress she was continuously verbally assaulted by men. 'I had never realised before that a lady's dress, or even that of a respectable working-woman, was a *protection*', she wrote. 'The bold, free look of a man at a destitute woman must be felt to be realised.' When staying at a casual ward she learned that the lecherous male porter had a key to their dormitory. When she complained, she was told that at another workhouse 'the portress left the care of the female tramps to a man almost entirely', and it was accepted that 'he did what he liked with them'. On another occasion, when sleeping outdoors, she was approached by a man who 'began to talk in a familiar and most disagreeable manner. He asked me where my husband was, and insinuated that I had been leading an immoral life' before suggesting that she spend the night with him in exchange for a share of his breakfast. After five days of treatment like this from the men she encountered, Higgs concluded 'I should not care to be a *solitary* woman tramping the roads.' At the time, Higgs was travelling with a female companion, but she found herself being warned by other women that if she tramped for any length of time it was necessary 'to take up with a fellow'.[14] Many women did, and therefore accepted the sexual advances of other vagrants in order to seal a relationship. Their 'free' behaviour was then used as further proof to reinforce the belief held by the police and the press that 'all vagrant women were prostitutes'.

When Ellen Stanley visited a number of female casual wards, she heard stories from the women similar to those told to Mary Higgs. In her account, Stanley relates the story of 'Cranky Sal', a 'grey-haired woman' whose face had been disfigured by a stroke. One day she noticed Sally had acquired a black eye. When Stanley enquired how she got it, Cranky Sal claimed it was 'because I would not let a man do as he liked with me'. She explained that she had been on the New Cut in Lambeth when a 'decently dressed' man offered to buy her a pennyworth of whelks and a twopenny pie:

> Then we strolled along, and stopping at a doorway he offered me a shilling. He said that would get a lodging for the night . . . and he asked me if I was going to take his money, and I said, Oh no! I don't do business like that, and he gave me a violent blow.

When Sally approached a policeman for help he laughed at her and joked 'that the man must have a strong stomach to fancy such as me'. She met with a similar response from another officer, 'who . . . refused to listen, and pushed [me] from the pavement into the middle of the street'. Stanley was moved by Sal's plight and questioned her about how she managed to survive on the streets. She replied, seeming uncertain herself of how she managed to cope:

> It is hard to tell you. I do not do anything really bad. You know what I mean; I beg and pick up what I can, and go about anywhere for a bit of food or a night's lodging. Sometimes

I make do on what they give me at these places here; sometimes
I get a few pence given me.[15]

The selling of sex was not the sole means available to the
female vagrant for acquiring sustenance and shelter, nor was it
central to her ability to survive. Even if she did resort to it,
'casual prostitution' among older women who did not possess
the physical allure of their younger counterparts frequently
did not involve penetrative intercourse but rather manual
stimulation or a grope up her skirt. Much of the era's alarmist
writing about impoverished and homeless women focused on
the young who turned to prostitution, without taking into
consideration that older women faced a slightly different set of
circumstances. For such women, there were other options.
When work could not be had, begging, even among beggars
themselves, could yield the pennies, cup of tea or piece of
bread needed to survive another day. As social commentators
marvelled, charity was 'frequently derived from the lowest
orders'; the most lethargic old female vagrants were tended to
by 'the energetic, prosperous mendicant' who 'is called upon
to give to those who are his inferiors in his profession'.[16]
George Sims remarked, 'Friendly leads, whip-rounds, and
benefits are nowhere so common as among the labouring
classes whose earnings are precarious . . . the street-hawker or
the dock labourer flings his sixpence into the hat extended for
a poor cove he has never seen in his life without a second
thought.' Among the homeless who frequented the lodging
houses these charitable practices were a way of life. Sims
writes that if a man came into such a place 'who has not the
four pence to pay for his bed' and 'his woes appear real, round
goes the hat in a minute, and the other lodgers pay for his
night's rest'. Food, too, was divided among poorer lodgers and

'a man, seeing a neighbour without anything, will hand him his teapot, and say, "Here you are, mate," ' and offer him the leaves for a second brew.[17] Although not everyone was fortunate enough to have their bed and tea bought every night, such a tradition of lending assistance was invaluable to a tramp.

Polly's experiences of tramping would not have differed from those of other women. Initially, life on the street would have been shocking and distressing, and then gradually accepted with resignation. It is no wonder that by the time she was arrested in Trafalgar Square in 1887, after nearly six months of vagrancy, she had evolved from a respectable, well-behaved Peabody tenant into a disorderly, foul-mouthed menace.

Following her hearing on 25 October, Polly was 'released on her own recognisances', but was instructed that she must go into the workhouse or face arrest.[18] On this occasion, she complied and went directly to the nearest one on Endell Street in Covent Garden. From there she was transferred to the Strand Union Workhouse in Edmonton, where she remained until December when, unable to bear the conditions any longer, she discharged herself.

Invariably, no sooner had she given up the regimentation of institutional life for one of tramping than she was reminded of its mid-winter hardships. On 19 December she turned up once more at the gates of Lambeth Union Workhouse, but it seems there was some discrepancy as to whether she still belonged to the parish. After passing Christmas inside the workhouse, the one day of the year where inmates were fed a proper dinner of roast beef and plum pudding, Polly was sent on her way. Now uncertain of where in London she might legally call her home, Polly began to wander north of the river, towards Holborn. She passed several nights in the casual ward at Clerkenwell and managed to scrape together the pennies for three nights at a lodging house in Fulwood's Rents, a dingy court off Chancery Lane, in the area she had known so well as a child. When she had run through what small amount of money she possessed, she handed herself over to Holborn Union Workhouse. Tramping in the cold and damp of January had obviously taken its toll and Polly soon fell ill, at which point she was transferred to the infirmary in Archway.[19]

While under Holborn Union's care, the Guardians, in accordance with the Poor Law, had to determine if Polly actually belonged there, or if some other Poor Law Union should be footing her bill in their own workhouse. After Polly had recovered, she was interviewed on 13 February 1888 when it was decided that she should be sent back to Lambeth, the Union that had only just turned her out.[20] On 16 April she was dispatched like a human parcel to Renfrew Road Workhouse. Shortly after her arrival there, Polly stood in front of the matron, Mrs Fielder, who eighteen months earlier had placed her in service. One might imagine a scene of sighing and scowling from both sides. Lambeth Union did not want her there, and were prepared to offer her another placement in domestic service, perhaps in the hope that this time there would be a better outcome.

Mrs Sarah Cowdry of 16 Rosehill Road in Wandsworth, south London, had made it known to the Lambeth Guardians that she and her husband would be willing to take a woman from the workhouse into their home as a servant. As observant Baptists, the Cowdrys adhered to the concept of Christian duty; not only did they seek to lend assistance to those less fortunate, but they also wished to set a moral example within their home and community. As Chief Clerk of Works to the

Metropolitan Police, Samuel Cowdry had undoubtedly acquired a certain understanding of the city's social ills, and, perhaps in response, he and his wife had committed to a life of abstinence from alcohol.

On the morning of 12 May, Polly Nichols arrived at the Cowdrys' comfortable middle-class home with nothing more than the clothes on her back. As the only servant in a household occupied by the couple in their early sixties and an unmarried niece in her twenties, Polly's duties would not have been especially demanding. She would have been expected to clean the rooms and cook the meals, but would also have enjoyed her own attic room and bed, which must have seemed a luxury after her months tramping or suffering in the workhouse. As Polly had no attire befitting her station as a housemaid, Mrs Cowdry would have had to provide her with at least one, if not two changes of clothes, a decent bonnet and shoes, a nightdress, caps, pinafores, a shawl, a pair of gloves, undergarments and a variety of other accoutrements such as a hairbrush, hair combs and pins. No middle-class mistress wanted her maid to appear ragged before her visitors.

During her first week at 'Ingleside', as the Cowdrys called their home, Sarah probably suggested that Polly write to her family and inform them of her whereabouts. Her mistress brought her paper and a pen and Polly, perhaps for the first time in two years, gathered the courage to address her father:

> I just write to say you will be glad to know that I am settled
> in my new place and going alright up to now. My people
> went out yesterday and have not returned so I am left in
> charge. It is a grand place with trees and gardens back and
> front. All has been newly done up. They are teetotallers and
> very religious so I ought to get on. They are very nice people

and I have not much to do. I do hope you are all right and the boy [Polly's eldest son who was then living with his grandfather] has work. So goodbye for the present.

Yours Truly,
Polly

Answer soon please and let me know how you are.[21]

What ensued over the course of the next two months at the house in Wandsworth is unknown. In the beautiful warm days of summer, Polly's life might have felt like a paradise when compared to what she had known on the streets and in the casual wards. She had access to the gentle peace of the Cowdrys' garden; she wore clean clothes and had vermin-free hair. There would have been three meals a day; dinners that included meat, fruit, puddings and foods she may not have tasted since she parted from her family. She had a real bed, an employer who wished to help her, and no fear of drunken attacks in the middle of the night or abuse from the staff of the casual ward. She may also have been marched to chapel regularly, required to say her prayers and study her Bible, made to feel ashamed of who she was and how she had led her life. At the Cowdrys' house, Polly had no company beyond her master and mistress and their niece, Miss Mancher, who would not have been inclined to chat with her or share jokes and secrets. With no other staff or companions, her days and nights must have seemed bitterly, if not painfully, long and empty. There were too many hours in which to pine for what had been lost to her. Then, of course, there was also the matter of drink and whether or not at that point in her life it was possible for her to live without it.

On 12 July, Sarah Cowdry sent word on a postcard to Renfrew Road Workhouse that Polly Nichols had absconded from their home with clothing and goods worth £3 10s. Polly had evidently packed up the belongings that Mrs Cowdry had provided for her – the dresses, the bonnet, the shoes, the pinafores and everything else – and taken her leave.

It is doubtful that she had any plan in mind when she crept out of the servants' entrance at Ingleside. Living an itinerant existence meant that Polly had grown accustomed to catering to her immediate needs. Returning to the workhouse would not have been on her agenda. With a variety of goods at her disposal she would have gone first to a pawn shop or a dealer of used clothing and turned a few of Mrs Cowdry's charitable gifts into ready cash. Although she would not have received the full worth of these items, she would have had enough money at her disposal for food and board at lodging houses for at least a couple of weeks. Her next stop was then likely to have been a public house.

With a pocketful of change, it's not surprising that Polly becomes untraceable from the middle of July until 1 August, on which date she spends a night at Grey's Inn Casual Ward, along her tramping route to Whitechapel.[22] Here she knew there was a wealth of cheap lodging houses, which would allow her to spin out her hoard of coins as long as possible. Of all the establishments she could have selected, Polly decided to take a bed at Wilmott's Lodging House at 18 Thrawl Street. Unlike many other such businesses in the area, Wilmott's catered to female lodgers only; for a solitary woman, tramping alone, this would have been the safest accommodation available. At Wilmott's, which housed up to seventy women, Polly shared what was described as 'a surprisingly clean' room with three others. This included an older woman named Ellen Holland, with whom she also occasionally split the price of a double bed.

Holland, who came to know Polly over the three weeks she was resident there, was the only person who appears to have formed anything like a friendship with the lonely woman. Ellen described her roommate as 'melancholy' and said 'she kept herself to herself', as if 'some trouble was weighing upon her mind'.[23] There were no acquaintances in the area that they shared in common and she knew Polly to have no male companions, 'only a female with whom she ate and drank for a few days', as was usual practice among vagrant women.[24] Holland also did not deny that Polly drank and that she had seen her 'worse for it' a couple of times.

Polly Nichols's last movements are largely told through the testimony that Ellen Holland offered at the coroner's inquest into her friend's death. Unfortunately, as there are no official transcripts of this hearing, and all inquest documentation has been lost, the only accounts that exist to paint a picture of events are those that appear in contemporary newspaper reports. Naturally, these summaries rapidly scribbled down by journalists in the courtroom are riddled with errors and inconsistencies. When written up as newsworthy stories, they were further shaped and embellished to suit the needs of the specific paper – sometimes to heighten sensation, sometimes to chop down a tale to fit the available column inches. Syndicated pieces were then sent out to smaller newspapers across the country. Journalists there, including some who had never even travelled to London or visited Whitechapel, cannibalized these stories, fabricating quotations and even interviews. Misinformation took root in the public consciousness as readily as it does today.

According to Ellen Holland, Polly remained at Wilmott's until roughly 24 August, when it seems her funds had begun to run short. It was common practice for deputy lodging-house keepers to extend credit for a night or so to regulars; however, as Polly was not especially well known, this kindness was not offered and she was turned out. Once more, Polly was back on the street, tramping and reduced to acquiring a few coins and lodging where she could. Holland believed she had spent some time around Boundary Street in Shoreditch and a few nights at another lodging house called the White House in Whitechapel, on the notoriously wretched Flower and Dean Street.[25] Until about 12.30 a.m. on 31 August, Polly had been drinking in the Frying Pan, a pub on the corner of Thrawl Street. She was quite intoxicated when she left and, in spite of having drunk away her doss money, thought she would try to secure a bed at Wilmott's, which she preferred to other lodging houses. The deputy lodging keeper was not in the habit of handing out beds to penniless drunks and so sent Polly on her way. As she left, she attempted to hide her disappointment with a laugh and a sharp comment that she would 'soon get her doss money'.[26]

At shortly before 2.30 a.m. Ellen Holland, who had been returning from watching a large fire at Shadwell dry dock, encountered her former roommate moving down Osborn Street towards the Whitechapel Road. Polly was not in a good way. She was staggering and couldn't walk straight. When Ellen stopped her, Polly slumped against a wall. Greatly concerned for her friend, Ellen kept her chatting 'for about 7 or 8 minutes', in which time she claimed to have attempted to convince Polly to return to Wilmott's with her. However, Polly's encounter with the deputy keeper earlier must have firmly convinced her that they would not allow her back that night. Polly bemoaned the fact that she had no money and appeared anxious that she had to 'make up the amount for her lodgings', though, as she could barely walk, this did not seem likely.[27] 'I have had my lodging money three times today and I have spent it,' she said to Holland with drunken remorse, but for Polly, this predicament would hardly have been a new one.[28] The prospect of not having a bed for the night may not have been welcome but it was by no means a situation to which she was unaccustomed.

Ellen Holland repeated this story to the police and then told it again at the coroner's inquest, where journalists were in attendance to hear all the details. However, before they had even listened to it fully, both the authorities and the press were certain of one thing: Polly Nichols was obviously out soliciting that night, because she – like every other woman, regardless of her age, who moved between the lodging houses, the casual wards, and the bed she made in a dark corner of an alley – was a prostitute. From this starting point, the police and press would form their theories about the killer. Initially, two possibilities were forwarded: the first was that the murder was committed by a 'high-rip gang', or group who extorted money from prostitutes; the second, which later gained more traction, was that a lone 'prostitute killer' was behind the crime. In both cases everyone was certain, without so much as a single shred of actual evidence to reinforce their convictions, that Polly Nichols was a prostitute.

These assumptions subsequently had a hand in crafting the direction of the entire investigation, the coroner's inquest and the way that the story was reported in the newspapers, even though virtually everything stated by the three witnesses who knew Polly most intimately – Ellen Holland, Edward Walker and William Nichols – appears to counter the preconception that she was engaged in prostitution. At times the coroner's inquest becomes a moral investigation of Polly Nichols herself, as if the hearing was in part to determine whether her behaviour warranted her fate.

When Polly last spoke to Ellen Holland on that night of 31 August, she made it clear to her friend that she disliked her new accommodation at the White House. When Ellen asked her where she was staying, Polly claimed 'she was living in another house together with a lot of men and women'. This was also variously reported as 'a house where men and women were allowed to sleep'.[29] The comment was made in contrast to the lodgings available at Wilmott's, which were single sex and which she preferred. In reference to the White House, Polly stated that 'she didn't like to go there', and that 'there were too many men and women'. She wanted to return to Wilmott's and promised Ellen that it wouldn't 'be long before she was back'.[30]

On several occasions in the course of her testimony, the coroner posed questions to Ellen Holland about her friend's moral character in the hope she would make an incriminating statement about Polly's assumed profession. At each juncture, Ellen makes it perfectly plain that Polly was not what they insinuated. When asked if Ellen knew what her former roommate did for a living, Holland claimed she did not know. She answered similarly when pressed over whether Polly stayed out late at night.

'Did you consider that she was very cleanly in her habits?' he enquired.

'Oh, yes; she was a very clean woman,' she replied.

The coroner then took the opportunity once more to probe Ellen over her comment that Polly intended to find the money for her lodgings.

'I suppose you formed an opinion of what that meant,' he interjected.

'No,' Ellen Holland stated adamantly, before reiterating that Polly was intent on returning to her women-only lodging house.[31]

So absolute were Holland's statements that a number of newspapers, including the *Manchester Guardian*, paraphrased her examination simply by stating, 'the witness said she did not think the deceased was leading a fast [or immoral] life; in fact she [Nichols] seemed very afraid of it'.[32]

It is hardly surprising that those most intent on shaping Polly's character into something insalubrious appear to have been the newspapers. Whether through sloppy note-taking, the mishearing of testimony or deliberate embellishment, journalists frequently twisted statements to cast a shadow over Polly's moral character. When the coroner enquired of Edward Walker about his daughter's behaviour when she lived with him in the wake of her marital breakdown, he asked if Polly 'was fast'. According to the *Morning Advertiser*, the *Evening Standard* and the *Illustrated Police News* his response was, 'No; I never heard of anything of that sort. She used to go with some young women and men that she knew, but I never heard of anything improper.'[33] However, the *Daily News* in its paraphrasing inserted something far more suggestive. 'She did not stay out particularly late at night,' Walker is claimed to have said, while also purporting to add, 'The worst he had seen of her was her keeping company with females of a certain class.'[34] Whether Walker actually said this is debatable, as there are at least two competing versions of his testimony. Similarly, the coroner's attempts to goad William Nichols into elaborating on his wife's character only succeeded in casting doubt over his own behaviour in light of his marriage breakdown. When asked why he discontinued Polly's 5-shilling maintenance payments, he claimed that in the two-year period since their estrangement she had been living with 'another man or men'.[35] This provided the newspapers with all the evidence they required to judge Polly for being an adulteress and a fallen woman; however, Nichols never once asserted that his wife was making a living as a prostitute.

When the story first broke, before anything substantial was known about Polly's life, almost every major newspaper in the country carried a piece stating, 'it was gathered that the deceased had led the life of an "unfortunate",' in spite of also reporting that 'nothing . . . was known of her'.[36] In order to validate their assessment of her lifestyle, the papers set about slanting the slender facts available. Polly's comment to the deputy keeper at Wilmott's – 'I'll soon get my doss money, see what a jolly bonnet I've got now' – before gesturing to a hat that no one claimed to have noticed before, was used to insinuate the illicit method she used to acquire money.[37] Whether or not this was actually said to begin with is as questionable as the context. Polly's 'jolly bonnet' was just as likely to have been one she had acquired from the Cowdrys a month earlier and planned to pawn so she could return to a familiar bed at Wilmott's. However, the truth of this, like so many other details surrounding her final hours and her death, will remain unknown. Like Ellen Holland, whose name the journalists could not even bother to confirm or record correctly, Polly was just another impoverished, ageing, worthless female resident of a Whitechapel lodging house.[38] There was nothing else the police, the coroner, the newspaper scribblers or their readers needed to learn about her.

Ellen Holland remembered the clock on Whitechapel Church striking half past two when she parted with her friend. She watched Polly, in her jolly straw bonnet edged with black velvet, sway off in the direction of Whitechapel Road and disappear gradually into the darkness.

At that hour, Polly would have known that her chances of begging money for her doss were slim. With her head spinning from drink and exhaustion, she wandered, stumbling through the network of East End streets. She steadied herself against walls and the sides of buildings, feeling her way through the night, groping for a place which might become a bed: somewhere with a step or a slightly recessed doorway. The cavities beneath stairs, landings in communal buildings, the semi-private yards that lay just beyond unlocked gates: all made places to attempt slumber. Polly would have learned how to locate a suitable spot; yet, as she was relatively new to the neighbourhood, the locations of Whitechapel's secret sleeping corners would be as of yet unrevealed to her. It is likely that she did not even know the name of the road onto which she had turned. The barest flickers of light from a window or a distant lamp would have guided her down Buck's Row. She passed beyond a set of flat-fronted brick labourers' cottages, which offered no convenient nooks or porches until the kerb dipped and the wall became a gate, set back slightly from the footpath. She may have pushed on it to find that it refused to give way, or simply slid down with her back against it to rest. Her heavy head would have slumped, and her eyes eventually shut.

But for the postcard she wrote to her father in the final few months of her life, we have been left no clear glimpse into Polly Nichols's thoughts. Ellen Holland saw in the woman who slept beside her something deeply melancholic: a personality folding in on itself, private, alienated and grieving. However, from these rough outlines, a faint but distinct pattern of a woman can be defined. There is enough here still from which to draw conclusions, to understand her not as a fiction, but as a person. Polly had been born between printing shops and presses, against the very backdrop where some of the most famous Victorian stories were fabricated. In death she would become as legendary as the Artful Dodger, Fagin or even Oliver Twist, the truth of her life as entangled with the imaginary as theirs. She had been brought into the world on the Street of Ink, and it is there, riding on its column inches, its illustrated plates, its rumour and scandal, that she would return: a name in print.

❧

On 1 September 1888 William Nichols had prepared for the worst. Uncertain of what he was about to encounter, he felt he should dress appropriately and attired himself in mourning: a long black coat, black trousers, a black tie and a top hat. It was raining that day, and he must have felt physically sick as he stepped into it and unfurled his umbrella, turning his back on his door on Coburg Road, where he lived with Rosetta and their children.

He was to meet Inspector Abberline at the mortuary and view the body of the woman it was supposed was his wife. It had been three years since he'd seen her and he had no inkling of where she had gone in that time, though he could have hardly anticipated such a shocking turn of events. The police inspector warned him that it was likely that he might have some difficulty recognizing Polly, but that they were hoping he would be able to provide a positive identification. He then escorted Nichols through a rear door and into a yard, across which stood a modest brick shed. The men stepped inside, where a plain pine coffin sat. Nichols removed his hat and braced himself as the lid was pulled back.

Even with her injuries, with the stitched-up gash across her throat and the deep cuts along her body, William Nichols knew his wife. He recognized her small, delicate features and high cheekbones. Her grey eyes, though vacant, were familiar to him, as was her brown hair, which in the years since they had last met had become streaked with silver. This was indeed Polly, as he used to call her, the woman who he had married and once loved dearly. It was Polly, the woman who had borne six of his children, who had comforted and coddled them, who had nursed him in times of illness, the woman with whom he had shared laughter and at least a handful of joys for sixteen years. It was Polly, who at eighteen had once been his girlish bride, and held her father's arm as she walked down the aisle at St Bride's Church. They had been happy, even if it had been only for a short while.

Abberline noticed that the colour had drained out of Nichols's face. He was noticeably shaken by the sight and then broke down.

'I forgive you as you are.' He addressed her as if she were merely sleeping and the brutish cuts on her body had not ended her life. 'I forgive you on account of what you have been to me.'[39]

It took William Nichols some time to compose himself. The coffin lid was moved back into place, and Abberline showed the grieving husband back across the yard and into the station.

Annie

c. September 1841 – 8 September 1888

5

Soldiers and Servants

T HE NEWSPAPERS DESCRIBED THE rain as torrential. It poured in buckets. It drenched everything. It seeped through woollen cloaks and coats; it cascaded from the brims of hats. This was chilling February rain which was certain to bring chest ailments and fevers to those who persisted in standing in it, yet it was remarked that none of the spectators' 'spirits were in the least damped'. They came in the thousands, pressing against the rails of Buckingham Palace and lining the route to St James's. Most of the assembled were, as the *Morning Chronicle* writes, 'generally of the working classes'. They 'scrambled and pushed and squeezed' in order to best position themselves to catch a glimpse of Queen Victoria and Prince Albert in their wedding attire.[1] Young men scaled trees, and were promptly yanked down by policemen. On several occasions, the assembly threatened to move onto the parade route but were held back by detachments of horse-mounted Guardsmen, their shining breastplates partially covered by their scarlet winter capes. At the appearance of a cortège of carriages, there was a sudden surge of excitement. Loud whoops and cheers were followed by cries of 'God save the Queen!' The crowd heaved forward, reaching out their hands to touch the vehicles and the horses, to spy the bright blue eyes of the royal bride. The troopers of the 2nd Queen's Life Guard advanced against them, cracking their whips above the heads of the masses, holding the line 'with a mixture of firmness and good humour which won the approval of all present'.

It was for this: for the spectacle of such pageants, for the pride of serving in the cavalry and one of the most prestigious regiments in the country, for the thrill of sitting tall on a mount in polished boots, that George Smith, just fifteen in 1834, left his home in rural Lincolnshire and came to London. Three years earlier a recruiting sergeant had come to the nearby village of Fulbeck and enlisted his elder brother Thomas in the 2nd regiment of the Life Guards. As a young boy, George could scarcely wait to join him. When he appeared at Regent's Park Barracks, he was still underage, but the regiment nevertheless enlisted this enthusiastic recruit. They taught him to ride like a cavalry trooper, and how to shine his breastplate and clean his helmet. He learned the strict routines of army life quickly: how to stand, march, salute, how to discipline his body so he never slouched or 'loafed about'. George and his brother were recruited because they were strong, healthy country lads of sturdy physique perfect for sitting astride a mount. According to his army records, he stood at 5 feet 10 inches when he enlisted, with a fair, clear complexion and brown eyes. The regimental barber cut his light brown hair short, but, because George was a trooper in the cavalry, he was permitted to cultivate a fine moustache.

Under the guidance of the 2nd Life Guards, George came of age. His position in the household cavalry secured him a seat in the front row of history. He witnessed the passing of the Georgian era when he served at the funeral of King William IV, and the birth of the Victorian age at the coronation of the new queen in 1838. On 10 February 1840 he was there to participate in the state ceremonies on the occasion of her marriage, guarding his monarch against the crowds.

On that day, when Londoners crowded into the streets and celebrated the marriage of their monarch, it is likely that a 22-year-old servant called Ruth Chapman was among them. Little is known about the Sussex-born young woman who, like so many others, left home to work in the capital. Her family at least thought it wise to baptize her at fifteen before sending her off into the wide world with all of its manifold temptations. What good it did her is questionable, for by the time of the Queen's nuptials she had already met and formed an attachment to a trooper of the 2nd Life Guards.

It is possible that she and George met somewhere near to his barracks on Portman Street. A relation of Ruth's worked for a Sussex family who lived on nearby Clifton Place, where she too may have been employed. Hyde Park, notorious as a venue for flirtation between soldiers and servants, lies just in between. According to the journalist Henry Mayhew, it was often in the parks when housemaids and nursemaids walking to and from their place of work were exposed to 'the all powerful redcoat' and 'succumbed to Scarlet Fever'. Soldiers were by no means immune to the impact their dashing uniforms and well-groomed military air had on members of the opposite sex, and deployed it to their advantage. As the army actively discouraged marriage among enlisted men and low wages meant the average private 'could not afford to employ professional women to gratify his passions . . . he is only too glad to seize the opportunity of forming an intimacy with a woman who will appreciate him for his own sake, and cost him nothing but the trouble of taking her about occasionally'.[2] More importantly, where the army was concerned, a monogamous relationship with a decent working-class girl 'was unlikely to communicate some infectious disease to him' and would keep him away from prostitutes.³ Such arrangements may have served the ordinary soldier well, but it placed the object of his affection in a difficult if not a potentially ruinous position. By January 1841, Ruth found herself in just this situation.

The precise day on which Annie Eliza Smith was born in early September 1841 is unclear. Having borne an illegitimate child, her mother may have attempted to hide many of the facts of her birth. The circumstances in which Annie arrived could not have been entirely happy for Ruth, who would have lost her employment as her pregnancy advanced and would have found herself dependent upon meagre and unreliable handouts from George. In the eyes of society, and the army, Ruth had become a 'dollymop': a soldier's woman who, while not quite falling into the category of 'professional', was deemed a sort of 'amateur' prostitute. Fortunately, the army's position on dollymops remained a pragmatic one, so long as only six out of every hundred enlisted men in a regiment were permitted to marry. In the field, such women would have been known as camp followers and allowed to earn their keep by taking in the regiment's laundry. While the cavalry remained in barracks they were often called upon to perform the same duties. One trooper's woman remarked that she made ends meet by doing 'a little needlework in the day-time' as well as 'some washing and mangling now and then to help it out'. She, much like Ruth, lived in a room near to the barracks, for which she paid a shilling a week.⁴

For five months after Annie's birth, Ruth's position remained a precarious one, especially as she soon found herself pregnant with her second child. Regardless of George's affection for her, there remained the ever-present possibility that he might be posted abroad, a circumstance known to be the death knell of many romantic attachments between soldiers and the women they hadn't married. Had fate taken this turn, Ruth would have been left with no financial support, two children and a soiled reputation. When placed in such a position, it was conventional for dollymops to remain loyal to the regiment and seek another protector from within it, or from within the barracks, although this remedy was not without consequences; in doing so they committed themselves to a career in prostitution. Fortunately, on 20 February 1842, two years after they had begun courting, George received permission to marry his sweetheart. Whether it was George's expressed wish or the thoughtful intercession of his commanding officer, the date of his nuptials was then backdated by two years on his military records. Should anyone have enquired, George and Ruth's wedding had taken place in the same month and year as that of Queen Victoria and Prince Albert.

From the day of their first acquaintance through all their subsequent years together, the army would completely dictate and define the lives of George, Ruth and all of their children. Although marriage ensured that Mrs Smith was now 'on the strength', or included as an official regimental wife, this did not necessarily make for a more comfortable life. While the army would have provided Ruth and her children with half-rations and permission to reside within the barracks, life there was not healthy or pleasant. Designated married quarters were not provided until the 1850s and so newly-weds had to make do with corners of the communal barracks room, screened off with hanging sheets and blankets. Women dressed and undressed, lay in bed, washed, gave birth and breast-fed surrounded by single men, who also strode about half-naked, swearing, jeering and singing lewd songs. Sanitation was not much better. When a national inspection of barracks was made in 1857, the dwelling spaces were revealed to be in appalling condition. Many dormitories were set over the stables and ill-ventilated. Dampness and poor lighting was the norm throughout, as were insufficient washing and latrine facilities. In some barracks large barrels were used as communal chamber pots, which were emptied and then used for bathing. Kitchen facilities, too, were found wanting. Most of these contained no ovens, which had a significant impact on the diet and health of military men who subsisted largely on boiled food.

However, there were some benefits to families who 'lived on the strength'. Savings banks were established to allow soldiers to put aside small sums, medicines from regimental supplies were made available to sick men and their families, while all ranks and their dependents were given access to the barracks' library. Most importantly, by 1848, families were allocated a small allowance for suitable accommodation outside of the barracks, which, while not necessarily offering them many comforts, did at least afford soldiers and their wives privacy and homes of their own. This would have proven especially timely to the Smiths, whose number continued to expand through the decade. Shortly after Ruth and George's marriage in 1842, a brother, George William Thomas, joined Annie and her parents. He was followed by Emily Latitia in 1844, Eli in 1849, in addition to Miriam in 1851 and William in 1854.[5] Annie and her siblings were able to make use of what was considered one of the greatest benefits of life on the strength: the regimental school.

More than twenty years before a system of mandatory state schooling was implemented in 1870, the sons and daughters of families on the strength were required to attend organized lessons funded by the army. In part, this facility was provided to remove children from the 'idleness and vice' of barracks life, which was deemed 'incompatible with decency', particularly where girls were concerned. However, the army also wished to reward enlisted men for their service by demonstrating their care for the education and welfare of the next generation. The regimental schools not only sought to instil notions of discipline, duty and respect in line with military ideals, but to provide children with 'the means of making themselves useful and earning a livelihood'.[6] Most regiments regarded attendance as compulsory, or families were threatened with being struck off the strength. At the same time, they also expected soldiers to pay for the privilege of educating their children, so the family budget had to be stretched accordingly. George would have been charged twopence a month for Annie to attend, and then one penny for each of her siblings who joined her.

The curriculum offered at the regimental schools was similar to that offered at civilian charity institutions. The schools were divided into classes for infants and those for grown children. The younger children were taught by a schoolmistress in the morning, while the elder children of both sexes were instructed by the schoolmaster. Following dinner, they were separated, with the boys remaining with the master and the girls joining the schoolmistress for more gender-specific occupational instruction. By the standards of the first half of the Victorian era, all children received a fairly rigorous education. The infants were taught spelling, reading and singing, a curriculum that was then expanded to include lessons in writing, diction, grammar, English history, geography, arithmetic and algebra. Under such a regime, Annie would have received an education far superior than that offered to the majority of her working-class peers, both male as well as female. As a girl, she would have also benefited from afternoon lessons in 'industry'; specifically in every type of needlework from embroidery to clothes making, crochet and knitting. By these means, girls would acquire the skills that would not only render them useful to the regiment in mending and making garments, but also would assist them in acquiring work when their schooling was complete. The only complication with this scheme was the peripatetic nature of army life which brought frequent interruptions to a child's education as their family moved between postings.

Although George and his family were never made to endure the hardships of a foreign posting, neither were they able to grow too comfortable in their domestic surroundings. Regiments were rotated between barracks often at short notice. While moving and organizing new lodgings near to barracks on Portman Street, Hyde Park and Regent's Park would have involved the inconvenience of relocating a few miles in one direction or the other, travelling to another posting in Windsor, more than 20 miles outside of the city, would have involved a great amount of upheaval and expense. In the course of George's service with his regiment, from the 1840s through to the early 1860s, the family lived at no fewer than twelve addresses between London and Windsor.

One of the curious aspects of growing up as the child of a soldier in a socially prestigious regiment was that life became an awkward balance between two disparate worlds. The world of the cavalry, with its aristocratic officers and its proximity to the royal family, brought opportunities to witness, even from afar, an existence of status, privilege and wealth beyond the daily experience of most working-class children. Annie's girlhood was spent between Knightsbridge, with its elegant stucco-fronted villas, and Windsor, in the shadow of the royal family's residence. The sight of landaus filled with ladies in expensive silk bonnets and titled gentlemen whose uniforms clanked with medals would have seemed an ordinary occurrence. As too would have a glimpse of Queen Victoria, or a royal prince trotting through Windsor Great Park on horseback. When Ruth and her children stepped from behind the doors of their temporary homes, they walked along clean, broad, well-lit streets, comparatively free from signs of want. They inhaled the fresh air of Hyde Park alongside the perfectly accoutred members of high society twirling their parasols. From a young age, Annie would have been taught to take pride in her father's position and to adopt his love of Queen and Country as her own. Regimental values of honour and dignity would have been inculcated as well. How Annie stood and spoke and comported herself, while not making her appear privileged, would have demonstrated that she understood the rules of appropriate conduct and was aware of her place within her surroundings. These skills were to remain with her, so that even as an adult she gave the impression that she had come from a good family.

However, while Annie might have gazed at the opulence of court life, the realities of her daily existence and her living conditions were those of a working-class child. The few privileges her father's position brought were tempered by the meagreness of his salary. While the Smiths lived in Windsor, they rented lodgings on Keppel Terrace, a road whose houses had been constructed and decorated 'at considerable expense' in order to appeal to 'small, genteel families'. Each three-storey property with its 'Portland stone mantels, rich cornicing' and 'fine views over the River Thames' was comprised of 'two parlours, three bedrooms and servants' quarters' in which three army families lived, while sharing a kitchen and lavatory facilities.[7] The quality of some of their housing in Knights-bridge was at times even worse.

Hidden between Knightsbridge's 'fine mansions and respect-able abodes', and no more than a moment's walk from its exclusive shops, existed a small pocket of 'insalubriousness' across the road from Hyde Park Barracks. 'From Knightsbridge Green all along the High Road was a succession of music-halls, taverns, beer-stores, oyster saloons, & cheap tobacconists' that was deemed 'a disgrace to any portion of London'.[8] Here also was situated some of the only housing affordable to the fami-lies of enlisted men. When it was possible, the Smiths lived at a distance from these establishments. In 1844, they took a small cottage on Rutland Terrace near to the Brompton Road, but as the century progressed, rents in the better areas increased and pushed regimental families into the densely populated streets between two of the most notorious music halls: the Sun and the Trevor Arms. Raphael Street ran east to west, just on the fringe of this carnival of iniquity, and although its housing stock had only been completed in the past couple of years, its homes had already been carved up and portioned out to mul-tiple families on lower incomes. In 1854, the Smiths were living at number 15 with at least two other families, each of whom occupied two rooms.

In the late spring of that year, just when the weather had turned milder, the London newspapers began to write of an alarming rise in the number of cases of scarlatina, or scarlet fever. This was soon followed by reports of outbreaks in Isling-ton, Knightsbridge and Chelsea, though journalists attempted to offer some reassurance to readers by stating that 'the dis-ease' was 'principally among the labouring classes'. On 3 May the *Daily News* wrote that a coachman who lived near the very wealthiest of society in Eaton Mews South had watched as 'malignant scarlatina carried off all five of his children in nine days'. It continued to warn readers that the outbreak 'was very bad in this district'. The tragic stories of what was now declared an epidemic continued through the summer. 'Scarlatina increases weekly,' wrote the *Morning Post* on 27 July. 'The . . . disease has visited some families with severity, and . . . an instance is reported in which three children died of it in the same family within 6 days.' In early June, the London Fever Hospital proclaimed a crisis when 'upwards of 100 patients' were admitted for scarlet fever alone. What then exacerbated the situation was the arrival of a second epidemic: typhus.

Whereas scarlet fever, a flu-like streptococcal illness characterized by a red rash, predominantly affected children, typhus spread among young and old without distinction. Commonly known as 'camp fever' or 'gaol fever', the disease was spread through the bites of fleas and lice harboured by clothes, blankets and bedding shared between people in close quarters. Like scarlet fever, those afflicted with typhus also suffered from a high fever as well as a red rash that spread across the body. Eventually, in fatal cases, the infection moved into the brain. In mid-May, both epidemics arrived at Raphael Street. An infant named John Fussell Palmer, not quite eighteen months old, was the first to die of scarlet fever. How rapidly the disease crept through the porous plaster walls and crowded rooms along the street is unknown, but shortly after the Palmer child fell ill, sickness came to settle in the Smiths' home. Miriam at two and a half would have come under twelve-year-old Annie's eye, when her mother was busy with her newborn, William. At that age, Miriam would have been toddling about the family rooms, giggling and prattling, turning over chairs and getting underfoot. A fever and sore throat, flu-like aches and much crying replaced this. When the rash

Annie

appeared, there would have been no doubt as to what had
befallen her. She suffered until 28 May, and was buried quickly
on the following day. In the time Ruth and George were nursing their youngest girl, William too had succumbed to the
rash and fever and died five days later, at the age of five months,
on 2 June. After carrying away the two youngest, seven days
later scarlet fever took its next victim: Eli, aged five.

What George and Ruth thought when their eldest son,
George Thomas, who had just turned twelve, began to sicken
cannot even be imagined. Like the others, his fever raged for
two weeks, and a rash spread across his body. When they buried his brother Eli, he lay in his bed, his condition worsening.
As families of enlisted men were not permitted to call upon
the services of the regiment's physician, the Smiths were
forced to summon a doctor whose fees they could hardly have
afforded. George Thomas was diagnosed with typhus. He
struggled with it for three weeks, before expiring on 15 June.

In the span of only three weeks, death had carried away
four of the Smiths' six children. The enormity of such a tragedy is almost inconceivable to modern, Western sensibilities,
particularly as their lives might have been spared had they
lived in an era of antibiotics. However, George and Ruth were
powerless in the face of incurable illness. The death of children was simply an unfortunate but unavoidable aspect of life,
though it did not render the experience any easier, either for
the parents or for the two surviving siblings, Annie and Emily.
Long after the event, the calamity continued to cast deep
shadows over the lives of those who had endured it.

Somehow Ruth and George found it in their hearts to move
forward. Two years later, in 1856, a daughter, Georgina, was born
in Windsor. She was followed by another Miriam – Miriam
Ruth – in 1858. In the midst of this, Annie grew into a teenage girl

with wavy dark brown hair and an intense blue-eyed stare. At about the time her mother's arms were once again filled with a newborn, Annie would have been nearing her fifteenth birthday. Traditionally this was considered the age when a girl's education would have been complete and she was able to contribute to her family's income with a full-time wage. For a large number of teenage girls this meant entering domestic service, which was regarded in many instances as a rite of passage, when a young woman took on the burden of supporting her younger siblings, often at the expense of leaving behind her family home. While removing herself from the protective parental eye posed potential moral dangers, domestic service was still viewed more favourably than factory work, which failed to impart any skills to a young woman that would prove useful in her future married life. As a result, between 1851 and 1891, nearly 43 per cent of women between the ages of fifteen and twenty went into service. As Ruth had Emily at home to assist with the younger children, it would have been appropriate for Annie, as the eldest, to begin making contributions to the family income as a live-in domestic.

Whether or not it was the first position she held, by 1861 Annie Smith was working as a housemaid for William Henry Lewer, a successful architect who lived at numbers 2–3 Duke Street, in Westminster, an area that served as home to a number of designers and engineers. Several doors down, at numbers 17–18, lived the great creator of railways, bridges and tunnels Isambard Kingdom Brunel and his family. As long-term residents of Duke Street, the Lewers and Brunels, who shared professional interests, would have also known one another socially. It is likely that Annie and her fellow housemaid, Eleanor Brown, as well as the Lewers' housekeeper, Mary Ford, would have at least recognized the Brunel family, if not had the privilege of waiting upon them in their master's drawing room.

In 1861, Annie was the most junior of the three women who tended to 67-year-old William Lewer and his bachelor brother, Edward, a retired stockbroker. Although all three would have worked from 5 or 6 a.m., sometimes until the very early hours of the morning, Annie's chores would have been the most arduous. Sometimes described as a 'maid-of-all-work', servants in small households were expected to perform every task, from cleaning dishes three times a day to hauling buckets of coal up flights of stairs, making the beds and lighting the fires in the grates. At the Lewers' home, Mrs Ford, the housekeeper, may also have doubled as a cook, whereupon Annie would be required to assist, not only in the preparation of meals but in serving them as well. Even in a home of two elderly gentlemen, Annie's list of jobs would have rarely allowed her a spare moment. When she wasn't dusting, or clearing out fireplaces, she was scrubbing the floors, beating rugs, drawing water for baths, polishing boots or mending clothes. If the Messrs Lewer did not have their dirty linens sent out to one of London's many commercial laundries, then the strenuous work of washing, rinsing, wringing and ironing would have fallen to Annie as well. For their hours of toiling, housemaids were remunerated poorly. Mrs Beeton, in her *Book of Household Management*, published in that year, suggested that Annie, as a maid-of-all-work, should receive an annual pay of between £9 and £14, and if William Lewer supplied her with an allowance to purchase her own supplies of tea, sugar and small beer, this figure would be reduced to between £7 6s. and £11.[9] Employers believed this minimal sum was justified, as they were paying for the young woman's room and board. In the Lewer household, where space appears to have been plentiful, Annie and Mrs Ford had their own rooms above the architect's office at number 2 Duke Street, while Eleanor slept in the attic at number 3. For Annie, who had spent her entire life sharing two or at most three rooms with her family, the privacy she enjoyed in William Lewer's servants' quarters must have seemed strange and wonderful.

When Annie began her life as a live-in domestic, she would have expected to see very little of her family. A housemaid's time off was granted at the discretion of her employer and most servants could expect no more than a day or even a half-day away from their duties each month. An hour or so on Sunday for attending church was also permissible. However, these restrictions would have made it difficult for Annie to travel to and from Windsor, where the Smiths were based until 1861.

For roughly twenty-one years, the army had beaten out the march to which the Smith family had moved. For Ruth as well as for George, the regiment – and the families and officers who comprised it – had formed the defining framework of their lives. This unique, closed, clan-like community, which migrated together between the barracks – who had shared housing and meals, whose children had been schooled together and grown up as if they were cousins, who had consoled one another, and lent each other money – would leave an indelible stamp on each of the Smiths' sense of identity. This was especially true for George, who as he entered his forties would be forced to contemplate retirement and his future prospects beyond the barracks. The 2nd regiment of the Life Guards had been as much a family to him as had his wife and children. So closely were the two intertwined that he chose to name his youngest son in recognition of those under whom he served. On 25 February 1861, Fountaine Hamilton Smith was born at

6 Middle Row North, a short distance from Raphael Street, where George and Ruth had parted with their three boys in 1854. Perhaps George found some relief from this tragedy that same year, when John Glencairn Carter Hamilton (later 1st Baron Hamilton of Dalzell) became one of his captains. Whatever support Hamilton provided, whether financial, emotional or spiritual, George never forgot his kindness. Neither was he able to forget the bond he had forged with another of his commanders, Captain Fountaine Hogge Allen, whose death in November 1857 must have affected him profoundly. It is likely that Fountaine's birth signified to George the approaching end of his career, and inspired in him a desire to commemorate those men and experiences that had shaped his person.

As a loyal servant of the regiment who had earned himself four distinguishing marks for good conduct, George was judged to be a suitable candidate to become a valet to his commanding officers. According to army regulations, cavalry officers who were not already attended by a civilian were permitted to employ a 'soldier servant' from within the regiment to maintain their military kit and uniforms, as well as to care for their physical appearance and to manage the administrative details of their daily lives. As Mrs Beeton explains, the valet's purpose is to tend to their masters' needs by 'dressing them, accompanying them in all their journeys' as well as acting as 'the confidants and agents of their most unguarded moments'; more specifically, this amounted to 'brushing his master's clothes, cleaning his top boots, his shooting, walking and dress boots; carrying up the water for his master's bath, putting out his things for dressing, assisting him in dressing, and packing and unpacking his clothes when travelling . . .'[10] Although Mrs Beeton points out that many gentlemen preferred to shave themselves, a valet must be prepared to perform this task too, as well as to regularly trim his master's beard and moustache.

Among the hierarchy of servants, the role of gentleman's valet was a trusted and prestigious one. No other servant was permitted such an intimate insight into their employer, from their physical weaknesses to their secrets and thoughts. In order to have been selected for such a position, George would have been judged to possess 'polite manners, modest demeanour, and respectful reserve' in addition to having 'good sense, good temper, some self-denial, and consideration for the feelings of others'.[11] In 1856, Roger William Henry Palmer, a Crimean War hero who had returned to Britain after his participation in the Charge of the Light Brigade, exchanged his commission in the 11th Hussars for one in the 2nd Life Guards. When it came to selecting a valet from among the men in his new regiment, Palmer spotted the necessary qualities for a 'gentleman's gentleman' in Trooper Smith.[12]

The benefits of George's association with a man who was not only lauded as a military hero but who would eventually succeed to his family's Irish baronetcy were many. Valeting excused him from parades and barrack responsibilities, including the universally disliked guard duty. It entitled him to live in the officers' mess where he received better food – and sometimes wine as well. Increasingly, especially after Palmer was elected as a Member of Parliament, George's duties would take him away from army life altogether and into the exclusive realm of country houses, shooting parties and government. As Palmer spent much of his time as a commissioned officer travelling between his family estates in County Mayo, George would have had the opportunity of seeing Ireland and the opulent interiors of its castles and manors. Then, in 1862, George Smith, the son of a Lincolnshire shoemaker, would go to Paris.

The year before, George had begun valeting for another officer in his regiment: Captain Thomas Naylor Leyland. So much had Leyland come to value his 'soldier-servant' that when he chose to marry and exchange his commission for one in the Denbighshire Yeomanry, he asked George to leave the 2nd Life Guards and accompany him.[13] This opportunity would have required a good deal of deliberation, but had arrived at a time in George's life when common sense demanded that he take it. Leyland was offering George a paid position that would place him alongside the butler and cook within the top rank of his household servants. He could expect to receive £25 to £50 per year, in addition to his army pension of 1s. 1½d. per day. As a middle-aged man from the working classes, George could hardly have done better for his family than this.

On 19 March 1862, less than a month before his forty-third birthday, Trooper George Smith became Mr Smith. He bid farewell to his associates, the barracks and the regiment that had made him, and set off to accompany Thomas Naylor Leyland to Paris where the latter proposed to marry his fiancée, Mary Ann Scarisbrick, at the British Embassy before embarking on their honeymoon through France.

From about the end of 1861, it appears that Ruth and George decided to settle the family more permanently in Knightsbridge, near to Leyland's palatial, art-filled mansion: Hyde Park House. This was conveniently situated in the area that Ruth knew best, near to the barracks, as well as being within a short walk from George's brother Thomas, who had also retired from the regiment and returned to the family occupation of shoemaking. Much like Annie, it is likely that George saw little of his family while engaged in domestic service, and this estrangement from his wife and children, as well as from all that he had known in the 2nd Life Guards, began to bear down on him. A valet, when not tending to his master, would have had time to himself – to read, to think; and without the immediate distractions of family or regiment, there were surely many subjects George did not wish to ponder. Undoubtedly, the deaths of his four children were among them.

On 13 June 1863, Captain Leyland had agreed to act as steward at the Denbighshire Yeomanry Cavalry Races in Wrexham. This was to be a large and convivial social gathering, which included a grand dinner for the officers and their ladies. The evening before, members of the regiment and their guests arrived in town and retired to their lodgings. While his master resided in officers' quarters, George shared a room at a pub, the Elephant and Castle, with another member of Leyland's staff. As they extinguished the light that night, George appeared his usual self, and 'quite cheerful'. The next morning, between 7 and 8 a.m., the servant called out to George, to remind him of the time. 'It's all right, I'm not asleep,' he answered, though he made no attempt to get out of bed. Less than an hour later, when George had still not appeared, the landlady went upstairs and much to her horror discovered Leyland's valet 'with his throat cut, in a shocking manner, with a razor lying by him covered with blood'. George was dead by the time they had found him on the floor, 'with only his shirt and drawers on'. [14]

That day, which had been intended as one of sporting amusement, immediately soured into one of shock and dismay. When informed of the horrible news, Thomas Naylor Leyland rushed to the scene and 'was much affected' by what he beheld. However, so that the races would not have to be abandoned, the coroners assembled that afternoon and presented a verdict of 'suicide by cutting his throat with a razor while labouring under temporary insanity'. [15] There was also the suggestion that George had been drinking, a problem to which he had succumbed quite seriously since leaving the army.

Notwithstanding the unfortunate turn of events, Leyland still appeared on the turf that afternoon to watch the horses run, though it cannot be imagined that he derived much pleasure from it.

He later paid the expenses of George's funeral.

There is no record of what occurred when Ruth and her daughters received the news. Fountaine, who was only two, would never know his father. The pension to which George had been entitled would have expired with his death; in the mid-nineteenth century the law did not permit widows to claim on behalf of their deceased husbands. Overnight, the family would be bereft of an income, other than the money that Annie sent home or that her sister Emily may have earned.

Curiously, a situation that might have led Ruth and her young children into the workhouse did not end with such misfortune. By the following year, Ruth had returned to an address where the family had once lived in 1851: 29 Montpelier Place, situated in the respectable, lower-middle-class Knightsbridge neighbourhood that they had come to know as home.[16] With three floors, including a basement kitchen and larder, as well as a ground-floor parlour that spoke of middle-class pretensions, this was certainly the most comfortable house the family had occupied. It is unlikely that Ruth would have been able to afford the rent on such a property without assistance. After George's death, Leyland would have paid what was owed of his valet's quarterly wage to his wife, and, given the tragic circumstances, it would not have been uncommon for an employer to have included a donation to his widow. Ruth invested the money she received wisely and, following the lead of many of her neighbours, took the lease on this adequately sized home and let out rooms to lodgers. The full kitchen and scullery below stairs also enabled her to make some extra income by taking in laundry.

Due to its affordability and its location close to the mansions of Knightsbridge, Montpelier Place and the surrounding streets were a haven for those in domestic service. Housemaids, butlers, valets and footmen filled the census returns for the area between the 1860s and 70s. Additionally, the street's position near to a number of mews meant that more than ten addresses on Montpelier Place alone were occupied by coachmen and grooms. Among them was a young man named John Chapman.

Little is known about the man who appeared one day at the door of 29 Montpelier Place and enquired about lodgings. Although he and Ruth shared the same surname, there is no apparent connection between the two families, though this commonality must have endeared his landlady to him from first acquaintance. Born in 1844, John hailed from a family of 'horse-keepers' in Newmarket, Suffolk. This centre of racing and horse-breeding would have given Chapman an immersive education in the needs and care of these animals. He and four of his brothers, having started their lives as stable assistants and grooms, brushing, feeding and exercising horses, eventually worked their way through the ranks to become coach drivers. By the second half of the 1860s, John had come to London to pursue his trade, probably in the employment of a family.

It might be imagined that Annie met her mother's lodger in the kitchen of the family home, on one of the few days away from her place of work. Or perhaps Annie was residing at home when John came into their lives. Either way, something blossomed between them, though it is impossible to say what, exactly. Annie, at twenty-seven, was not yet married, a situation not unusual for a woman who had spent her 'eligible years' in domestic service. But at this age she knew that to refuse an opportunity to marry might mean passing the rest of her days as a spinster, a person universally regarded with pity. With the exception of Fountaine, who was still a boy, the Smiths were now a family of women, headed by a widow. The addition of a man who might earn a steady livelihood and act as paterfamilias would have been most welcome. This would have been Annie's great moment: a chance to make a success of her life, to become everything society intended for her; not just a helpmate to her family, but the mistress of her own home and, most importantly, a wife and a mother.

6

Mrs Chapman

LIKE MANY VICTORIAN NEWLY-WEDS, Mr and Mrs John Chapman made an appointment to have their photograph taken. They had dressed in their Sunday finest for the occasion. John removed his hat when they arrived at the Brompton Road studio, and the couple were shown to a corner where a suitable backdrop had been unfurled beside some furniture. Either they or the photographer had chosen the scene: a pleasant outdoor image featuring a set of garden steps leading to a church in the distance. The canvas was flanked by drapery and intended to look as if the sitters were posing before a large picture window. Annie was placed at the centre, upon a chair, while John was directed to stand beside her and to lean with casual authority against a wood and plaster plinth. As this was a photograph commemorating the start of a new marriage, the photographer rested a Bible on Annie's lap. Annie, a wife and would-be mother, was to be the family guardian of all that was sacred in the state of matrimony: fidelity, fecundity, compassion, meekness, servility and cleanliness of body and soul.

When the photographer removed the camera's lens cap and exposed the negative to the light, he caught Annie and John as they were in May 1869. Mrs Chapman was no stranger to the fashions she saw displayed along the pavements of Knightsbridge and the tree-lined promenades of Hyde Park. As she sits against the back of the chair, the shape of her corset is visible from beneath her dress. Her gown, in a check pattern with small black buttons along the front of her bodice and dark piping around her cuffs and shoulders, is draped about her tapered bell-shaped crinoline, very much à la mode in 1868–9. Although the Chapmans were not wealthy, Annie's dress does not lack ornamentation. In addition to her wedding ring, little gold hoops hang from her ears, and a large ornate brooch sits at her throat, while her waist is cinched in by a dark belt with a prominent gilt clasp. John, too, in his frock coat, one leg crossed and an arm leant with easy confidence on the furniture, displays the gold chains and fobs of that essential piece of coachman's equipment: his pocket watch. Although neither Annie nor John might be considered conventionally handsome by the standards of their era, both convey an air of assurance. From beneath a broad forehead framed by fashionably plaited dark hair, Annie's large blue eyes stare intently at the camera. John matches her expression with one of pride and a stern, down-turned Victorian mouth.

As having one's image recorded in daguerreotype had become a privilege widely available by the middle of the nineteenth century, the Chapmans might have chosen to celebrate their union cheaply and simply. For 5 shillings, it was possible to order a set of three cartes de visite, small 2½-by-3-inch photographs pasted on card. The less prestigious studios, which catered to the better-off working classes, offered customers a very plain image without furniture or backdrops, but John and Annie aspired to own a photograph that spoke more of their hopes for a prosperous future life, and they were willing to pay for it. The picture they ordered was a cabinet photograph, a larger size intended for framing, to be set on a mantel or side table in a middle-class parlour.

The couple had been married on 1 May of that year at All Saints Church on Ennismore Gardens in Knightsbridge, the place where the family had attended services since Annie had been a girl. It is likely they and the wedding party walked from Montpelier Place, Annie proudly parading through the neighbourhood on her bridal day. Emily signed as Annie's witness, and John was attended by his colleague, a fellow coachman called George White, with whom the newly-weds are believed to have shared a house at 1 Brooks Mews North, shortly after they were married.[1]

Annie, the daughter of a gentleman's valet, had done well to have married a gentleman's coachman. John Chapman was not a hackney-cab driver, the sort known to loaf about in the pubs with a glass of brandy, to speak in strings of swear words and frequently spend the night asleep in the back of his cab; nor was he a hassled omnibus driver, who hauled common working people east to west or north to south. A private coachman was one employed by a wealthy family as the head or second driver of his master or mistress's vehicles. The primary coachman would be given charge of the larger, prestigious carriages such as the barouche, which required two horses, whereas the second coachman would drive vehicles drawn by a single horse. Much like the position occupied by Annie's father, her husband's role as coachman placed him near to the top of the servants' hierarchy. Unlike most other domestics attached to a household, the coachman was granted a certain degree of independence. If married, he and his family were expected to live in the mews adjacent to or above the stables, where he could keep watch over the groom's activities and maintain his master's vehicles and horses. Although he might opt to dine with the upper servants in the housekeeper's room, he more regularly took his meals alongside his wife, in their own home. In London, where some extensive residences had their own mews and stabling, a coachman might live rent-free, or in other cases an allowance would be granted that would permit the coachman to choose his own lodgings, provided they were nearby.

In the 1860s, John might have expected to have earned between 35 and 80 pounds per year depending upon the social standing of his employer. This sum did not include tips, which would have further padded his wages. Employers were also expected to provide their coachmen with at least one or two sets of stable dress for labouring and one livery (or uniform) that included two pairs of boots and two hats – as these were known to blow away in inclement weather. These benefits would have allowed John's family a slightly better quality of life. Money could be set aside, which might then fan the flames of the couple's aspirations.

Socially, much like the family of the gentleman's valet, the private, London-based coachman and his dependants occupied an awkward no-man's land within the territory of the working classes. Described as 'one of the most important and comfortable' within a retinue of servants, the coachman 'presides over a little establishment of his own; his horses and coach, as well as the stables, are all tended by "help" ', while he 'looks forth from his elevated position with an aspect of stolid gravity'.[2] A private coachman's privilege was known to give his family, and especially his wife, delusions of grandeur. Mayhew comments that most coachmen boasted that their positions meant their spouses did not have to work, as they 'can keep [their] wives too respectable for that'. Some families were well enough resourced to hire a maid of their own, or even to send their daughters to boarding school. However, these trappings of middle-class life rubbed against realities of their accommodation in the narrow mews, strung with laundry lines and smelling of stables. Still, their humble homes, usually with three or four rooms, one of which was designated as respectable parlour, were located in some of the country's most aristocratic districts.

This was especially true for John and Annie. In the first eight years of their marriage, John worked for a family in Onslow Square, an employer who lived near Jermyn Street, in St James's, and 'for a nobleman on Bond Street'.[3] Their little houses sat in the shadows of imperial London, a short stroll from the imposing gentlemen's clubs of Pall Mall and the gates of Buckingham Palace. Annie's daily walks would have taken her past the twinkling, gas-lit shop windows of Piccadilly and Bond Street and through the Burlington Arcade, with its colourful displays of the latest hats, shoes, walking sticks, glassware, jewellery, lace, watches, cigars, flowers and wine. The busy thoroughfares rattled with the conveyances of statesmen and society beauties, en route to Westminster or the rooms of the newly built Criterion for tea. It is likely that Annie was more than just a spectator of these pleasures, but partook of them as well. John's salary would have afforded a few purchases: gloves, a nice bonnet, a book from Hatchard's, a peek at the wonders of the Egyptian Hall or the Royal Academy at Burlington House.

While life in London held many benefits for a private coachman, John's work could come and go like the tide. Employers who engaged staff while they dwelt in the capital were often there only for a few years or a season or two. An ideal situation would be a more permanent one, with a landed family whose main residence lay outside London. Given the series of tragedies to have befallen the Smiths, it is likely that Annie and John remained in London on account of her reluctance to part with her mother and siblings. As John was the only adult male in the family, he too may have come under pressure to oversee the interests of Ruth, Emily, Georgina, Miriam and young Fountaine, who had only recently won a place as a boarding pupil at the Grey Coat School in Westminster. Even after their marriage, the couple returned regularly for visits and slightly longer sojourns at 29 Montpelier Place. In 1870, rather than summoning Ruth to assist her in the birth of her first child, Annie returned to the sanctuary of her mother's home in anticipation of the first pangs of labour. On 25 June, she delivered a little girl, whom she gave the name of Emily Ruth, the two women with whom she shared the closest bonds. By 1873, this child was joined by a sister, Annie Georgina.

Much as she had done on the occasion of her marriage, Annie would later insist on having photographs taken of her little girls. At the end of 1878, Annie dressed eight-year-old Emily Ruth in her best clothes: a tartan dress with a large bow at the neck and a set of buttons running down the front. She put her in a pair of striped stockings and boots and tied a ribbon at the top of her shoulder-length brown hair. A final touch: a large necklace of girlish beads was strung about her neck before her mother took her down the Brompton Road to the studio of Wood & Co. The photographer, who was an expert in coaxing even the worst-behaved children into position, got the wan, delicate-looking Emily to lean her elbow against a writing table, as if she were posing in a schoolroom. Three years later, this exercise was performed again with Annie Georgina. While bringing the child on a visit to her grandmother, Annie dressed her youngest daughter in the handed-down frock and beads her sister had worn and went down the Brompton Road to the Sutch Brothers' studio. She showed the photographer Emily Ruth's picture and instructed him to pose a slightly more robust-looking Annie in precisely the same manner, though against a different backdrop. When placed side-by-side, in a frame, the daughters, both captured at the same age, in the same clothing, gazed towards one another.

The timing of the first of these pictures was significant in that it marked a change in the Chapmans' fortunes. It is likely that a copy of Emily Ruth's photo was intended for her grandmother, as by the beginning of 1879 John had accepted a position as the head coachman to Francis Tress Barry, a gentleman of considerable wealth with a country estate in Berkshire. The Chapmans could not have hoped for a more promising opportunity.

Like many nineteenth-century industrialists, Francis Tress Barry had come from a relatively ordinary upper-middle-class family. Born in 1825, he completed his schooling at sixteen and entered directly into the world of business. After having established himself as a merchant in northern Spain, Barry began to explore the possibilities available in the copper mines of Portugal. It was here that he made his fortune and eventually became the head of his own successful mining firm, Mason and Barry. The honours and sinecures that he required to rise in society soon followed. In 1872 he was made the Consul General for the Republic of Ecuador and in 1876 he was created Baron de Barry of Portugal. However, acquiring similar recognition in Britain demanded a good deal more patience and strategy. It was not until 1890 that he was elected an MP for Windsor, and nine years later was granted a baronetcy by Queen Victoria.

Barry was a savvy entrepreneur and his purchase of the estate of St Leonard's Hill in 1872 was an obvious move designed to place himself and his family under the nose of the queen. The 62-acre estate in Clewer, a village at the periphery of Windsor, was said to 'yield one of the noblest views of the castle from its eastern lawn'. Additionally, it boasted of over '230 acres of old park and forest', home to 'gigantic oaks, stately beech, elm, fir and Californian redwood'. The property also came with an impressive pedigree. Its manor house had been built in the eighteenth century for Maria, Countess Waldegrave, and later came into the possession of the Earls Harcourt. However, when Barry acquired it, his intention was to create an elegant and impressive stately home in the most modern fashion. His vision was placed in the hands of architect Charles Henry Howell, who set about constructing an industrialist's palace in the modish French-chateau style. While Howell maintained some of the original eighteenth-century rooms, he rebuilt much of the house and added many uniquely late-Victorian features. When guests entered the Mexican-onyx-lined central hall of St Leonard's Hill, they were greeted by an imposing staircase and frescos depicting scenes from Grecian mythology. There were grand reception rooms: a dining room, large and small drawing rooms, and, through a set of mahogany doors, a winter garden. Upstairs contained six suites of bedrooms, and, as Japanese decor had become the rage, Barry had an entire suite created in this style. On the ground floor, he would be able to entertain lavishly with a billiard room, a smoking room and a card room, as well as a library. As Barry wished St Leonard's Hill to have only the most modern conveniences, an early central-heating system was installed, as well as conventional fires, gas lighting, hot running water, toilets and two hydraulic service lifts. Such a residence could not have been managed without a full complement of employees and so Howell created a downstairs service area large enough to accommodate a staff of thirty servants.

John Chapman had been hired not only to drive Francis Tress Barry's coach, but to maintain and supervise the running of his stable block, which, like his employer's house, was a considerable affair. The stables were built in a similar style to the mansion and intended to house no fewer than thirty horses and several vehicles. Upon assuming his position, John became the master of two grooms, four stablemen and a second coachman. The handling of the stable's accounts, and the ordering of feed, supplies and equipment, also fell into his charge. As Barry was one of the wealthiest and most prominent landowners in the area, John's duty was to represent him from atop his employer's highly polished carriage, in a tall hat, shining boots and with a clean-shaven face. To most villagers and inhabitants of Windsor, Barry would only ever be known by his passing coach, and his coachman had to ensure his master left an impeccable impression.

John's position of prestige at St Leonard's Hill entitled him and his family to live in the coachman's house, across the yard from the stables. For Annie, who had been accustomed to life in London's mews, this was a significant improvement. The coachman's cottage was a house of a different scale, consisting of a sitting room or formal parlour, a living room, where the family would dine and spend most of their time, a kitchen, scullery, wash house, larder and three bedrooms.[4] The family photographs in their neat frames would now have a proper room in which to be displayed.

If it had been Annie's aspiration to officially enter the middle class, then their arrival at St Leonard's Hill facilitated this. With a reasonably sized home and a comfortable income, Mrs Chapman would have hired a charwoman or a day maid to assist her with her more laborious home-making tasks. Once the family had settled into their new life, the Chapmans sought to place nine-year-old Emily Ruth in 'a highly respectable' young ladies' school in Windsor.[5] When not at school, Annie and her children had the use of Francis Tress Barry's parkland and forests in which to wander and amuse themselves, and should the coachman's wife wish to visit the shops in Windsor, she would have the use of one of the estate's 'fly' carriages to convey her into town.

The sense of having successfully scaled a rung up the social ladder was an achievement of which Annie grew proud – even, on occasion, boastful. In the spring of 1881, Annie brought her children on a visit to 29 Montpelier Place. Her sojourn at her mother's house happened to coincide with that year's census. When John, still at St Leonard's Hill, was asked to provide his 'rank, profession or occupation', he did not hesitate to describe himself as a 'coachman, domestic servant'. Mrs Chapman, on the other hand, claimed she was 'the wife of a stud groom'. While it is entirely possible that John's responsibilities had been extended to include the purchase and breeding of racing stock for Barry, Annie's identification of herself as such points to grander ambitions. The landed gentry venerated stud grooms. As the manager of a man's racehorses, his knowledge of equine flesh and his ability to breed winners rendered him a type of oracle. The stud groom had his master's ear and his respect, and, with this, the divide of the classes might be slightly breached. A stud groom stood apart from the others in a stable; he might be invited to carouse with other sporting gentlemen, taken to race meets, and asked to dine with his master. In this, he would become something more than a coachman ever could; he would become a confidant of the upper ranks of society.

Francis Tress Barry also understood that the nearer a man placed himself to the social class above him, the better chance he had of manoeuvring into it. Since the completion of St Leonard's Hill in 1878, Barry had made a concerted effort to announce his arrival with rounds of dinners and gatherings. He took his place among the established landowners of Clewer – Sir Daniel Gooch, Sir Theodore Henry Brinckman and Edmund Benson Foster – but in the end, it was not necessarily Barry's conviviality that won the friendship of Edward, Prince of Wales and Princess Alexandra, but rather the location of St Leonard's Hill, just 4 miles from Ascot Racecourse.

On 15 June 1881 Barry obligingly gave his house over to the royal party for Ascot week. Among those hosted at St Leonard's Hill were the Duke of Cambridge, the Earl and Countess Spencer, the Countess Lonsdale, the Earls of Fife and Clonmell, Rear Admiral the Honourable H. Carr Glyn and his wife, and a number of the Prince of Wales's wealthy associates who enjoyed the turf and his fast living. Two visits to the races in semi-state were planned for the Tuesday and Thursday, to be followed by a series of private entertainments, including a picnic and boating party at nearby Virginia Water, and a modest ball at St Leonard's Hill for 'some of the parties in the neighbourhood' on the second to last night.[6] This week-long house party would have been months in the planning and while John would have been occupied with juggling the carriages and horses of the royal guests, Annie would have been able to watch the spectacle from afar.

On each occasion, the royal cortège set out for Ascot from the house in five open-topped landaus led by 'Her Majesty's bay and grey horses sent from the Royal mews at Windsor'.[7] Flanked by outriders and postilions in livery they proceeded down the drive and through Windsor Forest as all the estate looked on at the excitement. The sight of their return in the afternoon would have been no less thrilling: the ladies in their frilled, feathered, flowered bonnets and veils; Princess Alexandra's unmistakable curls; the Prince of Wales beneath his hat and triangular beard, fat and bored. Later in evening, they might be seen walking about Francis Tress Barry's grounds, trailing bustled skirts and shadows behind them. St Leonard's Hill had done the trick for Barry and drawn him firmly into the prince's circle.

The royals and their retinue would be back for further dinners and events, shooting parties and races. The sounds of merry-making, music and laughter would have blown down from the house to the nearby coachman's cottage: the cottage where Annie's children slumbered in their own bedrooms, the cottage with a sitting room, the cottage that had brought constancy and what should have been contentment. This might have been Annie's story in its entirety; it might have ended in quiet, middle-class comfort on a gentleman's estate with the Chapmans carefully saving their pennies to pay for their children's schooling and John's retirement to a little house in Windsor. Their girls might have grown up and married middle-class men: a shopkeeper, a clerk, even a solicitor. The courses of all of their lives might have ended quite differently had Annie Chapman not been an alcoholic.

7

Demon Drink

IN 1889, A LETTER from a confirmed teetotaller and committed Christian appeared in the *Pall Mall Gazette*.[1] Throughout the nineteenth century, newspapers were accustomed to receiving correspondence such as this from the many adherents of the Temperance Movement, which sought to restrict the sale and consumption of alcohol. However, this letter differed from those offering the usual condemnation and biblical quotes. It was written by a parishioner in Knightsbridge, a woman by the name of Miriam Smith.

'Just before I was six years old, my father cut his throat, leaving my mother with five children, three girls older, and one [child] younger than myself,' her missive began. She then went on to provide details of how she and her sisters came to sign the abstinence pledge, in which they promised to forgo the use of all 'fermented spirits'. All but her eldest sister had committed themselves to this path. 'We tried to persuade the one given to drink to give it up. She was married and in a good position. Over and over again she signed the pledge and tried to keep it. Over and over again she was tempted and fell.'

Annie's struggle had been a lifelong one. Miriam suggested that her sister had inherited 'the curse' of alcoholism from their father, and that her problem began 'when she was quite young'. How young, precisely, she does not say, but it is likely that Annie's discovery of the pacifying effects of the bottle may have corresponded with the loss of her siblings and her placement in service shortly thereafter. Alcohol's presence in daily life was ubiquitous, if not almost unavoidable. Any middle-class house, aside from those that had adopted abstinence, would have had brandy, sherry, sweet wine or some form of spirit on hand to imbibe as a 'tonic' for anything from a headache to a cold, a fever, a toothache, or to rub on the gums of teething children. Spirits and medicine were almost interchangeable: a hot brandy and water was taken as a sleep aid, to ward off the chill, and to dispel malaise. The principal ingredient of most shop-bought curatives for everything from coughs to rheumatism was alcohol. The 'dose' and the 'dram' might even taste and smell identical, and, but for the fact that medicines often contained an additional addictive substance such as laudanum or cocaine, their frequent usage usually ended similarly – in dependency.

Like many for whom drinking becomes an issue, Annie, in the early years of her disease, when she was still a servant, may not have even perceived that her consumption had become a problem. During the mid-nineteenth century, working-class amusement still revolved around the convivial drink and the camaraderie to be found in the neighbourhood pub, where servants would congregate during a spare hour or on their day off. Habitual drunkenness was only an issue when it impinged on an employee's ability to perform their job; however, by the 1870s, when the concept of addiction had been identified, it took on more sinister implications. Drunkenness, especially when it was noticeable and public, came to be seen as a reflection of a person's degenerate character: their 'intemperate' nature, their poor judgement, their moral weakness, their idleness. More significantly, conspicuous inebriation was something that became associated with the poor and the 'uncouth' working classes. Those who wished to affect a middle-class identity, like Annie did after her marriage, would have attempted to conceal or deny their growing dependency. This was easily accomplished when one had a stock of medicinal brandy, cordials or whisky on hand in a cabinet, or a headache meant a trip to the high-street chemist for a little bottle of spirit laced with laudanum. In a pinch, the baby's gripe water might be drunk, with no one being any the wiser.

For a time, Annie would have been relatively successful in hiding her addiction within the confines of her home, though not from her family. Often the tendency to drink was precipitated by a sense of loneliness, especially, as one commentator remarks, 'in young wives whose husbands are away all day'. Curiously, this was the paradox of upward social mobility: a wife who doesn't have to work, who can afford a maid and whose children are at school, has to find some way of distracting herself. As a coachman, John's very early and exceptionally late hours would not have made for much sociability at home, if indeed he returned home. His work was liable to take him on lengthy excursions, which would have left Annie quite isolated, especially after the Chapmans had moved to St Leonard's Hill. It was suggested that middle-class women in such circumstances often 'acquired the habit of "nipping"' in order to ward off their melancholy spirits. By the last quarter of the nineteenth century, the appearance of 'ladies' saloon bars' meant that having a wee 'nip' in public might also be veiled with respectability. Moralists complained that it was 'now the regular thing for women to go in and have a drink when shopping', and it was not unusual to see a well-dressed woman joining her husband or son for a tipple. As London boasted twenty thousand pubs by 1870, there would have been no shortage of opportunities for Annie to have taken 'refreshment' either inside or outside her home.

It was perhaps Annie's drinking and a desire to remove her from the temptations of city life that played a role in John's decision to accept Francis Tress Barry's offer of a position at St Leonard's Hill. Unfortunately, so long as his wife desired drink, it would never be entirely out of reach. Far from her mother and sisters, Annie was likely to have felt a greater sense of isolation and boredom, which would have only increased her itch to self-medicate with alcohol. The public houses of Windsor were easily accessible during an excursion to the shops, as were the drinking establishments of Clewer and Dedworth villages, only a short stroll from home.

The practicalities of keeping Annie away from drink was but one of the challenges the couple faced in their life together. Miriam Smith's letter to the newspaper reveals that over the course of her sister's marriage, she gave birth to eight children, though 'six of these have been victims to the curse [of alcohol]'. Annie's first child, Emily, bore the appearance of a healthy infant, but by the time she was eight, began to suffer from epileptic seizures. Emily's illness may not at the time have been associated with her mother's addiction, but today such disorders have been linked to maternal drinking during pregnancy. On 5 March 1872, Annie gave birth to a second daughter, Ellen Georgina, who lived no more than a day. The following year, Annie Georgina was born with what is now recognized as Foetal Alcohol Syndrome, the physical characteristics of which – small, wide-set eyes, a thin upper lip and a smooth ridge that runs below the nose to the top lip – are clearly distinguishable in her childhood photograph. Annie's two little girls were briefly joined by another; Georgina, born on 25 April 1876, who only lived until 5 May. Shortly before the Chapmans left London, Annie gave birth to George William Harry in November 1877.[2] The infant was born sickly and died eleven weeks later. Annie was soon pregnant again and delivered Miriam Lily on the St Leonard's Hill estate on 16 July 1879. She survived a week less than her brother and died in October. On 21 November 1880, John Alfred arrived. This boy, the last of the Chapmans' children to be born, suffered from paralysis.[3] As Miriam's letter suggested, it was obvious to Annie's family, and perhaps to Annie too, what lay at the heart of this series of tragedies. Late-nineteenth-century science had already begun to uncover and make known the links between maternal alcohol consumption and the dangers it posed for children. As early as 1878, one medical journal asserted that substantial evidence had been gathered to prove that 'drunkenness in the parent before and after birth has more effect on infant mortality than all other causes'.[4] The realization that her drinking was likely to have been behind the suffering of her children may have pushed Annie deeper into despair at her inability to control her impulses. By 1881, the difficulties she experienced in remaining sober while also caring for an infant with a disability may have lain behind her prolonged visit to her mother when John Alfred was about four months old. While in London, it is also believed Annie sought to place her son in an appropriate hospital for children.

At the time of Annie's visit to 29 Montpelier Place in the early spring, her sisters, Emily Latitia and Miriam, had set up as dressmakers in their own home at 128 Walton Street, a road that ran to the rear of the recently expanded Harrods department store. According to Miriam's account, she and her sisters had become Presbyterians as well as embraced teetotalism after 'hearing a sermon on Christians and Total Abstinence'.

The complete rejection of alcohol was a stance that resonated particularly with those balanced precariously on the edge of middle-class life. It also went hand-in-hand with the popular philosophy of 'self-help', which blamed poverty on an individual's own behaviour and lack of responsibility for their choices in life. By eschewing alcohol, not only could a hard-working man or woman save money, but build a better life for themselves and their families, a creed to which Annie's sisters not only subscribed, but through which they prospered financially. Signing the 'abstinence pledge' in the presence of one's family or a member of the clergy was viewed as a solemn promise to adhere to the principles of teetotalism, and all that accompanied it: a restriction of one's impulses, a moderation of desires and a conscious effort at moral improvement. What becomes obvious from Miriam's letter is that Annie desperately did want to give up drink, but found it almost impossible. Her sisters had convinced her several times to take the pledge, they prayed for her and with her in her difficulties, but could not get her to adhere to it permanently. It is likely that during her visit in 1881, they were able to witness how desperately she struggled, and the degree to which the disease had truly taken hold.

In the following year, her battle with addiction came to a head. Towards the end of that November, her eldest daughter, twelve-year old Emily Ruth, began to sicken. When the child's high temperature gave way to a spreading red rash, Annie would have recalled the signs and symptoms of scarlet fever, the disease that had devastated her family when she was a girl. The doctors came and went, and eventually informed Emily's mother that her child was afflicted with meningitis, which bore similar traits and was no less life-threatening. It appears that Annie did not deal well with her daughter's raging illness. As the days passed and Emily's condition worsened, Annie drew support from her usual source: the bottle and the stultifying haze its contents threw across her distress. When her daughter died on the 26th of that month, Annie was not present at her bedside. Instead, the wife of a local farm labourer, Caroline Elsbury, who may also have charred for the Chapman family, tended to the girl in her dying moments.[5]

At some point, prior to the autumn, Annie had begun to acquire a reputation among the local police and Windsor magistrates for public drunkenness. She had been found wandering between the villages and along the roads from the St Leonard's Hill estate. From all accounts, the coachman's wife did not make for an ugly drunk, but rather, a sad, sullen, quiet one, weighed down by her heartache. During that final week of November her pain would have been unbearable.

It is unknown for how long Annie had absented herself or where she was eventually found; ensconced in a public house or swaying down the road in Clewer in search of respite. Whatever the circumstances, her behaviour was enough to raise serious alarm among her family. On the 30th, the same day that the Chapmans buried their daughter, Annie's sisters, Emily and Miriam, paid an urgent visit to the Spelthorne Sanatorium, on the outskirts of London.

In 1879, growing public concern about the societal impact of alcoholism gave rise to the Habitual Drunkards Act. The law, which sought to offer rehabilitation for alcoholics as opposed to punishment in prison, was responsible for the establishment of asylums or sanatoria for the treatment of those 'who by a means of habitual intemperate drinking of intoxicating liquor is dangerous to . . . herself, or to others, or incapable of managing . . . herself, and . . . her affairs'. Patients were to be admitted into these 'retreats' either voluntarily or 'upon the application of their friends' and were required to spend at least a month but no more than two years in treatment. Spelthorne Sanatorium in Feltham was one such institution, designed especially for the treatment of women, predominantly of the middle class.

On 9 December 1882, the entry in the Spelthorne Sanatorium log book reads: 'Mrs Chapman arrived – brought by her sister from Windsor'. As Miriam's account asserts, Annie agreed to enter this 'home for the intemperate . . . of her own accord'. This process involved writing a formal letter of application to the head of Spelthorne, which was then witnessed by a J.P. As Francis Tress Barry, her own landlord, held that title in Berkshire, it is possible that he may also have had some hand in her admission for treatment.

It is likely that the Misses Smith had been told of Spelthorne before their sister was in urgent need of its support. Its founders, the Antrobus family, who lived in Knightsbridge, would have drawn their charitable cause to the attention of local clergy, who spread the word among their parishioners.[6] As alcohol dependency was viewed in part as a weakness of the will, the type of rehabilitation offered at the sanatorium was largely spiritual in nature. However, in addition to prescribing daily attendance at chapel, the programme also sought to correct the habits of mind and body. Spelthorne's setting on four acres, surrounded by yew trees and country lanes, was believed to be the sort of clean, uplifting and health-promoting environment that also improved the spirit. Its facilities and dormitories, situated within 'a fine old country house', were decorated with 'gaily-striped counterpanes, suitable pictures and texts' and 'plain yet shining furniture' intended to draw 'the mind away from thoughts of debasing self-indulgence'.[7] The institution's 'patients' (a term used in place of 'inmate' so as not to 'wound the pride') were encouraged to walk and amuse themselves on the grounds when not cultivating the two kitchen gardens, or working in the laundry, washing, drying and ironing their and their fellow patients' clothes. Any form of idleness was to be discouraged, as it often gave way to cravings. Instead, the women were allowed to read and encouraged to produce crochet and needlework, which would be displayed during inspections by their board members and donors. When women had demonstrated a suitable level of progress, they would be reintroduced slowly to the outside world and its temptations. This would usually involve escorted walks through the local area or even shopping excursions to nearby Hounslow. Inmates were also given regular treats, such as 'musical evenings' or group outings to London, presumably to stave off fits of melancholy and despair, to which married patients were especially prone.

Annie had committed herself to a year-long programme of treatment. According to the log books, her time at Spelthorne was relatively quiet. Her name isn't recorded among the occasional troublemakers, the women who found giving up alcohol nearly impossible, who tore their clothing, destroyed furniture, or who lashed out in violence. She was permitted visitors as well. On 30 December, shortly after she arrived at the sanatorium, the log book records that 'Mrs Chapman's husband called to see her'. John must have been very worried about his wife to have begged leave from his obligations to the Barrys during the height of the Christmas social calendar. It was he who was paying the expense of her treatment, at a cost of 12 pence per week.

Shortly before she was discharged, in November 1883, it appears that Annie was permitted to make a short visit home, perhaps to assess her readiness to resume her old life. She seems to have passed this simple test and returned on the 14th to Spelthorne to complete the final month of her programme. She was officially released on 20 December in the company of one of the nursing sisters, Laura Squire, who, it is recorded, 'took Mrs Chapman to Windsor to join her husband'.

That Christmas and New Year period would have been a joyful (and dry) one among the Chapman family, now four in number. As Miriam writes, her sister 'came out a changed woman – a sober wife and mother, and things went on very happily'.

The story which Annie's sister then goes on to relate sounds almost apocryphal: like a cautionary tale from a teetotaller's handbook. Several months after Annie's reunion with her family, John was stricken with 'a severe cold'. As 'his duty compelled him to go out', he 'took a glass of hot whiskey' in order to fortify himself against the poor weather. With a bottle under the roof of her own house, it was remarkable that Annie managed to resist temptation for as long as she had. John 'had been careful enough not to have it in her presence'. He 'drank it and came to kiss her before departing. In that kiss the fumes of alcohol were transmitted and all the cravings came back.'

According to Miriam, that kiss quite literally brought about the death of everything Annie had fought to achieve.

She must have turned over every room for that bottle. It did not matter in the end whether she found it. 'She went out' and 'in less than an hour was a drunken mad woman'.

Annie's failure, after more than a year of progress, completely devastated her. 'She never tried again,' lamented her sister. Annie said to her, in words that are redolent with the profound suffering of the chronic alcoholic, 'it was of no use, no one knew the fearful struggle . . . unless I can keep out of sight and smell, I can never be free'.

John had arrived at this realization as well. His wife's return to her old habits found her once more wandering stupefied through the St Leonard's Hill estate. In the past, the Barrys had been lenient with their coachman and his wife's problems. Her residency at Spelthorne may have come about as a result of a gentle ultimatum issued by the family. Now that they moved in society's highest circles, they could not afford the embarrassment of harbouring a notorious and unpredictable inebriate on their grounds. Spelthorne was intended to cure Annie, and the failure of this plan was the last straw. Francis Barry made it known to his coachman that he would not indulge Mrs Chapman any longer. Either John was to remove her from his home or Barry would dismiss him.[8]

Although John had served his master since 1879, it is unlikely he would have received the sort of reference necessary to acquire another job as well-remunerated or prestigious. As the father of two children, one severely disabled, it was necessary that he consider their long-term welfare.

The decision to separate appears to have been an amicable one, but not without heartbreak for both parties. John's devotion to his wife, in spite of her affliction, demonstrates nothing short of genuine love. It would have been out of character for him to have simply cut adrift the mother of his children and, in her fragile state, set her loose into the world. As placing Annie at Spelthorne had involved her entire family, so too would they have a role to play in deciding what now was to become of her. When John made arrangements to pay Annie a maintenance of 10 shillings a week, it was almost certainly with a view to having her return to her mother's home. Back at 29 Montpelier Place, Ruth as well as Annie's siblings would be able to keep watch over her. Ten shillings a week, some of which would have assisted Ruth in keeping her daughter, would have gone a long way towards buying some comfort and a few of the middle-class luxuries to which Annie had grown accustomed: perfumed soaps and inexpensive pieces of jewellery. She would be better off with her sisters' devotion, John would have reasoned, and perhaps might even stand a chance of recovering. With the support of her beloved family, Annie might just be all right.

8

Dark Annie

ALTHOUGH JOHN'S SCHEME HAD been well-intentioned, it lasted little longer than it took for Annie to arrive in London. Whether it was a matter of weeks or days, Annie would have found it impossible to live under the auspices of her family. Neither her mother nor her sisters would have tolerated her drinking. The shame of her affliction, the shame of her inability to cure herself of it and, now, the shame of having failed as a mother and a wife, would have made a relationship with them almost impossible for her to bear. Miriam writes that her sister had told them 'she would always keep out of our way' but that 'she must and would have the drink'. Ultimately, Annie, like so many addicts, chose a life without those she loved, rather than a life without the substance she craved.

In previous attempts to recount the events of Annie Chapman's life, one of the greatest oversights has always been a failure to examine how someone who had lived on a country estate in Berkshire or who had resided in Knightsbridge ended up in Whitechapel. This alteration in circumstances would not have happened overnight, as both geographically as well as socially it is not a natural trajectory. A sudden slip into financial hardship would not have necessitated a relocation from Knightsbridge in the west of the capital to the slums of

Whitechapel in the east. The East End did not possess a mon-
opoly on cheap lodgings; they, along with destitution and
criminality, could be found in large and small pockets throughout London. If Annie had found life insufferable at her mother's
house, she needn't have travelled any further than the streets
across from Knightsbridge barracks to find a 4-penny-a-night
lodging house or a room for 5 shillings a week. Had she wished
to avoid her family altogether, she might have strayed further
afield to the down-at-heel neighbourhoods of nearby Chelsea,
Fulham or Battersea, or ventured into the centre of London,
to Marylebone, Holborn, Paddington, St Giles, even to Clerkenwell or Westminster, or south of the river to Lambeth,
Southwark or Bermondsey. There was no obvious reason why
Annie, who had passed most of her life between Knightsbridge
and the West End of London, would have had any cause or
inclination to move to a part of town with which she had no
familiarity; unless, of course, she knew of or accompanied
someone there.

In the late nineteenth century, Notting Hill, which lay just
across Hyde Park and to the west, had become notorious for its
working-class housing and deprivation. While many of its
streets are marked in black on Charles Booth's poverty map
and are condemned in the notebooks of Booth's social research-
ers as 'hopelessly degraded', others are simply described as
being occupied by the working poor: residents whose windows were covered with 'dirty curtains' and whose children
wore 'threadbare clothes'.[1] Notting Hill's proximity to the
area of the city Annie knew best, while also lying beyond the
immediate reach of her family, would have made the location
a likely place for her to have settled. Here, she might maintain
herself quietly, collecting her weekly allowance from the post
office, while living in a single room and pursuing her drinking

undisturbed. As an addict in a new community, it would not have been long before Annie discovered fellow-travellers among her neighbours, especially in the local beer houses and pubs. While at one such establishment it is likely that she became acquainted with a man whom her friends would come to call 'Jack Sievey'. 'Sievey' or 'Sievy', it seems, had acquired his name on account of his profession as a wire or iron sieve-maker. Little more is known about him other than that he had a connection with Notting Hill and that he and Annie eventually became a pair, almost certainly on account of their shared love of drink.

It is difficult to fathom the emotional despair to which Annie must have succumbed when agreeing to part with her husband and children, and after turning her back on her mother and siblings. As one whose family subscribed to religious teachings and who strove to maintain respectability, Annie would have perceived her fall as an unredeemable one. According to the era's definition of womanhood, she had failed. She had proven her inability to mother her children, to maintain a home for her husband or to care for anyone, even herself. The female drunkard was considered an abomination, one who allowed 'their most brutal and repulsive penchants to come to the surface', one who 'abandons herself to sensuality, and who . . . becomes unsexed in her manners'.[2] Perversely, it was the self-recognition of her disgrace that kept the 'female inebriate' drinking 'in order to drown her shame'. Although her transgressions may not have been of a sexual nature, Victorian society conflated the broken woman with the fallen woman. The woman who had lost her marriage and her home through her moral weakness was viewed with no less abhorrence than the woman who had engaged in extra-marital sex. A woman who was 'drunk and disorderly', who embarrassed herself in public, who demonstrated no regard for her appear-ance, who did not have a respectable home or a husband or family to regulate her conduct, was judged to be as much of a degenerate as a prostitute. They became one and the same: outcast women. Just as was the case with Polly Nichols, Annie's precarious position as a lone woman demanded that she find a male partner, despite the fact that she was still legally married. Whether or not she wished to throw in her lot with another man, her circumstances compelled her into what society would consider a state of adultery. However, as Annie was already considered morally ruined, this no longer mattered.

It would have been on account of Annie's ties to Sievey that she followed him to Whitechapel during the second half of 1884 in search of work. Since her arrival in that part of town, all that remained of Annie's identity – the daughter of a guards-man, the wife of a gentleman's coachman, the mother of two children, the woman who strolled through Mayfair and Hyde Park, who sat proudly for her photograph in gold hoop ear-rings and a brooch – was left behind in west London. Annie was only ever known as Sievey's wife – Annie Sievey or Mrs Sievey – and, occasionally, as 'Dark Annie', on account of her wavy brown hair, now streaked with grey. Annie did not speak much of her past, so that even her new friends, includ-ing the kind and loyal Amelia Palmer, the wife of a former dock worker, were told only scant facts. When asked about chil-dren, Annie gave mocking answers, that she had a son who was unwell and 'in hospital' and a daughter 'who had joined the circus', or 'who lived abroad in France'. She told no one but Amelia the truth, that she had been separated from her hus-band who lived in Windsor, and that she had a mother and sisters with whom 'she was not on friendly terms'. Amelia remarked that in spite of this, her friend remained 'a very respectable woman' whom she 'never heard use bad language'. She also described her as 'straightforward' and 'a very clever and industrious little body' when she was sober.[3]

According to Amelia Palmer, the two friends met when Annie and Jack Sievey lived in Dorset Street in Whitechapel. Although Dorset Street would not be crowned 'the worst street in London' until the 1890s, its reputation for despair and degradation preceded this. Even in the decade before, it was composed almost exclusively of the cheapest, filthiest lodging houses and 'furnished rooms'. Journalists and social reformers who visited it remarked that it was thronged with criminality. Even Charles Booth, who had walked nearly every byway of the capital, wrote in a state of near-disbelief at what he witnessed: 'The worst street I have seen so far, thieves, prostitutes, bullies, all common lodging houses.' The local police inspector who escorted him echoed his sentiments: 'In his opinion [this is] the worst street in respect of poverty, misery, vice, of the whole of London. A cesspool into which had sunk the foulest & most degraded.' He went on to remark that even Notting Hill or Notting Dale (as the poorest part was known) 'is not so bad as this. Notting Dalers . . . were very poor, shiftless & shifting; always on the move, poor tramps who might stay a month in the Dale and then move on doing the round of the London casual wards & ending up again in the Dale.' Dorset Street, he said, was different, it 'might be stirred but its filth will always sink again in the same spot'.[4]

At the time when Annie and her 'new husband' had come to live there, most of Dorset Street was owned by two landlords, John McCarthy and William Crossingham, each as ruthless and unprincipled as the other when it came to managing their crumbling, vice-teeming property portfolios. 'Mr and Mrs Sievey' were known to have inhabited lodging houses on the street, primarily number 30, where Amelia and her husband also lived, but when the pair had managed to reserve some money, they would rent a furnished room instead. While these rooms offered more privacy than a communal lodging house, many believed their condition to be 'infinitely worse'. For 10 pence a night, tenants might have a poorly ventilated room or one with broken windows, rotting wooden floors and ceilings with holes. Hot water was out of the question, and a stinking, malfunctioning toilet might be found at the top of the stairs or in the yard behind. The minimal furnishing was, according to a journalist from the *Daily Mail*, comprised of 'the oldest furniture to be found in the worst second-hand dealers in the slums. The fittings . . . are not worth more than a few shillings.'[5] Annie's new situation would have been a far cry from her parlour and living room at St Leonard's Hill. The recognition of this would have required still more drink to dull the memory and the emotions. The true tragedy of Annie's situation is that, unlike the majority of women by whom she was surrounded, she needn't have lived in such reduced circumstances on 'the worst street in London'. Jack Sievey would have brought in an income, and failing that, they could always rely on her 10 shillings a week, which would have paid for a better room elsewhere, as well as for food and coal. Instead it paid for alcohol – at least until December 1886.

It was in that month, quite without warning, that the weekly payments suddenly stopped. According to Amelia Palmer, Annie was so alarmed by this that she sought out her 'brother or sister-in-law' who she believed 'lived somewhere near Oxford Street in Whitechapel' in order to learn the cause.[6] John, she was informed, had fallen gravely ill. This news shook her so deeply that she determined she must see her husband and set off on foot to Windsor, in the midst of winter. She covered just over 25 miles in two days, trekking through west London and out beyond Brentford into the frozen countryside along the Bath Road. When it grew dark she sought shelter at the casual ward at Colnbrook. Treading this road, Annie would have had ample time to fret over her coming encounter, and worry about her children, even to feel heartsick at the thought of returning to Windsor and revisiting her past. All the while, the fear of arriving too late would have plagued her.

Staying the night at the casual ward set her back at least a morning, as she would have been required to pick her share of oakum in exchange for her bed.[7] When departing, she faced another 5 miles to New Windsor, the area she had known as a girl, off what was then called the Spital Road.[8]

Before she had set out, Annie had learned of John's retirement due to ill-health, six months earlier. Relations had informed her that he no longer lived on Francis Tress Barry's estate, but rather he had taken a house on Grove Road, where he lived with the children for a time. However, being uncertain of his precise address, Annie stopped at the Merry Wives of Windsor, a pub on the corner of the street, and enquired after her husband. The publican distinctly recalled the visit from what he described as 'a wretched-looking woman having the appearance of a tramp'. Annie told him that she had 'walked down from London' because she had 'been told that her husband, who had discontinued sending her ten shillings a week, was ill'. She then hardened her expression and claimed 'she had come to Windsor to ascertain if the report was true and not merely an excuse for not sending her the money as usual'.[9] The publican pointed her in the direction of John's house: 1 Richmond Villas, Grove Road, and 'did not see her again'.

What then occurred is unknown. Presumably, Annie

arrived prior to John's death on Christmas Day, though she did not linger long enough to witness it. At the time, he was being nursed by Sally Westell, an elderly friend from the nearby almshouses.[10] This reunion must have been a bitter one indeed. Annie's addiction and the collapse of their marriage had felled John completely. Shortly before his death at only forty-five, Miriam describes him as 'a white-haired, brokenhearted man', who, whether she knew it or not, also seemed to have taken to drinking. His death is cited on account of 'cirrhosis of the liver-ascites and dropsy'.[11]

John's death devastated Annie. Whatever mercenary reasons she had cited for marching to Windsor and back, her interest in seeing her husband was more than purely financial. When she returned to Dorset Street, she cried as she recounted the details of her ordeal to Amelia.[12] Annie would never be the same again. 'After the death of her husband,' her friend recalled, 'she seemed to give way altogether.'

Whether it was on account of losing the extra 10 shillings or because Annie had grown morose and mournful, Jack Sievey decided he was done with John Chapman's widow. In early 1887, he left her to return to Notting Hill. Now without either a husband or a common-law protector, Annie found herself truly unsupported. As few women found it easy to survive in the slums without a male companion, it became imperative that she find one.

For a time, she seems to have taken up with a hard-drinking pedlar of chapbooks called 'Harry the Hawker' who also inhabited the lodging houses of Dorset Street, but this relationship did not last long. As Amelia described, Annie was not happy; increasingly physically unwell, she was becoming 'a pitiful case', her life marked by 'drink and despondency . . . hunger and sickness'.[13] Certainly by 1887 she had begun to suffer from what appears to have been tuberculosis, which, according to George Bagster Phillips, the Divisional Surgeon of Police, had been long-standing at the time of her death and had begun to affect the brain tissue.[14] Although ill, Annie remained assiduous in her attempts to earn an income. According to Amelia, 'She used to do crochet work, make antimacassars, and sell matches and flowers.' Saturdays were spent 'selling anything she had' at Stratford Market, a hub for small traders who came from all over the surrounding countryside and East End. In the late summer of 1888, in spite of her deteriorating condition, Annie still insisted that she intended to join the annual migration into the fields of Kent to go hop-picking, if her sister would send her some boots.

Not surprisingly, it was during this unfortunate period of her friend's life that Amelia Palmer seemed to worry most about her. Curiously, Amelia claims that she 'was in the habit of writing letters for her friend' to 'her mother and sister' who she seemed to recall 'lived near Brompton hospital'.[15] This statement raises a number of questions as to why Annie, who was able to read and write, would permit this. Was she at times too unwell to write, and in need of money, or was she simply too ashamed to do the asking? Miriam in her account of events asserts that Annie would never disclose her address to them, undoubtedly on account of both shame and a fear that they might attempt to thwart her drinking. Nevertheless, although she remained estranged from them, Annie found it impossible to isolate herself from her family altogether. Miriam writes that, on occasion 'she used to come to us at home . . . we gave her clothes and tried in every way to win her back, for she was a mere beggar.'

The Smiths were heartbroken at the path Annie had chosen for herself, and do not seem to have refused her small amounts of financial assistance when she requested it. However, her younger brother Fountaine may have offered her slightly more than this. In his rather confused testimony at the coroner's inquest, Annie's sibling seemed to indicate that he had met with her on two occasions: first on the Commercial Road, and then, in what seems to have been an unplanned encounter, in Westminster. In one instance, Fountaine states he lent her 2 shillings, while in another that he gave her this money. What the newspapers do not report, however, is that, like her, Annie's brother was also an alcoholic, though one who had at least temporarily held down a job as a manager in a printer's warehouse. In truth, Fountaine may have seen more of his sister than he was willing to indicate, both to the public and to his family. As someone who was equally fond of the bottle, her brother would have been a softer touch and good for standing her a drink or two. Neither would chastise the other for their weaknesses, and, in a family of teetotallers, Fountaine's behaviour would have been subject to as much scrutiny as Annie's. The 5 pence that she procured from 'her relatives' on 7 September 1888 is more likely to have come from Fountaine, who lived nearby in Clerkenwell (directly opposite St Bartholomew's Hospital), than from her sisters in Knightsbridge.

By 1888, Annie had also begun to benefit from a steadier relationship with Edward Stanley, a 'florid-faced' 45-year-old 'man of a respectable appearance' who worked for a local brewery.[16] Although Ted, or 'the Pensioner', as he was commonly called, claimed to have known Annie for two years, they had only begun their part-time cohabitation that summer. By then, Annie had become a regular at 35 Dorset Street, a lodging house known as Crossingham's, where she and Stanley would pass the weekends together. According to Timothy Donovan, the deputy keeper there, Annie used to wait for Stanley at the corner of Brushfield Street on Saturday, when the couple would go to the pub. Stanley usually remained with Annie until Monday morning, during which time he did what was expected of any Victorian man in the company of a woman: he footed their expenses, which included the cost of Annie's lodging until at least Tuesday morning. At the lodging house, Annie and 'the Pensioner' were recognized as a couple. Stanley even made it clear to Tim Donovan that he understood his relationship with Annie to be an exclusive one and, as a jealous partner, asked the lodging-house keeper to prevent her from becoming involved with anyone else. Interestingly, in the time that she knew 'the Pensioner', it was claimed that Annie had purchased some brass rings which she wore on her left hand. Only Stanley was confident in his description of them as being two in number: 'a wedding ring and a keeper' (an engagement ring), which he claimed was 'of a fancy pattern'.[17] Although these rings were not a gift from Stanley, it appears that Annie wished to affect an air of marital respectability.

Although Annie was by the standards of the nineteenth century considered both a 'broken woman' and a 'fallen woman', she was not a prostitute. According to the orders issued by the Commissioner, Charles Warren, on 19 July 1887, roughly a year before Polly Nichols's murder, 'the Police are [not] justified in calling any woman a common prostitute, unless she so describes herself, or has been convicted as such . . .' The order went on to state that although a police constable 'may be perfectly convinced in his own mind that she is such' he should 'not assume that any particular woman is a common prostitute' unless there are witnesses and proof to attest to this.[18] Just as in the case of Polly Nichols, there also exists no reliable evidence to suggest that Annie Chapman either worked as a prostitute or identified herself with the trade. Contrary to the romanticized images of the Ripper's victims, she never 'walked the streets' in a low bodice and rouged cheeks casting provocative glances from beneath the gas lamps. She never belonged to a brothel or had a pimp. Nor is there any evidence she was arrested or even cautioned for her behaviour. Following 'enquiries made amongst women in the same class . . . at public houses in the locality' the police could find not a single witness who could confirm that she had been among the ranks of those who sold sex.[19] Those who worked in the trade were generally well known, not only to one another but frequently to the police as well as to their neighbours and to local publicans. In impoverished areas where little stigma was attached to the sale of sex, friends, family and associates were not bashful about openly identifying a woman as a prostitute when she genuinely was one.

As the police were still of an opinion that the Whitechapel murders were committed by either a high-rip extortion gang or a lone prostitute-killer (believed at this stage to be John Pizer, known as 'Leather Apron'), it was essential that the victim be identified with the sex trade. Evidently, with no heed paid to Charles Warren's order of 19 July, the police of H Division simply wrote the word 'prostitute' into the space provided for 'occupation' on Annie's forms. Just as they had with Polly Nichols's case, the authorities began their inquiry from a fixed position: that Annie *must* be a prostitute, a stance which from thereon guided the direction of their investigation, as well as the attitudes and interrogations of the coroner's court.

The newspapers were not inclined to question this assumption either. As this murder occurred in the middle of the inquest into Polly Nichols's death, the press seized the opportunity to link them. These two similar killings, committed within weeks of each other, whipped the papers into a frenzy of excitement. The number of journalists in Whitechapel swelled. Murders sold newspapers and the editors had to spin out these stories for as long as they could. The papers wanted to capture the sense of 'moral panic'; they wanted interviews, site visits, opinion pieces and detailed coverage of the Chapman inquest. The result was a panicked pandemonium of writing far more extensive than that inspired by the Nichols case. A chaos of contradictory statements, derived from hearsay, badly transcribed notes and testimony reframed to fit particular journalistic angles, emerged in the newspapers. Yet again, as with Polly Nichols's murder, the official transcripts of what was actually said at the coroner's inquest, as well as most of the police documentation, does not survive; a definitive set of records is absent. As a result, virtually all that is known about Annie Chapman's life in Whitechapel is drawn from this morass of confused 'facts' reported in newspapers.

The coroner's court testimony of Amelia Palmer, Tim Donovan and the night manager at Crossingham's, John Evans, who appear to have been most familiar with Annie and her movements, vary markedly from publication to publication. When placed side by side, one account directly contradicts another. On 9 September the *Guardian* writes that Palmer stated, 'As a regular means of livelihood she [Annie] had not been in the habit of frequenting the streets, but had made anti-macassars for sale. Sometimes she would buy flowers or matches with which to pick up a living.' This claim was repeated in a number of syndicated northern newspapers, including the *Hull Daily News* and the *Eastern Morning News*. By contrast, on the 11th, *The Star*, which always seemed to opt for the most sensationalist angle, has Amelia claiming, 'I am afraid the deceased used to earn her living partly on the streets.' Other newspapers, including the *Daily Telegraph*, cite Amelia's testimony more ambiguously, and refer only to the fact that Annie 'was out late at night at times'. Some publications even omitted a reference to her mode of life altogether. As a definitive version of this statement does not exist, Amelia's actual words can't be confirmed and neither can they be used to support a claim that Annie prostituted herself.

Reports from Donovan's and Evans's testimonies contain similar vagaries. According to the *Morning Advertiser* on the 11th, John Evans is reported as saying 'I have known that the deceased was out at nights, but I have known only one man with whom she was associated,' and Tim Donovan as asserting that 'I could not say whether the deceased walked the streets.' Donovan was most likely telling the truth; it's unlikely that he had taken much notice of or interest in the daily activities of one of his many lodgers until circumstances forced him. Even when it's possible to pick through the journalistic inconsistencies for information that accords with a historical understanding of how impoverished women lived, Donovan's carefully crafted testimony does not provide much compelling evidence to suggest that Annie made her living by the sex trade.[20] In several publications it appears that Donovan was asked about Annie's associations with men, as was another witness, Eliza Cooper, who was known to have had an antagonistic relationship with Annie. Not only had Cooper recently come to blows with Annie over a borrowed bar of soap, but Annie had once been connected with Cooper's current partner, Harry the Hawker. Both the deputy keeper and Eliza assert that as far as they knew, Annie had only been associated with two men, Harry and Ted Stanley. However, Cooper later claimed to have seen Annie 'with several other men', though added 'she only brought them casually to the lodging house'.[21] If this were the case, then according to Tim Donovan's testimony, these men didn't get very far. In his testimony Donovan explained that Ted Stanley had instructed him 'not to let the bed' if Annie came to Crossingham's with another man. The deputy keeper maintains that he kept to his word and in his defence cited that 'As a rule [Annie] occupied a double bed by herself.'[22] Neither of the two witnesses were questioned about this discrepancy, nor whether Annie was successful in obtaining entry in spite of Donovan's alleged bar, or what she did in the event she was denied access. Neither is it known what Annie's relationship was to these men, and if they were as 'casual' as Annie's love-rival suggests. Even Charles Warren in his police order had recognized the difficulties in distinguishing a prostitute and her behaviour from that of other poor, working-class women. This was and remains especially the case when the context of a woman's actions, as well as her own voice, are completely absent from the story.

The Victorian newspapers ignored such fine distinctions. Stories were crafted on top of assumptions and the assumption was always that Annie Chapman was a prostitute. *The Star* confidently declares:

> We are able to see the kind of existence that women of CHAPMAN'S unfortunate class are compelled to live … Probably she did not rise until the shades of night enabled her to ply her hideous trade, and she then seems to have spent her time in passing from liquor shop to liquor shop with the fitting companions, male and female, of such orgies.[23]

But *The Star*, and other publications like it, failed to view Annie as an individual, rather than as part of 'an unfortunate class' into which all impoverished women regardless of age or circumstance were lumped. As the *Daily Mail* pointed out, 'No criminal centre is wholly criminal, and to represent even the lodging houses of Dorset Street as wholly inhabited by the utterly depraved would be wrong.'²⁴ Unlike what was suggested by *The Star*, Annie did not sleep all day in order to rise when 'the shades of night enabled her to ply her hideous trade'. She sewed, crocheted and was intent on earning money through what Amelia Palmer referred to as her own industry. Such depictions of her also did not take into account the state of her health. Annie was seriously, if not terminally ill with tuberculosis. In addition to taking tablets, she had two bottles of medicine and what appear to have been letters of prescription given to her during a visit to St Bartholomew's Hospital among her belongings recovered after her death. This, as much as her desire to spend the night with Ted Stanley, would explain her insistence on having an 8-penny double bed. Not only were these 'doubles' surrounded by a wooden partition that afforded a rare degree of privacy, but as Elizabeth Allen, a fellow lodger at Crossingham's, commented, 'an eight-penny bed' carried 'with it greater advantages than those accorded by a four-penny . . . doss. The lodgers having the cheaper bed . . . were expected to turn out earlier in the morning.' Towards the end of her life, Annie would have valued an extra hour in bed before she was put out on the street at midmorning, feverish, aching and racked by coughing fits.

In the last few months of her life, as her health deteriorated, Annie became increasingly dependent on Ted Stanley to fund the cost of her lodgings. When he stayed with her on the weekend of 1 September, he gave Annie enough money to pay for her bed until Tuesday, as he usually did. On that afternoon, Amelia Palmer spotted her friend 'looking very pale' and walking slowly beside Spitalfields Church. Annie confessed to her that she was feeling ill and thought she might go to the infirmary. She was completely penniless and 'had not even had a cup of tea that day'. Amelia gave her tuppence and instructed her not to buy rum with it. She next saw Annie on that Friday, the 7th, lingering on Dorset Street, looking just as unwell as she had earlier in the week. Amelia asked her if she would be going to Stratford to sell her crochet work. 'I am too ill to do anything,' Annie answered wearily. When Amelia returned to the spot, ten minutes later, she was quite alarmed to see that her friend had not moved from where she stood. Annie hadn't a penny on her and was too sick to earn the sum she so urgently needed for a bed. 'It's no use in my giving way,' she said to Amelia, recognizing the gravity of her situation. 'I must pull myself together and go and get some money or I shall have no lodgings.'[25]

One of the mysteries that the journalists covering Annie's story seemed unable to solve was the issue of where precisely she had gone during that week. Timothy Donovan confirmed that when she left 35 Dorset Street on that Tuesday afternoon, the 4th, he did not see her again until Friday. It is believed that Annie went to the infirmary at St Bartholomew's Hospital, but as her name does not appear on the in-patients register, it is likely she was examined by a doctor and sent away. Similarly, her name is absent from existing casual-ward admissions registers, and if she did go to such a place, this would only have accounted for two nights. On the whole, this is not inconsistent with Annie's past behaviour, as there is no evidence that she ever stayed in a London casual ward or workhouse – almost certainly because such a sojourn would have entailed going without a drink. According to a study conducted by the 1904 Vagrancy Committee, those truly addicted to alcohol preferred sleeping rough to the restrictions they faced when placing themselves into the care of institutions.[26]

As Annie never sought shelter from her siblings and no one

among Whitechapel's lodging-house-keepers or residents came forward to claim that she regularly slept anywhere other than Crossingham's, it is unlikely that she did. Yet, at the same time, Elizabeth Allen asserted that Annie only ever had money enough to stay '3 or 4 nights a week' at 35 Dorset Street, the period that she spent with Ted Stanley. Logically, this would imply that Annie had no bed at least three nights out of every week.

It is unrealistic to suppose that an impoverished, sickly addict, whose primary concern was finding money for drink, would have had a regular bed every night. According to the social commentator Howard Goldsmid, Whitechapel, like the Embankment, Hyde Park and London Bridge, was, 'night after night, thronged with dossers, who have no money for a night's shelter'. He witnessed many who slept 'crouched in a doorway, or huddled in a heap upon the pavement'. 'Dozens of homeless creatures, male and female' whom he described as 'hungry, ragged men and women' congregated near Christ Church, Spitalfields, where they might be found 'hanging onto the railings, or crouching down by the walls', while others half-leaned and half-lay on the low rail-topped wall that surrounded the buildings. Goldsmid comments that most of these people had been turned out of their usual lodging houses on Thrawl Street, Flower and Dean Street and Dorset Street because they couldn't produce their doss money. 'When you enter the kitchen of a doss-'ouse, it would be a mistake to suppose that all the people you meet there are going to spend the night under its roof,' he writes.

Many of them are reg'lar'uns, who, in consideration of their constant patronage are permitted to spend the evening, or a portion of it, before the blazing coke fire, for though the deputy will give no trust, he knows better than to offend a regular lodger. As the evening wears on, however, these poor wretches become restless and moody. They pace the floor with their hands in their otherwise empty pockets, glancing towards the door at each fresh arrival to see if a 'pal' has come in from whom it may be possible to borrow the halfpence necessary to complete their doss money. At last, their final hope being gone, they shuffle out into the streets and prepare to spend the night with only the sky for a canopy.[27]

On the night of 7 September, Annie Chapman was faced with just this scenario. According to Timothy Donovan, Annie reappeared at Crossingham's that afternoon and, after explaining that she was unwell and had been to the infirmary, asked if she could sit downstairs in the kitchen. Donovan granted her request, but in the early evening (about the time when she encountered Amelia) she went out again. By around midnight, Annie was seen back in the kitchen, asking a fellow lodger, William Stevens, to fetch her a pint of beer from a nearby pub. In doing so, she seemed to indicate that she had 'been to her relations' and managed to beg 5 pence. That money, which might have paid for a bed, was quickly converted into drink. After she finished her pint with Stevens, she set off to the Britannia, a pub on the corner of Dorset Street and Commercial Street. Having taken her fill, Annie returned once more to Crossingham's kitchen and ate some potatoes. By then it was about 1.45 a.m., the time when Donovan began to clear the kitchen of those who did not have the pennies for their doss. He asked the night watchman, John Evans, to go downstairs and do the collecting. Annie came up short, but went to Donovan's office to make a special pleading for her usual bed, number 29.

Interestingly, a point that never emerged in the press, but which Tim Donovan revealed to the police, was that Annie had specifically 'asked him to trust her' for that night's doss money. This 'he declined to do'.[28] Had this incident become common knowledge, it's likely that Donovan would have faced an even worse backlash from the public for his role in Annie's demise. 'You can find money for your beer, and you can't find money for your bed,' were the words the deputy keeper is said to have spoken in response to her request. Annie, not quite willing to admit defeat, or perhaps in a show of pride, responded with a sigh, 'Keep my bed for me. I shan't be long.'

Ill and drunk, she went downstairs and 'stood in the door for two or three minutes', considering her options. Like the impecunious lodger described by Goldsmid, she too was likely to have been contemplating from whom among her 'pals' she might borrow her doss money. However, when she set off down Brushfield Street towards Christ Church, Spitalfields, it was more probable that Annie had reconciled herself to spending 'the night with only the sky for a canopy'.

Her thoughts as she stepped out onto Dorset Street, as the light from Crossingham's dimmed at her back, are forever lost. The route she wove through the black streets, and to whom she spoke along the way, will never be confirmed. All that will ever be certain is her final destination.

Twenty-nine Hanbury Street was typical of most of the dwellings in the area. At least a hundred years old and three-storeys high, it consisted of eight decaying rooms, inhabited by seventeen people. As rooms were rented out individually, no one had much concern for the communal spaces: the passages, stairway, landings or the yard behind which formed part of the property. Neither the gate to the yard nor the door to the building were locked, and an assortment of people came and went through this public (though concealed) space at all times of the day and night. According to the police as well as to the residents, the location was well-known among the street-wise inhabitants of the area. Occasionally, 'the yard was used for immoral purposes' by 'strangers', and was just as regularly occupied by rough sleepers.[29]

Over the past two years, Annie, like any of Goldsmid's dossers, would have become acquainted with the best corners, the most inconspicuous doorways, and the least traversed passages in which to lay her head. The yard adjacent to 29 Hanbury Street was not a place Annie stumbled upon accidently in the early-morning hours of 8 September, but a familiar space that she would have sought for its solitude. She would have known about the gap between the house's steps and the fence. It was an ideal spot in which to curl up with her back against the wall, and she would have been relieved to find it vacant.

Of the many tragedies which befell Annie Chapman in the final years of her life, perhaps one of the most poignant was that she needn't have been on the streets on that night, or on any other. Instead, she might have lain in a bed in her mother's house, or rested in her sisters' care, on the other side of London. She might have been treated for tuberculosis; she might have been comforted by the embraces of her children. At every turn there had been a hand reaching to pull her from the abyss, but the counter-tug of addiction was more forceful, and the grip of shame just as strong. It was this that pulled her under, that had extinguished her hope and then her life many years earlier. What her murderer claimed on that night was simply all that remained of what the drink had left behind.

Sometime around 8 or 9 September, the Smith siblings, Emily, Georgina, Miriam and Fountaine, received some truly dreadful news. Whether a police constable had paid them a visit or they had read a story in the newspaper, the realization that their sister had been the victim of a brutal murder would have devastated them. Emily, Georgina and Miriam could not bear to tell their elderly mother that the child she had lost to alcohol had been killed, and that her death had been so gruesome and dehumanizing. They smothered their grief as they held the hands of Annie's two children, who would never know the fate that had befallen their mother. The pain and humiliation her sisters suffered as story after story appeared in the papers, calling Annie a prostitute and describing her degraded life, cannot be imagined. For three devout women, the shame of this and the need to keep silent about their suffering would have been almost more than they could withstand.

As the man of the family, the worst tasks, those that required a public face, fell to Fountaine, who, in addition to his sorrow, carried in his heart his own private turmoil. He, like Annie and their father, was also an alcoholic. Perhaps without his family's knowledge, he had seen Annie only recently, handed her a few coins and probably shared a few drinks. It was Fountaine who identified the torn, ragged body of his elder sister and stood before the coroner. His distress on this occasion was so great that he was hardly able to make his voice audible.

Fountaine Smith was not made of strong stuff. He buckled under this misfortune and as he fell he grabbed for the one thing he knew would provide him with immediate though fleeting relief: the bottle. Within a month of the harrowing ordeal of his sister's death, Fountaine suffered a breakdown. After stealing money from his employer to buy drink, he lost his job as a warehouse manager. Friends intervened and found him another position, but Fountaine's misery followed him here too. One day, unable to cope, he filled himself with alcohol and his pockets with his employer's funds, abandoned his wife and two children and disappeared.

A week later, the family received a letter from Gloucester; Fountaine had walked into a police station and surrendered himself. 'Oh, my darling wife, it is all the cursed drink,' he wrote at the bottom of his confession. 'For God's sake don't let the children touch it.'

Annie's brother was taken back to London and tried at Marlborough Street Magistrates' Court, where he was found guilty and sentenced to three months' hard labour at Millbank Prison. Upon his release, Fountaine resolved to start his life again and took his wife and children across the Atlantic to settle in the dust and heat of Texas.

Elizabeth

27 November 1843 – 30 September 1888

9

The Girl from Torslanda

THE CANDLES SPREAD A warm yellow light through the wood-panelled rooms of the farmhouse. They and the hearth fire worked together to cast out the darkness of a late Swedish November, a time when the skies shift swiftly between shades of grey and the black of night. In one room of the four that belonged to Gustaf Ericsson, his wife, Beata lay on her back, labouring with their second child. Three years earlier, she had brought a daughter, Anna Christina, into the world. On this occasion, the farmer would have hoped for a son to assist him in managing the livestock and bringing in the harvests. He had no such luck; on the 27th of that month in 1843, little Elisabeth's newborn cries filled the couple's bedroom.

The Ericssons were more fortunate than many who tended the land in Torslanda, the area that lay roughly 16 kilometres to the west of the city of Gothenburg. Although Elisabeth had been born during a period of drought which had begun in the 1840s, the family were relatively prosperous. Not only could Gustaf Ericsson afford to cultivate fields of grain, flax and potatoes, but he also owned a barn, several cows, pigs, chickens and a horse. The clapboard house in which Elisabeth, her elder sister and eventually her two younger brothers, Lars (born in 1848) and Svante (born in 1851), were to share was considered spacious, with a large kitchen in which the household took their meals, a sitting room, and at least three bedrooms arranged on the ground and upper floors.

As a farmer's daughter, Elisabeth would have been initiated into the routine of agricultural life as soon as she was steady enough on her feet to carry pails and gather eggs. When older, she would have assisted with the basic chores of milking, tending the chickens and pigs, making butter and, as was traditional in Swedish households, learning how to distil aquavit, the alcoholic liquor which was offered at mealtimes. In the winter months, the mornings would begin many hours before dawn, when she, her sister or mother would rise in what felt like the middle of the night and light the fires and lamps. In the summer, the men and women would work in the fields long into evening, beneath an almost never-ending twilight. Where previously farmers' wives would have toiled alongside their husbands, by the middle of the nineteenth century the availability of cheap labour meant that the more demanding tasks could be performed by hired help, thereby leaving Beata and her daughters to tend primarily to affairs within the home. Notwithstanding this privilege, daily rural life was fairly egalitarian. Little distinction was made between master and servant: 'They all sat at the same table and ate off the same plate,' reminisced one of the era's farm hands, who also recalled that everyone in a household 'did the same jobs, and the daughters of the farmer shared the bed with the maids'.[1]

In the small rural settlement of Stora Tumlehed, they also prayed together. Sundays in the conservative, Lutheran community were for church and a close study of the Bible. As the head of the household, Elisabeth's father would have been expected to shepherd not only his family but also his hired help in their daily religious duty. Prayers would have punctuated the day: before meals, before bed, and upon waking, offering thanks to the Lord for seeing his sheep safely through the long night.

It is unlikely that Elisabeth ever conceived that her experience might depart from the constant rhythm of farm life: the turning of the seasons, the cutting of the fields, the freezing of the earth, the thaw of the ice, the sowing of seeds. As a girl, little was expected of her beyond a mastery of housekeeping, child-care and basic animal husbandry, all of which she could learn from assisting her mother. Her minimal schooling reflected this. Rural parents often considered an education, which distracted their children from the business of agriculture, to be 'superfluous knowledge'. While by the mid-nineteenth century each parish was required to establish a common school for local children, the learning that was offered extended little beyond reading and arithmetic, as well as writing for the boys. Among Lutherans, the ability to read was considered of prime importance, as the study of the Bible and the understanding of catechism lay at the centre of all devotions. Elisabeth and her siblings would regularly make the near hour-long walk to the church in Torslanda to receive the necessary tutelage in scripture in order to prepare them for their confirmation.

As children, they were taught the Small Catechism from Martin Luther's 1529 *Book of Concord*, which sets out the tenets of the Lutheran faith. Elisabeth's instruction included the memorization of the Ten Commandments, the Apostles' Creed, the Lord's Prayer, the Sacrament of Holy Baptism, the Office of the Keys and Confession, and the Sacrament of the Eucharist. However, as it was also necessary that all members of the faith possess a thorough comprehension of God's word, her education would have included an analysis of scripture and a regular drilling by the parish priest and her father in its meaning.

'What are the Ten Commandments?' the priest would ask.

'The Ten Commandments are the law of God,' Elisabeth would be expected to answer.

'How did God give His Law?'

'When God created people, He wrote the Law on their hearts. Later he arranged the Law in Ten Commandments, wrote it on two tablets of stone, and made it known through Moses' would be the anticipated response. Such statements would then be bolstered with corresponding quotes from scripture.

'What is the sixth commandment?' Elisabeth was asked on numerous occasions.

'One shall not commit adultery.'

'What does this mean?'

'We should fear and love God so that we lead a sexually pure and decent life in what we say and do, and husband and wife love and honour each other. Carnal relations are reserved for matrimony and we should not give into base lusts,' she would have been taught to respond.

By these means, Elisabeth was prepared to assume her role as a committed member of the faith. At the age of fifteen, on 14 August 1859, she stood before the congregation in the ancient cottage-like church at Torslanda and was confirmed. In doing this, Elisabeth demonstrated she was prepared to enter the adult world and, armed with a strong knowledge of the word of God, to face the trials and temptations that awaited her.

Just over a year later, and a month before her seventeenth birthday, Elisabeth Gustafsdotter set out for Gothenburg to seek employment as a servant. In 1857, Anna Christina had undertaken the half-day's walk to the city for the same purpose. In Sweden, as in other European countries, it was traditional for young women to gain experience of domestic life beyond the confines of their homes and communities. For many, the years prior to marriage spent in the kitchens, the nurseries or scrubbing floors under the auspices of other women functioned as a type of apprenticeship before they assumed command of their own households. This period of labour also offered girls the opportunity to earn dowries, or money to assist in purchasing the clothing, linens and other items they would require for married life and childbearing. For young women from rural communities like Elisabeth and her sister, a move to the city also increased their prospects of finding a suitable husband. While the daughters of land-owning or land-leasing farmers were raised alongside agricultural labourers and those of a lower social status, marriage between the classes was actively discouraged. In an urban centre, filled with the sons of craftsmen and small shopkeepers, the opportunities for finding a more appropriate spouse were greater.

In this regard, Anna Christina was especially fortunate. Not only was she able to secure a place working in the home of Bernhard Olsson, a shoemaker, but after seven years of service, in 1864, she married her master, a situation that was not uncommon when employer and servant were of a similar class.[2] In many cases, elder siblings already established in service were able to assist younger sisters in obtaining positions, sometimes within the same household. It is likely that Anna Christina had some influence in obtaining work for Elisabeth in Gothenburg. According to her residency records, Elisabeth was living in Majorna, a working-class suburb of Gothenburg, by 5 October 1860 and four months later, in February, her name appears officially on the census as a maidservant to the family of Lars Fredrik Olsson.[3]

Like Anna Christina's employer, Lars Fredrik Olsson and his family were not wealthy, but rather members of the more comfortable lower-middle class. His employment as a *månad-skarl* implied that he performed the role of a caretaker, possibly for the block of apartments in which the family lived on Allmänna Vägen, a hill slightly elevated above the port.[4] Olsson's fortunes appear to have been on the rise, and by the 1870s he had purchased further property in Majorna.

The social line that divided Elisabeth from her employer would have been a relatively thin one, but as the Olssons' prospects were improving, they would have been keen to demonstrate their resources to their neighbours and associates. As female labour in Sweden was extremely cheap and the Servant Act made it compulsory for those who did not have an income through land to find employment in service, families with even meagre means were able to hire girls to work in their homes. Lars Fredrik and his wife Johanna were able to afford two: Elisabeth, and Lena Carlsson, who would have shared a bed in a loft space above the family's rooms. Indeed, how much work might have been found to occupy two women as well as their mistress in the maintenance of a handful of rooms and the care of the couple's three- and four-year-old sons is questionable. Nineteenth-century Swedish commentators often remarked that lower-middle-class families frequently employed more servants than there were tasks to occupy them. Art historian Henrik Cornell, reflecting back on his childhood, recalled a middle-class wife who busied her bored, under-employed maids by making them carry wet linen through the rooms in order to catch the dust before it settled.[5]

Swedish law was fairly explicit about the relationship between a master and mistress and their employee. While the employer may have had an obligation to house, feed, clothe and tend to a servant while ill, in return a servant was expected to offer complete obedience. 'Unfounded discontent over the food' or 'treating a fire or the master's property in a careless way' were grounds for dismissal, as was the 'visiting of inns or other places where alcoholic beverages were served'.[6] Once such agreements were struck, they were considered binding, and a servant was required to work out her term of employment, unless both parties agreed to dissolve the contract.

Why precisely Elisabeth's term of employment with the Olssons was dissolved in early February 1864 is likely to remain a mystery. Census records indicate that on the 2nd of that month she moved no more than a short walk along the cobbled streets of brightly painted clapboard buildings to the neighbouring district of Domkyrko.[7] When the clerk who added her name to the register asked her occupation, she told him that she was a servant, but the address where she was employed along with the name of her master or mistress was not recorded. It is possible that this was simply an omission, an oversight on the part of the clerk, or perhaps it points to something else: that Elisabeth herself was uncertain of her future and into whose hands she was placing it.

Allmän Kvinna 97

IN THE NINETEENTH CENTURY no household could operate effi-
ciently without female labour, yet bringing unknown young
women into a home was a risky business. Most employers
knew the dangers of hiring girls from outside the city. Still,
there was a preference for them: the ruddy-cheeked daughters
of yeomen who smelled like grass and goats, who had not yet
learned how to dissemble or steal, who had been raised in
close-knit communities where the parson presided over everyone's business. Urban girls, having been exposed to avarice and
licentiousness, who had witnessed the worldly ways of their
betters, were considered more corruptible. While city girls
might appear untrustworthy, their country sisters seemed
innocent and vulnerable. Living in alien surroundings, in the
households of complete strangers, they were prone to homesickness and loneliness. Their inexperience of metropolitan life
rendered them perfect victims for the unscrupulous. Although
it was a master or mistress's responsibility to keep them from
harm, frequently the injury that they encountered came from
within the very place where they were employed.

Servants, who were not allowed to enter beer houses or
spend a night outside of their master's home without permission, were given virtually no opportunity to form relationships

with members of the opposite sex beyond their household or immediate community. Their interactions with other servants from the homes of their employer's friends and family, or with other workers such as grocers, butchers, bakers and those making deliveries, were brief (though often flirtatious and familiar). Young women like Elisabeth who lived cheek-by-jowl with the family who employed her could be as much a temptation to the male members of the household as they were to her. For men of all ages, sexual liaisons with one's servant – who would have intimate knowledge of his habits, who may have made his bed, washed clothes and filled his baths – were considered commonplace occurrences. Whether or not she encouraged the advances of the master or his son, his brother, cousin, friend or father, there were plenty of opportunities for her to find herself alone, to be coerced, overpowered, or to give in to mutual desire.

While service was believed to be the making of a young working-class woman's character, becoming sexually entangled with a man beneath her master's roof was more often than not the undoing of it. Such relationships were regularly cited as being a factor that eventually drew women into lives of prostitution; 'the housemaid of a pharmacist or a surgeon might be seduced by her master's assistant; a lodging-house maid by a student, a commercial traveller or officer . . . a hotel servant by a regular guest; a young clerk might seduce his parents' servant-girl' and so forth.[1] Often, a woman's lover would promise to look after her and many made good on their word, establishing their mistresses in lodgings, which might be a single room or an entire house, depending upon his resources. Some lived alongside their paramours, posing as married couples; others visited only on occasion. Some relationships continued for many years, if not for a lifetime, but many more fell apart within weeks or months. While the nineteenth-century double standard enabled men to walk away from such attachments, it often devastated the lives of the women, who were left to bear the crying and gurgling consequences.

Elisabeth has taken to her grave the name of the man who altered the course of her life with his lust. It will be never be known whether her first encounter with him was consensual or forced, where it occurred or under what circumstances. All that is known is that through April 1865 she continued to describe herself as a servant, though her name is untraceable on any of the Gothenburg censuses. A likely explanation is that she did not remain long in her new position as maid before taking up lodgings with or paid for by a lover. In such cases, the regular practice was to conceal the true nature of the relationship by assuming her lover's surname, becoming for propriety's sake, for however a short a period, his wife.

In Gothenburg, maintaining a semblance of respectability while living in sin was done not merely to satisfy the landlord and the neighbours of one's character, but to hide from the law and the suspicions of the police. Until 1864, extra-marital sex and illegitimate pregnancy were illegal, punishable offences. Additionally, in 1859 a law that regulated prostitution in the city was introduced in order to quell the spread of venereal disease, specifically syphilis. The new legislation was a threat to any woman living in a potentially compromising situation.

In this large port city, with a growing population of over one hundred thousand, and foreign ships dropping anchor daily along the Göta River, the authorities were greatly concerned about how easily this debilitating illness could be communicated through the civilian population and spread through the military. Sweden took its cue from other European nations, such as France and Germany, who, when faced with a similar threat, had instituted a series of strict laws designed to regulate the sex trade and ensure the health of the women who practised within it. Britain too saw the benefits of introducing such measures in its port towns, and in 1864 passed the first of its Contagious Diseases Acts.

While the methods of enforcing regulation varied between countries, the concept which they all shared was that women in the sex trade should shoulder the blame for the transmission of syphilis. It was believed that if the state could control the morally corrupt fallen woman, the instrument of the disease's spread, then the problem could be isolated. The male carrier was exempt from regulation. In Gothenburg, as in Stockholm, Paris, Hamburg, Berlin and cities throughout Europe, women who participated in the sex trade were required to register their names and addresses with the police and submit to regular gynaecological examinations to ensure they were free of disease. However, determining who exactly should be placed on this roll was down entirely to the whim of the prostitution police patrolling various neighbourhoods. Many women who were forced to enlist themselves were not selling sex, but were suspected of what the police described as 'lecherous living'.[2] According to the historian Yvonne Svanström, Gothenburg's system employed two separate lists: one consisting of the names of acknowledged prostitutes and the other comprised of suspected women – pregnant single women, women frequently seen alone with men, or out at night, and mistresses.

The police and her neighbours may have suspected Elisabeth for some time, but by March 1865 they became fairly certain that she was guilty of 'lecherous living'. She was then six months pregnant and unavoidably showing through her clothes. Whoever had got her into that condition was no longer present to shield her from the consequences. Where he had gone and with what means of livelihood he had provided her while she carried his child will never be discovered. At the end of March, when the wind was still sharp with ice, Elisabeth was ordered to appear at the first of what would become regular examinations of her genitalia by a surgeon at the police inspection house.

On her first visit her name, Elisabeth Gustafsdotter of Torslanda, was inscribed onto the official ledger as 'Allmän Kvinna' (Public Woman) number 97.[3] Elisabeth was required to provide certification of her birth and information about her past, such as where she previously worked, and where she lived. She was deliberately silent on these matters, stating only that she had been born the daughter of farmers and that she had come from the country to the town where she had worked as a servant. She was asked about her religious education as well and stated (incorrectly) that she was confirmed at seventeen.[4] The official recording her details then looked up at the young woman and assessed her appearance. He noted that she had 'blue eyes' and 'brown hair'. Her nose he described as 'straight' and her face as 'oval'; elongated, as opposed to round. With the exception of her swelling, maternal belly, he surmised that the 21-year-old woman had not been living a life of gluttony. She was 5 feet 2 inches, and he described her as having a 'slender' build.[5]

The rules that would govern her daily life would have been explained to her. She must attend the inspection house twice a week, on Tuesdays and Fridays, or face arrest and a fine or three nights in prison on rations of bread and water. She would not be permitted outdoors after eleven at night. She was required to 'conduct a quiet and silent life', which assumed she was a prostitute and solicited openly. Regulations prohibited her from loitering in the windows or doorway of where she lived and from 'calling out to passers-by'. She was required to 'dress in a decent way when appearing in public' and 'not to call attention to herself'. The humiliation that women must have experienced at being lectured in such a way, especially if they did not associate themselves with the sex trade, or if their crimes were not public ones, but a rape or a private indiscretion with a lover, must have been overwhelming. Regardless of the fact that her name appeared on what was colloquially referred to as 'the register of shame', Elisabeth continued to describe herself in her documentation that spring not as a prostitute but as a servant.

The routine of inspection was designed as much to chasten the city's 'public women' as it was to screen them. So as to avoid giving offence to the sensibilities of Gothenburg's respectable citizens passing along Östra Hamngatan, all suspected and known 'public women' were asked to enter the police building through a concealed passage at the back. Once inside, they were required to strip naked and form a queue. Sometimes, if the wait was a long one, they were ordered to stand in the outdoor courtyard, shivering in the cold, as the uniformed officers stood over them.

For a young woman who had been raised in a religious community and drilled in her catechism, the indignity of this experience would have been shocking. However, as Elisabeth was pregnant with an illegitimate child, it is likely that she, like so many women of her era, would have internalized the punishment as a justifiable one. Society and the church would have had her believe she had sinned against her parents, her community, herself and God. Her sense of disgrace is reflected in her reticence to reveal in her registration document further details of her circumstances. When asked about her parents, she did not hesitate to pronounce them both dead. While this was true of her mother, who had died of tuberculosis in August 1864, Elisabeth's father was still very much alive, but the shame of her predicament would have kept her from returning to him.[6] Anna Christina, too, who had married in May of that year, seems to have severed all ties with her sister, whom she may very well have regarded as lost to the family.

Since having her name placed on the police register in March, Elisabeth would have been subjected to this routine no more than a handful of times before it was discovered on 4 April that she had developed condyloma, or genital warts. The medical examiner recognized the meaning of this immediately: Allmän Kvinna 97 was presenting the symptoms of syphilis. She was committed immediately, under police escort to the Kurhuset, or 'cure house' – the venereal disease hospital.

By the time Elisabeth was placed on the police roll, her syphilis had already entered its secondary phase. The first presentation of the disease would have occurred roughly ten to ninety days after exposure and included the appearance of a tell-tale chancre, or painless sore, on the genitals, which would subside within three to six weeks. After this, Elisabeth would have begun to experience flu-like symptoms: a fever, swollen glands, a sore throat and then the eruption of a rash on her back, hands and soles of her feet. In this stage, victims also suffered from wart-like growths and lesions on their genitals. This secondary phase may have lasted for no more than several months or may have continued to plague the sufferer for well over a year. Although it is impossible to determine for certain from whom she contracted syphilis, the stage of the illness indicates that it may have been the father of her child. The sexually inexperienced, who would not have known to look for symptoms of the disease on their partners, were more likely than those established in the sex trade to become infected.

According to Elisabeth's records, she was kept in the Kurhuset until 13 May.[7] Far from being a sanctuary to where sufferers could retreat for a cure, Gothenburg's venereal disease hospital had a reputation for treating patients as prisoners. As those committed there were done so by order of the law, its attendants and nurses were allowed to use force and coercion to keep the patients locked in until they were pronounced cured. In 1855, the Kurhuset housed 133 women in its syphilis ward, many of whom shared beds due to overcrowding. During those times when the numbers of patients exceeded capacity, the inmates were simply made to sleep on the floor.

By the 1860s, two types of treatment for syphilis were advocated by the medical establishment. The first and most traditional involved the ingestion of mercury, as well as its topical application to chancres and lesions. The second and more modern theory favoured the use of other metals – gold, silver, copper – as well as bromine, iodine and nitric acid to be taken internally or applied in ointments. Both were hazardous to the health of the patient. Of these two methods, Gothenburg's Kurhuset appears to have favoured non-mercurial cures. Elisabeth, during her stay, was treated internally with hydroiodic acid, the main components of which are iodine and hydrogen, while her genital warts would have been dehydrated with a cream or cut off. After receiving this cure for seventeen days, Elisabeth went into premature labour. On 21 April she gave birth to a stillborn girl at seven months while under lock and key at the Kurhuset.[8] She did not cite the father's name on the birth certificate.

The trauma of Elisabeth's experience between the end of March when her name was placed on 'the register of shame' and 13 May when she was discharged from the Kurhuset cannot be underestimated. To have been publicly denounced as a whore, to have suffered the indignity of police examinations, to have discovered that she carried a potentially deadly and disfiguring disease, to have been incarcerated and subjected to excruciating medical procedures, to have suffered a miscarriage in a hostile environment and then to have been released onto the street with no relations to whom she could turn must surely have scarred her.

One of the consequences of a system that treated women suspected of 'lecherous living' no differently than it treated known prostitutes was to condemn them both to the same fate. Once a woman appeared on the police register she would not be able to procure respectable work. The only means by which she could then sustain herself would be to resort to the profession she had been accused of practising. It is not known how precisely Elisabeth came to join the ranks of the women who sold themselves on Pilgatan, Gothenburg's infamous 'street of many nymphs', but by October of that year, she cites it as her address.[9] As street-walking and open solicitation were prohibited by the police, Elisabeth would have resorted to plying her trade indoors, either at one of the area's several coffee houses which masqueraded as legitimate establishments, or from within a brothel, though the madams who operated these businesses would have been resistant to hiring women who had undergone recent treatment for syphilis. Trawling the coffee houses between Pilgatan and Husargatan, learning the unwritten rules that governed relationships between the various women, their clients and the owners of these businesses, would have been a steep learning curve. Elisabeth's life would not have been without violence or the fear that accompanied the threat of it. As her name at this period still fails to appear on the census roll for Haga, the working-class district in which she claimed to have lived, it is likely that she continued to use an alias when she brought men back to her lodgings. The place that she called home was most probably one of a large number of small cubicle-like rooms known as *luderkupor* (or 'whore closets') situated in the attics of many of the area's houses. These were specifically designed to be hired out to prostitutes and allowed them to earn a discreet but meagre living.

The incurability of the disease from which Elisabeth suffered was but one of many misfortunes to befall her and, undoubtedly, a good number of the men with whom she had sex. As the pathology of syphilis was not fully understood, it was erroneously believed that the afflicted were not contagious while there were no immediate signs of the disease. In spite of the determined efforts of the medical profession, a successful treatment for this devastating illness was not available until 1910 with the introduction of Salvarsan, and later with antibiotics. It is therefore not surprising that by 30 August, Elisabeth was once more manifesting symptoms of the disease. She was returned to the Kurhuset where she remained until 23 September. On this occasion, she was treated for a lesion on her pubis with applications of silver nitrate. Twenty-three days after her discharge she was admitted again on 17 October for another lesion, this time on her clitoris, and underwent a repeat treatment with silver nitrate before she was declared 'cured' on 1 November. The ensuing police examinations conducted on the 3rd, the 7th and the 10th attested that she was now 'healthy', though in truth she would never be.[10] At some point after this date, Elisabeth's syphilis would enter its latent phase. Although her symptoms would disappear and she would no longer be contagious, eventually, many years later, the disease would return for its destructive and terminal tertiary stage.

While the legal system had very little pity for those caught in a vicious circle of prostitution and disease, attitudes among some segments of the population were more sympathetic. Like many European nations, mid-nineteenth-century Sweden and its Nordic neighbours witnessed a groundswell of interest in the 'rescue' of fallen women. This work, which was largely undertaken through the Church by middle- and upper-class women, aimed to rehabilitate back into Christian life those who would otherwise have been lost to God. It was widely held that circumstance did not induce women into prostitution but, rather, it was a personal choice. Having strayed off the path, a fallen woman could also decide to return to it. This character reformation could be effected by turning 'a public woman into a private woman'; by bringing her back into the domestic sphere, the place scripture intended for good Lutheran women. Rehabilitation involved retraining as a housemaid or a laundress, learning how to clean, iron, cook, tend, sew and create traditional handicrafts. The Lutheran deaconesses who placed themselves at the vanguard of this work opened reformatory shelters and laundries and regularly made visits to red-light districts and venereal-disease hospitals as part of their recruiting mission.

It is likely that this is how Elisabeth was discovered by Maria Ingrid Wiesner. Maria was the wife of a German musician who had been employed by the Gothenburg Orchestra at the city's recently built New Theatre. Although not wealthy, the Wiesners, like the families of the fellow musicians who inhabited the clapboard block of apartments at 27 Husargatan, were accustomed to keeping a maidservant as a sign of social status. The decision to hire a fallen young woman may have come about as much as a result of the couple's financial position as it did from a sense of Christian duty. Only several months earlier, the orchestra had been disbanded for lack of funding and rather than return with his Swedish wife to his native Bohemia, Carl Wenzel Wiesner determined to remain in Gothenburg and make a living as an oboist. The Wiesners were without a maid, and as Maria was shortly expecting her first child, the assistance would have been welcome, especially as women from the police register might be hired only on a bed-and-board basis.

On 10 November, Elisabeth attended her regular health examination. Maria, in her bonnet and winter cloak, would have been waiting for her outside the inspection house to escort her to her new life. This offer of work, of a home, of someone who held out a hand in sympathy for her plight, was an exceptional stroke of good fortune. According to the law, it was also the only way, outside of marriage, in which a woman on the police register could have her name removed and thereby recover her life and reputation. What it was precisely that made Maria Wiesner choose Elisabeth from among the many faces at the Kurhuset will remain unknown, but it is possible that something in Allmän Kvinna 97's tragic story moved her. Perhaps it was because they were both of a similar age and both came from villages in the west of Sweden. Perhaps Maria, who had been married for two years, was in need of a companion as well as a servant. Perhaps, too, she saw in Elisabeth a religious devotion and a genuine desire to alter her fate.

The process of having one's name struck from 'the register of shame' required an employer to write a letter of surety to the police, vouching for the future character and conduct of the former public woman. On the 13th, three days after Elisabeth had followed Maria Wiesner to her first-floor apartment, her employer wrote, 'The servant-maid Elisabeth Gustafsson was engaged in my service on November 10 and I am responsible for her good conduct as long as she stays in my service.'[11] On the following day, Elisabeth was required to undergo one final health inspection. The doctor pronounced that her cure had been a success, and Allmän Kvinna 97 was no more.

It can only be hoped that Elisabeth's time working for the Wiesners at 27 Husargatan was a happy one. The owner of the building, Johan Fredrik Bergendahl, an army sergeant who had played trumpet in the orchestra with Carl Wiesner, appears to have favoured tenants with whom he had a personal connection. In addition to the Wiesners, Bergendahl chose another army trumpet-player, Frans Oscar Malm, and an army widow and her children as neighbours. This year, as the winter closed in and returned its heavy, cold darkness to the city, Elisabeth's once grim and painful existence would have been filled with candlelight, a hearth fire and music.

In the nineteenth century, it was music and art that drew all the disparate strands of society together. Although those who produced entertainment tended to hail from the working or 'artisan' class, those who participated in and sponsored cultural endeavours were frequently the wealthiest and most influential members of the community. Artists, like their well-endowed patrons, travelled internationally; they mixed with a variety of people of all nationalities and could gain access to the ears of those in power. It is likely it was through music that Elisabeth was given her next opportunity.

The commercial expansion of Gothenburg, which had begun in the eighteenth century, continued at a rapid pace throughout the nineteenth. The city's large port and access to raw materials such as timber and ore attracted a significant amount of foreign investment from the British who saw grand opportunities to make their fortunes. Families such as the Dicksons, the Keillers and the Wilsons started shipping empires. David Carnegie opened an investment bank, a sugar refinery and a brewery. Gothenburg soon became a draw for British master brewers, as well as for Scottish and English engineers, who were contracted to design railways and sewage systems. The British community exerted such a presence that Gothenburg soon acquired the nickname of 'Little London'.

Gothenburg's 'Little Londoners', who largely came from Scotland, were also some of the city's most generous philanthropists. James Jameson Dickson and his brother and father were personally responsible for raising the money to fund the Gothenburg Orchestra and played a vital role in the lives of the musicians. The leader of the Orchestra and director of Gothenburg's military band, Josef Czapek, Carl Wiesner's friend and employer, also served as the organist at the English Church, the very heart of the British community. It was likely to have been through this network that the Wiesners were made aware of a position for a maidservant wishing to travel with a British family back to London.

It is possible that in the time Maria had spent with Elisabeth they had discussed her feelings about what remained for her in Gothenburg. Although Elisabeth was now no longer on the police register or working as a prostitute, she need only step outside the door of the Wiesners' home onto Husargatan to see the faces of those who remembered what she had been. Each day, on a visit to the shops or to the market, she might encounter former clients, the owners of the coffee houses and the women who had shared her profession. The police, too, would continue to watch her. So long as she remained in the city, Elisabeth would never escape her past, and so the possibility of beginning again in London, as a housemaid to an affluent family, must have seemed a gift from providence.

Fate had already been generous; now it bestowed on her one

final offering. While she lived with the Wiesners, Elisabeth received what is believed to have been an inheritance of sixty-five crowns from her deceased mother's estate.[12] However, as Swedish law stated that women under twenty-five were not able to inherit money in their own right and that property belonged to a woman's husband after death, it is unlikely that this money was indeed what it at first appears.[13] The sum was a relatively small one that would have stretched to the purchase of items for her new life: clothing, shoes, hats, perhaps even a trunk for travelling. If Elizabeth did receive such a payment, it is likely to have been from a different source, perhaps from one wishing to make amends for the misfortune he had visited upon her. Gestures of this sort were common practice among men parting with their mistresses.

In early February, the snow lay thickly along the city streets. Gothenburg's canals were slicked with ice. At the port, on 7 February 1866, dock workers, sailors and passengers were swathed in wool and fur against the sharp cold. Elizabeth stood among them, preparing to board one of the London-bound ships whose funnels pushed towards the sky, pumping out warm clouds into the frozen air.

Five days earlier, she had filed her application for emigration to England and submitted a certificate of altered residence for the capital city. On her form she stated that she was travelling without her family. She had only recently turned twenty-two and would be the only Swede to emigrate to London that day.[14] She would not be travelling on one of the crowded immigrant ships which sailed via Hull, but in a certain degree of comfort with her new British employers. As she stood on deck or watched the peaks and domes of the city's skyline diminish through the windows, she could not have felt much remorse. Gothenburg had left a cruel mark upon her, one that would always remain, no matter where she called home.

II

The Immigrant

FEW MEN COMMANDED RESPECT in Sheerness like William Stride. He was the sort of sombre local figure at whom townspeople tipped their hats but were afraid to smile. Stride had done everything a labouring man in his position could to improve his life and clamber into the ranks of the property-owning bourgeoisie. He had begun his career around 1800 as a simple shipwright, but after decades of prudent saving and investment he came to make his money in the development of land and the sale of houses. By the 1840s, he was living in one of his own constructions, on an entire street of homes that bore his name: Stride's Row. In that time, he had risen from working at the docks to holding a position as a Commissioner of Sheerness Pier, and if anyone ventured to ask him to what he attributed his success, Stride would almost certainly have cited his devotion to God.

Shortly after his marriage in 1817, Stride converted to Methodism, a religion to which he adhered strictly throughout his life and which governed his every decision. In spite of his comparative wealth, Stride, his wife Eleanor and their nine children led an austere and abstemious life. For most of it, they and their expanding brood chose to inhabit one of the cottages on Stride's Row. According to the strictures of their faith, they would have eschewed any of the outward signifiers of affluence: no expensive clothing, no jewellery and nothing but the simplest furnishings. Rather than dancing, theatre and card games, the family would engage in a weekly day of fasting. Most importantly, in this small town of sailors and seaside amusement, there would be no alcohol. In spite of the fact that he was abundantly able to do so, William Stride never employed a live-in servant, even after the death of his wife in 1858.

It was into this prohibitive and restrained environment that John Thomas Stride was born in 1821. As the second eldest child, John was initiated into his father's profession and trained to become a carpenter. While the busy dockyards at Sheerness would have offered men of John's trade ample opportunities for work in the early part of his life, by the mid-nineteenth century, when iron replaced wood in the construction of ships, employment would have become more difficult to secure. It is likely that this contributed to the reason why John, unmarried at the age of forty, continued to live at home, caring for his elderly father and keeping watch over his youngest brother, Daniel, who appears to have struggled with mental health issues. That year, in 1861, a difficult situation at home may have come to a head when John caught Daniel stealing £6 11s. 6d. from his top drawer. William Stride would not have looked kindly on such behaviour and it is likely that it was his decision to denounce his son to the police. Daniel was arrested, imprisoned and tried at the Petty Sessions in March, where John refused to prosecute him and instead secured his release.[1] It was not long after this incident that the frustrated carpenter decided to leave Sheerness and seek work in London.

In the 1860s, any Londoner wishing to purchase a well-hewn set of dining chairs or a fashionable sideboard would have paid a visit to one of over seventy furniture-making establishments situated around the north part of Tottenham Court Road. The area, which spread from Marylebone Road eastward for over a mile to St Pancras Station, was filled with factories, warehouses and shops where the scent of freshly cut mahogany and oak perfumed the air. By the time John Stride arrived in London, the city's 'furniture district' was home to 5,252 employees working in every aspect of the trade, from upholstering to cabinet making to sales. Stride, with his box of carpenter's tools, would have been able to acquire work easily at one of the numerous workshops.

He also took lodgings within the area, in the home of Charles Leftwich, at 21 Munster Street, just off the Euston Road. Leftwich, who made his money as a lead merchant, a lettings agent and an occasional inventor of plumbing devices, was a respectable middle-class family man whose finances were not beyond taking in a lodger to fill a spare room. John, a single, middle-aged Methodist who was accustomed to quiet, teetotal living, would have made an ideal boarder. However, it is likely that the Leftwich family, tended to by their two servants, maintained a socially dignified distance. John, who would have left for work as early as dawn and returned late, would have taken his meals apart from the family; in his room or in the kitchen, or sometimes at Daniel Fryatt's coffee house at 6 Munster Street.

By the middle of the nineteenth century, the coffee house, often associated with the intellectual pursuits of the Georgian era, was experiencing a revival among all ranks of London's working men. Open from as early as 5 a.m. and until as late as 10 p.m., these establishments offered simple meals of chops, kidneys, bread and butter, pickles and eggs along with cups of sugared coffee. The latest newspapers and periodicals were also available to read or to hear read aloud, but no alcohol was served. Coffee houses became a retreat for those who had taken abstinence pledges or simply for men who wished to enjoy a convivial environment somewhere other than the pub. Factory workers and craftsmen, who once drank porter in the mornings, now stopped on their way to work for a penny roll and a cup of hot caffeine. On the way home, the busy atmosphere of the coffee house mellowed into something more restful. Patrons were encouraged to take their time amid the partitioned, dark-wood stalls, enjoying a plate of pork chops alongside their lightly stained periodicals. 'In the evenings these places become reading rooms,' writes one observer. 'They are convenient to thousands of persons who have not the comforts of domesticity at home. The good fire, the bright light, the supply of newspapers and magazines, and the cup of simple beverage, are obtainable for a few pence . . .'[2]

John Stride, without a wife or family and far from the familiarity of the Kentish coast, must have passed many an hour in this pleasant environment, conversing with Fryatt and contemplating the possibility of opening a similar establishment. As a man in his forties, John would no longer have been able to ignore the physical strains of slaving over a carpenter's bench or in a furniture factory six days a week. Like his father, he recognized the worth of investing hard labour in a business that might generate a larger and more comfortable income and one day support a wife and children.

As was the case with most skilled labourers, John's opportunities to meet women were limited by the length of his working day. Socializing would have occurred in pubs, public parks, music halls or at church events. Coffee houses, too, could offer possibilities.

Generally, women did not frequent these dark wood rooms that smelled of fat and brewing coffee and echoed with gruff male conversation. However, shop girls, servants and those who worked for a daily wage often came in for coffee and a penny bun while on an errand for their mistresses or passed their lunchtimes eating soup, fruit puddings and tapioca. This is most likely how John Stride came to meet a young house-maid from Sweden called Elizabeth Gustafsdotter.[3]

When she first arrived in London in the winter of 1866, Eliz-abeth lived nowhere near the busy, commercial surrounds of Tottenham Court Road, but in an elegant townhouse on the fringe of Hyde Park. At mid-century, few locations in the city were more synonymous with wealth and gentility than those streets encircling the beau monde's favourite spot for prome-nades. Although the identity of Elizabeth's employer and his family remains a mystery, their social status is not. Elizabeth would have taken her place among a household of servants, in the home of a prosperous, cosmopolitan family, not unlike the Dicksons, who travelled regularly between Sweden, Britain and Europe in the course of superintending their shipping, iron and timber empire. Although this would have been a presti-gious position in domestic service, the stakes were much higher for Elizabeth than they had been at any of her previous places of employment. Now part of a hierarchy of staff, she would have to submit to the governance of a housekeeper or a butler in a grand home spread over several floors, rather than a gene-rous, lower-middle-class mistress with a handful of rooms. This position would have come with an entirely new set of rigid rules: clean hands, an erect back, a silent tongue and eyes that never met those of her master or mistress. If or when she encountered a member of the family while traversing a hall or staircase, she would have been instructed to turn her face to the wall. The demands of the job, as well as the cultural differ-ences, when combined with the difficulties of learning a new language must have at times felt overwhelming.

When she had accepted the offer of a job in London, she had also determined to permanently settle in Britain. Although it was not required of every Swede who moved to London to register with the Swedish Church, it appears to have been an administrative formality for those who had applied for permanent residency in the UK. The journey from Hyde Park to the Swedish Church in Prince's Square in the East End of London would have been a time-consuming one for a servant allocated no more than one day off per month. By the time Elizabeth was able to make her way there, five months had elapsed since her arrival in the country. Ultimately, her errand appears to have been carried out at the behest of her employer in the course of preparing for a move abroad – which may not have appealed to her. Elizabeth, who could not write, gave her name to the clerk of the church who inscribed it onto the register, along with a note of her occupation and that she was single. At the same time, Elizabeth also expressed her intention to travel to Brest, in France, one of the centres of the shipping industry, and applied for a change of residency.[4] Whether she did indeed follow her employers to France is unknown as a line was later drawn through her application by another hand, perhaps before the intended departure or after a return to London.

The circumstances that led Elizabeth to eventually leave her position in Hyde Park are unclear, but a strange inference made during the coroner's inquest in 1888 hints at a possible scandal, not unlike that in which she found herself embroiled in Gothenburg. Commentators have remarked that Elizabeth had been blessed with beautiful features. Chief Inspector Walter Dew observed wistfully that notwithstanding her trials and tribulations, 'traces of prettiness remained in her face'.[5] As a young woman in London, with an exotic foreign accent, a high forehead and dark wavy hair, she would have caught the eye of many admirers. One of these, a policeman, courted her while she lived with her employers at Hyde Park, though due to the long hours she worked, this relationship failed to blossom. However, it would appear that someone closer to home may also have had a claim on her affections.

More than twenty years later, a witness at the inquest into Elizabeth's death was questioned about the details of his own romantic relationship with her. He implied that it was stormy. Michael Kidney said that he treated Elizabeth as he might a wife, regardless of the fact that she left him on several occasions. 'Do you know anyone else she has picked up with?' asked the coroner.

'I have seen the address of the brother of the gentleman with whom she lived as a servant somewhere near Hyde Park,' Kidney replied with what seems at first to be a strange non sequitur.

'That was not what I asked you,' the coroner responded. 'Do you think she went away with anyone else?' he clarified, referring to the period in which Kidney was involved with Elizabeth, not to an episode in the past, before he knew her.[6]

Why Elizabeth retained the details, not of the employer for whom she worked more than twenty years earlier, but of his brother, raises many questions. However, it is extremely revealing that Kidney volunteered the information in the context of being probed on the subject of men with whom his partner may have had a relationship. In what form this address appeared is also mysterious. As Elizabeth could not write, the details would have been inscribed by another hand and given to her. Perhaps it was a letter, written by the man himself, carefully preserved over the decades. Elizabeth had also obviously spoken of him and their history to Michael Kidney.

Twenty years is a remarkably long time to recall someone who had simply been the brother of her employer.

It may have been on account of this illicit attachment that Elizabeth eventually left the Hyde Park residence. Whatever the state of affairs, her employer (or perhaps his brother) provided her with a good enough reference to enable her to acquire employment elsewhere.

By the beginning of 1869, if not earlier, Elizabeth was working for a widow by the name of Elizabeth Bond. Mrs Bond, as she was known to her two servants, ran a genteel lodging house and let furnished rooms to a respectable clientele at 67 Gower Street, around the corner from the furniture warehouses and shops of Tottenham Court Road. A Swedish maid well-trained in a gentleman's household in Hyde Park would have conferred a certain sophistication on her establishment, though the drudgery of Elizabeth's chores would have been no different. While Mrs Bond and her widowed daughter Emily Williams took on the daily management of her business, Elizabeth and her fellow servant passed their days and nights trudging up and down the three flights of stairs with their scuttles of coal and buckets of water, their precariously balanced supper trays and piles of laundry. Those whose grates she scrubbed and beds she made were firmly of the middle class. Mrs Bond's lodgers at various times included a lecturer and fellow of Corpus Christi College, Oxford; a Prussian merchant of 'fancy goods'; a former brewer and his wife and daughter; a solicitor; and a widow 'living on independent means'. Among them between 1868 and 1869 were also a German musician, Charles Louis Goffrie, and his daughter, who lived and gave singing and piano lessons from Mrs Bond's rooms.[7] Once more, Elizabeth found herself among musicians, her days and errands lightened by the presence of melody and perhaps a remembrance of those who had once lifted her from adversity.

One day, when she was sent out to fetch provisions or visit the post office, Elizabeth may have stopped at a local coffee house for a spot of refreshment when she was noticed by a 47-year-old carpenter from Sheerness. It is impossible to say how their meeting occurred or how their relationship progressed, if John and Elizabeth's paths crossed on multiple occasions, on the street moving to or from work, or in the wooden stalls drinking a dark, sugared brew. Whatever the case, by the early months of 1869, they had become engaged.

Nothing is known about John Stride's appearance; if he was a man of commanding good looks, or plain and respectably turned-out. By his late forties, he was certain to have been turning grey. What, then, did a very pretty 25-year-old house-maid, who may have recently been the mistress of her rich employer's brother, see in a modest maker of furniture nearly twice her age? In her mid-twenties, Elizabeth knew that she would have to marry soon, and John, who had lived as a bach-elor for many years, would have been able to put money aside. Perhaps, too, after her tumultuous past, John's affections seemed genuine. She had experienced the harm men could do her and John Stride must have appeared to be a safe choice.

Interestingly, they were married neither in a Methodist chapel nor in a Lutheran church, but at Elizabeth's parish church, St Giles-in-the-Fields, with its lobster tail of a spire pok-ing through the London soot. On that day, 7 March 1869, Elizabeth stood before the altar with no one from her life, nei-ther family nor friend to act as her witness. While Daniel Fryatt signed his name to the register alongside that of his constant customer and companion, the church sexton was made to per-form this role for Elizabeth. There was nothing from her past that could intrude on her wedding day. She even chose to cite a false name for her father: 'Augustus Gustafsson'. Her experience was typical of an immigrant, one who wished no shadows or remembrances to fall upon this new chapter. How much her husband knew of her tragic life in Gothenburg and the disease she still carried within her is unknown.

The Strides' marriage marked another fresh beginning in both of their lives. Their union was sealed by the birth of a business venture and a move to another part of town: Poplar, roughly 6 miles away in the East End. This relocation would have been a well-considered one. John Stride's intention was to open a coffee house, but the possibility of carpentry work at the docks also offered a failsafe. The area's thriving dockyards employed over two hundred full-time labourers and during the 1860s were undergoing an extension project that linked the North London Railway with the port. John's brother George, a dock clerk, had established himself and his family there and it's likely that having relations nearby was an equal draw to a couple who expected to soon have children of their own. By 1871, the two Stride brothers were joined by a third: Charles, who had settled in Limehouse.

Within months of their wedding, the Strides had opened their new endeavour on Upper North Street, in the heart of what was called Poplar New Town. This grid of recently built nineteenth-century streets to the north of the waterside was a mixed area of modest villas, middle-class terraced housing and lodgings for labouring families. According to the writer Jerome K. Jerome, who lived there as a child in the 1860s, it was a place of contrasts, where 'town and country struggled for supremacy', where the surrounding marshes were still dotted with farms and where herds of goats and cows might be driven through the streets. 'Processions of the unemployed' moving between the docks and the workhouse were also a regular sight.[8]

In theory, the social composition of Upper North Street, with its grocers, apothecaries, dressmakers and butchers, was no different from Munster Street, where John had studied Daniel Fryatt's efforts at coffee-house keeping. The teachers, masons, servants, shipwrights and labourers who lived alongside the shopkeepers would have been the Strides' intended clientele rather than the workers at the dockside. The coffee house's position across the road from Trinity Methodist Chapel was also strategic. The outlay on the lease and the initial investment required to establish the business was presumably covered by savings, to which Elizabeth too may have contributed. It is possible that John employed his skills as a carpenter to create or improve upon the interior, which generally consisted of plain wooden stalls, varnished partitions and drop-leaf Pembroke tables. With Elizabeth's experience as a servant, she and John would have run their family business together. Charles Dickens describes the ubiquitous sight in working men's coffee houses of the 'neat waitress', who is 'economical of speech' but ever 'ringing the changes between her two refrains of "coffee and slice" and "tea and a hegg" '.[9] The coffee-hall owner's hours were long ones, but the couple were able to keep their own clock and, for the first time, Elizabeth's scrubbing, cooking, washing and serving would have been performed not for an employer, but for her benefit and that of her husband's alone.

The difficulties the Strides were likely to have encountered came from competition with pubs. In spite of the popularity of coffee halls, not every working man was prepared to abandon alcohol and the jolly camaraderie of the local public house. While the coffee house may have had its dedicated adherents, a business could rise or fall dependent upon its location; too many pubs and too few teetotallers could draw the shutters across even the most welcoming of coffee rooms. By 1871, the Strides had learned this the hard way and were forced to move their endeavour to 178 Poplar High Street, where they hoped to attract a better trade. The failure of this first venture would have come at a cost to the couple. In order to cover the financial loss, John appears to have returned, at least part-time, to his former calling, citing himself on that year's census not as a coffee-house owner but as a carpenter. Still, the Strides were not prepared to concede defeat and were just able to sustain their business.

In four years since they were married, there had been no children. If Elizabeth had pregnancies, then these had not been brought to term, most likely on account of her condition. While her syphilis could not be communicated to John in its latent stage, there was a high risk of miscarriage and stillbirth. In an effort to bury her past, Elizabeth may have been too ashamed to confide her secret to John. Bringing syphilis into the marital home was considered a social disgrace and a tragedy, but it was one for which errant husbands who visited prostitutes and who kept mistresses tended to be blamed. Medical texts generally addressed the problem from this perspective while partially exonerating the man for his conduct by claiming that the true root of the issue lay with the selfish immorality of those in the sex trade.[10] The possibility that a man might choose to marry a woman with a sexual past, who had been exposed to the disease, seemed unconscionable. Elizabeth's failure to become a mother in an era when a woman's identity and purpose was defined by this role would have been devastating to her, especially as society and the Church would have ensured that she shouldered the blame for her own misfortune. Elizabeth's upbringing would have inculcated her with the belief that this was punishment for her sinful life. How John and his devout Methodist family viewed the situation is uncertain. While Stride maintained contact with his brother Charles and his wife and children during the early years of his marriage to Elizabeth, it seems that they began to drift apart after 1872. The Stride family appears to have been a divided one, and at no point were the fissures more evident than in the wake of the death of their revered patriarch.

In the early 1870s, William Stride was approaching his ninetieth birthday. Stubborn and determined until his last, he never once missed a meeting of the Sheerness Pier Commission. However, by the end of the summer of 1873, his health had begun to falter. On 6 September he died in the home he still shared with his son Daniel, and was attended by his daughter Sarah Ann. For one who had played such a prominent role in the development of Sheerness, the obituary that ran in the local paper was rather sparing with its words. It described him only as one 'who was generally respected throughout the town'.[11] There appeared no catalogue of his great deeds or selfless acts of charity, and more revealingly still, no mention of a devoted and grieving family.

With the exception of Daniel, no one among the Stride children had dedicated more of their adult life to their father than John. If anyone had a reason to expect to receive something from William Stride's will, it was his second eldest son, who had forgone marriage until his forties, and remained in Sheerness at the expense of his income and future financial security in order to serve his family. However, when the will was read on the 30th of that month, it contained a number of surprises.

Daniel was handsomely rewarded with property. His father left him five houses on Stride's Row and two houses on

Victory Street, which included an additional 'plot of ground, a stable, a coal shed, a workshop and a garden'. William Stride's daughter, Sarah Ann Snook, who had made her life only three doors down from her father, was also favoured with two houses on Stride's Row. John's affluent brother, Edward, who had remained in Sheerness, trained as a surgeon and became the star of the family, was bequeathed a house on Stride's Row as well.[12] John received nothing, not even a mention or acknowledgement.

William Stride had played a vindictive game of favourites designed to send a clear signal from beyond the grave as to who among his progeny had pleased or dishonoured him. John's eldest brother, William James, who had been born deaf and struggled financially as a labourer in Sheerness all of his life, was similarly excluded, as were all the sons who had abandoned their father for London.

It cannot be a coincidence that John and Elizabeth were forced to sell the lease of their coffee house within months of William Stride's death. The collapse of their first endeavour on Upper North Street was likely to have left a debt, while a second failing business would only have increased their arrears. In order to keep his concern afloat John may have borrowed money, quite probably against the promise of inheriting property. When his father's will left him disappointed, there was nothing to be done but shut the door for good on his ambitions and attempt, however he was able, to keep a roof over their heads.

12

Long Liz

IT WAS NEARLY 8.00 P.M. The sky had darkened and the moon had risen over the flat, silvery Thames. On the evening of 3 September 1878, summer was in retreat and more than eight hundred passengers on board the *Princess Alice*, a pleasure cruiser filled with day-trippers and those returning from their holidays in Sheerness, were headed back to London. On deck, the ship's band played a rousing polka and couples gathered to dance and sing. Children chased one another across the slippery wooden floors. Gentlemen read their newspapers and watched the passing shoreline: warehouses, docks and factories disappearing into night's shadow. As they approached North Woolwich Pier, it never occurred to those lulled by the gentle evening and the music that they were moving directly into the course of the *Bywell Castle*, an 890-ton iron-clad coal freighter. By the time both ships realized a collision was imminent, it was too late. The sharp point of the *Bywell Castle*'s bow plunged knife-like through the *Princess Alice*, tearing directly through the engine-room and shearing the vessel in half. Both parts of the ship were sucked into the depths of the sewage-filled Thames within minutes, the panic-stricken clambering and clinging to its walls as it went under. The river was flooded with bobbing heads, gasping for breath and crying out to loved ones through the black water. Parents held tight to their drowning children, women's heavy skirts and metal bustles made it almost impossible for them to fight the pull of the tide. The *Bywell Castle* threw down ropes and lowered the few lifeboats they had on board, but were otherwise impotent in their efforts to save the lives of so many.

More than 650 died in the tragedy, the greatest loss of life sustained in any Thames shipping disaster. The number of survivors was never confirmed, though estimates placed it between 69 and 170. Those who lived faced the horrific task of helping to identify the dead who were daily pulled from the clasp of the murderous river. Entire families perished on the night of 3 September; children were left orphans, wives and husbands widowed; some had watched helplessly as their loved ones slipped beneath the waves.

The *Princess Alice* disaster traumatized London. The story spread furiously among the communities surrounding the East End docks. Many would have witnessed the events first-hand, seen the bodies, the wreckage, or listened with horror to the descriptions of those who had. As the impact of the tragedy was felt equally among those from Sheerness, the news would have landed especially hard on the Stride brothers in Poplar and Limehouse, who would have anxiously scanned the growing lists of the dead for the names of family, friends or neighbours. Elizabeth must have watched this with keen interest, taking in the magnitude of the calamity as tale after tale circulated in the newspapers and among those she knew.

By the time of the *Princess Alice* disaster, Elizabeth's own life was in turmoil. Following the collapse of the coffee house, her marriage to John had turned sour. The ensuing financial hardship and possibly other factors, such as the couple's inability to produce children, may have contributed to the friction between them. It is also likely that drink had begun to play a role.

In March 1877, eight years into their marriage, it appears that Elizabeth had left John. Although this was to be only a temporary separation, she had nowhere to turn, and rather than opting for the casual ward, chose to take her chances on the street. On the 24th, she was picked up by the police under vagrancy laws, either for begging or sleeping rough, and forcibly taken to the workhouse. After this experience, the Strides were reconciled, but their arguments and difficulties continued. Two years later, when John had fallen ill, Elizabeth appealed for aid from the Swedish Church, and in 1880, her name appears in workhouse records, once at Stepney Union in February, and a second time at Hackney Union in April, where the word 'destitute' was written beside her entry.[1]

It was during this period, if not as early as September 1878, that Elizabeth alighted upon an ingenious method of supporting herself. If John was not able to provide for them, then she would have to use her wits to survive. As the autumn of 1878 wore on, she had witnessed how horror stories about the victims of the *Princess Alice* disaster had led to outpourings of pity and offers of material compensation. The newspapers were filled with information about the generosity of Londoners who had raised more than £38,246 as part of a relief fund.[2] Victims, survivors and their families were urged to come forward with claims, and Elizabeth may have been inspired to do just this, inventing a sorrowful tale of her own. In the weeks following the calamity, many were playing this same game. On 29 September, a 21-year-old woman named Elizabeth Wood was sent to prison for a month after defrauding a Woolwich coffee-house owner on the pretext that she had survived the disaster but lost her family.[3] Similarly, the *Princess Alice*

Fund rejected fifty-five applications for assistance from 'those with no good reason'. Elizabeth Stride's name does not appear anywhere among the list of survivors, and unless she employed an alias, neither was she successful in acquiring charity from the relief fund. It's far more likely that her gains were made simply by peddling her story to concerned individuals.

Elizabeth's tale was an elaborate one, coloured with detail and drama designed to beguile the listener. She claimed that she had been aboard the *Princess Alice* with John and two of their nine children. She appears to have told some people that John was employed on the ship and she and her children were accompanying him that day. When the pleasure cruiser was struck, they were separated; John had attempted to save the children but he and the two young ones were snatched away by the river and drowned. Elizabeth, who found herself within one of the ship's collapsing funnels, saw that a rope had been dropped by the *Bywell Castle* and grabbed for it. In scaling her way to safety, she was kicked in the mouth by the man above her, which damaged her palate. Remarkably, she survived, or so she told her listeners. She went on to say that life as a widow was fraught with hardship. As she was unable to support her seven remaining children, they were placed into the care of an orphanage in south London run by the Swedish Church. In the end, she had been left with nowhere to turn but to a friend of her husband's, and there she still found herself in dire financial need.

Elizabeth may have knitted this story together from others she had heard, or lifted it wholesale from a person she had known. John Stride's wife had not borne nine children, or if she had, the true tragedy may have lain in the fact that none of these survived birth. She may have instead endured nine failed pregnancies, or perhaps she had simply borrowed the number from John, who was one of nine siblings. Whatever the case, in the ensuing years Elizabeth would retell this tale enough times to convince everyone around her of its veracity. It would be the first step in rewriting her history and reframing what would become a malleable identity. She would also use it to distance herself from her husband; during periods when she separated from him, she claimed he was dead.

In April 1881, the couple were again reconciled, though this time only for a handful of months. The census for that year finds their circumstances considerably compromised. When once they occupied several rooms above their coffee shop, their living space was now reduced to a single room in a house on Usher Road, in Bow. By December, John and Elizabeth appear to have agreed to part permanently. Like William Nichols and John Chapman, John Stride may have also consented to pay his wife a small maintenance as a formality of making their separation official. From this period, Elizabeth took up residence in Whitechapel, first on Brick Lane, and then, following a stay in the workhouse infirmary for bronchitis, at the lodging house to which she'd return repeatedly for the next six years: 32 Flower and Dean Street.

According to the writer Howard Goldsmid, 'Flowrydean Street' – as it was called by its habitués – was no 'rose by any other name', but rather 'one of the worst of the East-end slums' which smelled 'unwholesome' and looked 'uninviting'.[4] The Associated Press journalist who visited the street in 1888 described it in slightly more flattering terms, claiming that 'for the East End' it had 'a fairly presentable appearance'. He continued:

> One side of the street is mainly occupied by a huge pile of modern buildings, intended for occupation by the families of artisans, and rented almost exclusively by a colony of

middle-class Jews. The other side presents a far more dingy appearance. The brickwork of the houses is blackened with age, and doors and windows alike present the only too familiar aspects betokening the abode of the extreme poor.[5]

According to the article, all of the buildings on the dilapidated side of the street were registered lodging houses, and number 32 had beds for one hundred 'dossers'. While Goldsmid describes these dormitories as crawling with vermin, 'shamefully overcrowded, very ill-ventilated, and . . . foul-smelling and unhealthy', the AP journalist believed number 32 'seemed to look uncommonly comfortable' inside. Certainly, Elizabeth preferred it to other lodging houses and, over the years, came to regard it as a base.

In the time that she lived at 32 Flower and Dean Street Elizabeth supported herself through 'charring'. A charwoman, described as being 'the lowest trade of domestic – even lower than the maid of all work', was an occasional servant, who came to a home for a few hours to perform tasks for families who wouldn't otherwise be able to afford live-in staff. The charwoman was generally older than the housemaid, 'between 40 and 60', and usually, as evidenced by her 'dirty mob-cap, battered bonnet . . . tucked-up gown and bare, red arms', impoverished.[6] In addition to the 2 shillings she would have received for her work, Elizabeth might also have expected to receive food: toast and tea, scraps of the family meal or even a provision of sugar.

In the East End, the Jewish community, who comprised the majority of the population between Whitechapel High Street and Hanbury Street, were reliant upon the services of gentile charwomen to assist them during the Saturday Sabbath. Because religious custom forbade Jews from engaging in any form of work from sunset on Friday to sunset on Saturday, a charwoman was hired to light the fires, switch on gas lighting and to cook and serve meals. As recent immigrants who had escaped persecution in Russia, Prussia and the Ukraine, most families did not speak English, though Elizabeth learned to communicate with them in Yiddish. In fact, it is possible that she had acquired the rudiments of this language in Gothenburg. Haga, the working-class district where she had lived, was also the home of the city's Jewish community.[7] Working for Jewish families would have also offered Elizabeth the security of knowing that fellow immigrants were not usually eager to discuss their pasts, and therefore were unlikely to make many enquiries into hers.

Living apart from John, away from the West End and from Poplar, gave Elizabeth the opportunity to become whoever she wished. She had learned that shedding identities was as simple as moving somewhere new. While she resided in Whitechapel she was Elizabeth the widow and Elizabeth the disaster victim. The farmer's daughter had become a servant; the servant had become a man's mistress and a fallen woman; the fallen woman had become a prostitute, and then a rescued Magdalen. She had found herself an immigrant, the paramour of a rich man and the wife of a struggling carpenter. She had been a coffee-house keeper and a workhouse inmate. She was Swedish, but could speak English well enough to fool people. She may also at times have claimed to be Irish, and used the name Annie Fitzgerald. When she chose to, Elizabeth could even transform herself into another woman's sister.

In 1883, fate threw Elizabeth into the path of a woman named Mary Malcolm, a tailoress. It seems that the years spent squinting over a needle had ruined what remained of Mrs Malcolm's eyesight. Her attraction to the bottle probably did not help matters. One day, perhaps on the street or in a pub, she glimpsed Elizabeth Stride and was convinced it was her estranged sister, Elizabeth Watts. Mary had probably called out her sister's name, and Elizabeth had conveniently answered to it. The mistaken identity stuck, in part because Elizabeth Stride was all too pleased to use this new relationship to her advantage.

When the tailoress gave her account of events, she appears to have conflated the two women's stories, weaving the details she understood of Elizabeth Watts's life with those Elizabeth Stride told her of her recent past. She claimed that her sister was colloquially called 'Long Liz' and had lived with a man who ran a coffee house in Poplar. She also stated that she knew Elizabeth's husband had died in a shipwreck, though recalling the circumstances of this proved more problematic. As it happens, Elizabeth Watts's second husband had genuinely died as a result of a shipwreck on the Isle of St Paul, but these facts became entangled with Elizabeth Stride's lies about the *Princess Alice* disaster. Knowing that her real sister had led a chequered life, which included at least two marriages and a period spent in an asylum, Mary Malcolm was inclined to believe that the bedraggled, impoverished woman she had met was this same person.[8]

From the time Mrs Malcolm first encountered 'her sister', she claimed that drink was Elizabeth Stride's primary failing. She was always in need of money, and Mary 'had her doubts' about what she did for a living. However, as family, she felt compelled to assist her. For the next five years, the two women met at least once a week, sometimes more frequently. Mrs Malcolm handed over 2 shillings every Saturday at four o'clock on the corner of Chancery Lane. Occasionally she gave Elizabeth clothing as well. Regardless of how things may have appeared, Mary seems to have harboured suspicions which she suppressed or kept to herself. In fact, during the five-year period she met with Elizabeth, she insisted on keeping her at arm's length. Mrs Malcolm never invited her 'sister' into her home, and instead claimed 'I was always grateful to get rid of her.' When asked if her husband or anyone else had known about her meetings with 'her sister', she confessed, 'No, I kept that from everyone. I was so ashamed.'[9]

Mary Malcolm's shame may have stemmed in part from her persistence in maintaining the relationship with Elizabeth in spite of her doubts. So long as Mary did not scrutinize Elizabeth too closely, she could continue to fool herself, while Elizabeth successfully managed to hide from her the true circumstances of her life.

In October 1884, Elizabeth received word that John, whose health had been deteriorating for some time, had been admitted to the Stepney Sick Asylum. It is here that he died of heart disease at the age of sixty-three. He was buried on the 30th of that month, and within weeks, her life rapidly spiralled downward.

Certainly it is no coincidence that by 13 November, Elizabeth was arrested on the Commercial Road for soliciting.[10] That she was also charged with drunk and disorderly behaviour betrays her anguished state of mind. The desire to numb herself and rage at the world was a natural one. Frederick Merrick, the chaplain of Millbank Prison, observed that most of his female inmates 'loathed' selling sex on the streets and that 'their repugnance to it could only be stifled when they were more or less under the influence of intoxicating drinks'.[11] For her offences, the judge gave Elizabeth a prison sentence of seven days' hard labour. Following this, there is no evidence that she was ever arrested again for soliciting.

It was after John's death that Elizabeth met and took up residence with another man: Michael Kidney. Kidney was a dock worker who loaded and unloaded vessels and who also earned some extra income as a volunteer in the Army Reserve. He, in his mid-thirties, was several years younger than his new paramour, but always assumed from her appearance that they were roughly the same age. It is believed that the two met on the Commercial Road, though whether this occurred by accident or while Elizabeth was soliciting is uncertain. The relationship soon became a firm one, and the couple took lodgings together in a series of dingy furnished rooms, first on Devonshire Street and then on nearby Fashion Street. Like Elizabeth, Kidney enjoyed drinking to excess and he was no less angry or violent than her when intoxicated. In January and June 1887, Elizabeth made complaints to the police about Kidney's brutality, though, like many women faced with an abusive partner, later dropped the charges.[12] However, Elizabeth was by no means a passive victim in her relationship. According to Kidney, in the three years the two cohabited, Elizabeth left him twice but was gone, he estimates, 'altogether about five months'. 'She always returned without my going after her,' Kidney boasted, because 'she liked me better than anyone else.'[13] On the occasions when she did leave him, Elizabeth regularly sought out a bed at the familiar surroundings of 32 Flower and Dean Street. The couple's relationship was a complicated one, which was likely to have unravelled not only on account of Elizabeth's drinking and Kidney's violence, but also due to infidelity. By the end of their time together, Kidney was suffering from syphilis for which he received treatment at Whitechapel Infirmary in 1889. He would not have contracted this from Elizabeth, who was no longer contagious by the time she was living with him.

Interestingly, in the course of her many visits with Elizabeth, Mrs Malcolm had no inkling of these tribulations. She claimed that she never knew Elizabeth to be involved with a man and that she had only a vague understanding that her 'sister' was living in a lodging house, 'somewhere in the neighbourhood of the tailors and Jews at the East End'. However, she did know that Elizabeth was undone quite frequently by drink and that she had come before the Magistrate and 'been locked up' on account of it.[14]

From roughly 1886 until her death, there does appear to be a distinct change in Elizabeth's behaviour. Her arrests for drunken disorderliness and obscene language increase quite markedly. By the end of the summer of 1888, Elizabeth had been charged on no fewer than four occasions over three months. While this can undeniably be attributed in part to her dependency on alcohol, there may have been another contributing factor. It had been over twenty years since Elizabeth had contracted syphilis, and the disease would have potentially been entering its final, tertiary phase.

Neurosyphilis, or cerebral syphilis as it was known in the late nineteenth century, presents in a variety of different ways when the disease begins to attack the brain and nervous system. The French physician Alfred Fournier, who conducted a study of the progress of the disease, identified 'epileptic fits' as its first manifestation of the tertiary phase. Interestingly, Mary Malcolm mentions in her inquest testimony that Elizabeth had recently begun to suffer from these. These 'fits' confused her, as she had never known her sister to have epilepsy.[15] Apparently Elizabeth's seizures were so bad that there were occasions when the police had let her off charges on account of her condition. Had Elizabeth actually suffered from severe epilepsy throughout her life, it is unlikely that she would have been able to maintain her positions in service, or that Michael Kidney and others would have failed to mention it at the inquest. It is also unlikely that these were a sham. The police and magistrates would have seen every possible trick to avoid a prison sentence and would not have been easily fooled by this one.

In addition to seizures, neurosyphilis can also lead to paralysis in some and symptoms similar to dementia in others. A victim's memory may falter and the sufferer may become prone to hallucinations and delusions. Behaviour becomes erratic, if not irrational, inappropriate or violent. If Elizabeth was indeed suffering from the early stages of neurosyphilis then her heavy drinking was likely to have disguised these symptoms, or at least offered an easy explanation for her increasing episodes of violence and obscene language. It is also possible that the symptoms themselves drove her to further her alcohol intake in order to contend with feelings of disorientation or pain.

Whether or not Elizabeth's disease was to blame, her behaviour for most of the time she lived in Whitechapel was decidedly secretive and deceitful. The scam she perpetrated on Mary Malcolm, as well as her insistence that she was a survivor of the *Princess Alice* disaster, may have demonstrated to her the gullibility in human nature. In the manner of an experienced con artist, she appears to have learned how to milk this weak spot for financial gain. In her testimony, Mrs Malcolm mentions that Elizabeth had told her she had 'a hollowness in the right foot', caused by 'an accident when she was run over by a machine' three years earlier. She had told Mary that she intended 'to get some money' for it, but Mrs Malcolm could not say 'whether she ever got the money'.[16] However, after viewing Elizabeth's body she had noticed that the 'hollowness' had mysteriously disappeared, a situation for which

Mary could not account. Mary Malcolm also raised another peculiar incident. She claimed that Elizabeth had one day left a naked baby girl outside her door. 'I had to keep it until she fetched it away,' Mary continued. She was under the impression the infant was Elizabeth's child, which she had with a policeman.[17] Michael Kidney, when questioned about this, was entirely baffled. 'She never had a child by me and I never heard of her having a child by a policeman,' he commented.[18] The child was unlikely to have been Elizabeth's, but rather one she had acquired temporarily from an acquaintance or a baby-farmer for the purposes of begging.[19] The addition of an infant, swaddled, crying and hungry in its 'mother's' arms was a well-known ruse designed to tug on the heart and purse-strings of passers-by. Elizabeth later returned for the baby. When Mary asked after it again, Elizabeth lied that she had taken the girl to Bath, to live with the family of her first husband.[20]

Aside from Mary Malcolm, Catherine Lane, the wife of a labourer, was the only other person to claim to have known Elizabeth for a substantial period of time. Lane stated that she had met Elizabeth when Stride first came to stay at 32 Flower and Dean Street, around 1881–82. She saw Elizabeth nearly every day during that time. As the lodging house was the nearest thing she had to a permanent home, Elizabeth would make a habit of coming by to visit, even while she was living with Michael Kidney. However, given the constancy of their association, it's also surprising how little either Catherine or Elizabeth Tanner, the deputy lodging-house keeper at number 32, actually knew about Elizabeth's life. Neither knew her surname or her age. While Michael Kidney believed her to be in her thirties, she had chosen to tell Ann Mills, another resident at the lodging house, that she was 'over fifty years of age'.[21] No one seemed to know where she had been born. It appears that

Elizabeth had learned to speak English so well that some people could not even guess she was foreign. In addition to peddling her stories about the *Princess Alice*, Elizabeth told her friends that she was from Stockholm. Only Sven Olsson, the clerk of the Swedish Church to whom she applied regularly for charitable handouts, had a grasp of her true history from the details recorded in the church's ledgers. Sadly, in all of the time she spent in Whitechapel, Elizabeth's friendships appear to have remained ephemeral; even those who thought they knew her were kept at arm's length.

In late September 1888, Elizabeth returned once more to 32 Flower and Dean Street after she and Michael Kidney had what Catherine Lane described as 'words'. By now, Elizabeth was familiar with this cycle. She gathered her possessions and spoke to a neighbour, a 'Mrs Smith', whom she asked to look after a Swedish hymn book while she was away.[22] Possessions of value were never safe in a lodging house, and 32 Flower and Dean Street was no different. It was here, on the 26th, where the social reformer Thomas Barnardo claims to have encountered her in the communal kitchen, along with several other women. As a campaigner for children's welfare, Barnardo had come to speak with the women about their experiences with children in lodging houses and how their lot might be improved. Instead, the female residents were more eager to discuss the Whitechapel murders, by which they 'seemed thoroughly frightened'. At one point, a 'poor creature who had evidently been drinking exclaimed somewhat bitterly; we're all up to no good and no one cares what becomes of us. Perhaps some of us will be killed next! If anybody had helped the likes of us years ago we would have never come to this!'[23] With hindsight, Barnardo claimed that he believed the woman who spoke those words might very well have been Elizabeth

Stride. In truth, they all might have been Elizabeth Stride, and certainly Elizabeth strove to be all of those women – everyone and no one. She was anonymous: a woman with a mutable story, a changeable history, someone who had recognized that the world didn't care about her or what happened to her, and chose to use that as a weapon in order to survive.

The day of 29 September was no different from any other for Elizabeth. The whitewashers had been in to smarten up the walls of 32 Flower and Dean Street. She and Ann Mills had cleaned the rooms after the men had finished. For completing this task, Elizabeth Tanner gave her sixpence. Elizabeth then went out to the Queen's Head Pub on Commercial Street for a drink, where the deputy keeper saw her again. Tanner mentions in passing that Elizabeth had gone out to the pub 'without a bonnet or cloak', a point that would not have been lost on newspaper readers.[24] In the slums, those women who wished to show that they were available sexually often appeared 'in their figure', without items of clothing obscuring their appearance. However, it was equally known for women selling sex to dress 'gaudily' and for even the poorest to wear plumed and decorated hats. If Elizabeth had gone to the Queen's Head in order to solicit, she did not meet with much luck, as she and Tanner walked back to the lodging house together around six thirty. Presumably it was at this time when she may have paid the deputy keeper for her bed.

Just as the newspapers' reporting on Polly Nichols and Annie Chapman's last movements are riddled with contradictions and inconsistencies, the same is true for Elizabeth Stride. While some publications, like the *Western Daily Press*, affirm that she did pay Elizabeth Tanner in advance for her stay that night, others, like the *Daily Telegraph*, state the opposite. If Stride had paid for her bed, then her intention when she left number 32 later that evening was certainly to return. Knowing that she would be out for at least several hours, she asked Catherine Lane to mind a length of green velvet that she had acquired, perhaps with a view to pawning. Finally, before she stepped out of the door, she sought to smarten up her appearance and borrowed a brush to rid the muck from her only set of clothes.

Precisely where Elizabeth went and with whom is one of the more puzzling mysteries surrounding the deaths of the five canonical victims. As Elizabeth appears to have avoided telling anyone anything detailed about her current or past life, it is impossible to conclude what her designs were that evening. During the inquest no one was able to say if she was involved with a man or men other than Michael Kidney. No one was able to comment on her typical habits, which were her usual haunts and who might have been her regular companions, or if indeed she had any. Instead, her death merely left more questions about a woman whom no one could claim to have known at all. It is possible that Elizabeth may even have wanted it that way.

Only a handful of demonstrable facts are known about what she did that night. From the autopsy report, it seems that she had eaten some potatoes, bread and cheese. It is almost certain that she would have had a few drinks as well. At some stage in the evening, she had acquired a corsage or nosegay: a single red rose tied together with some maidenhair fern which she or someone else attached to her bodice. She also had been carrying some cachous, or hard sweets, for freshening the breath. Either these had been purchased for her, or she had enough spare change to buy these items. She had presumably gone out to socialize or to meet someone – possibly a pre-arranged occasion, or possibly not. She may have gone with the intention of soliciting, or in the hope of finding a longer-term partner – or both. At the time she was wearing what the *North London News* described as 'a rusty black dress of a cheap kind of sateen with a velveteen bodice over which was a black diagonal worsted jacket with fur trimming', adding that her black crepe bonnet was too large for her and that Elizabeth had stuffed the back of it with 'a folded copy of a newspaper . . . with the object of making the article fit closer to the head'. Interestingly, they also remarked that Elizabeth's mode of dress was 'entirely absent of the kind of ornaments commonly affected by women of her station'.[25]

In the wake of her murder, a number of people came forward claiming to have seen her that night, but due to poor lighting and the proven inaccuracy of witness perceptions, none of these claims are in any way verifiable.[26] Additionally, by the occasion of what came to be called 'the double event' – the murders of both Elizabeth Stride and Catherine Eddowes on the same night – the residents of Whitechapel were desperate to offer what assistance they could to end the killer's bloody rampage. With hindsight, the silhouette of any woman who had been seen in a doorway or on the street that evening with a man took on the form of Elizabeth Stride, an individual whose face they had never seen clearly and whom they didn't know. Of all of the purported sightings, only one may have possibly been Elizabeth.

At around 12.45 a.m., a Hungarian man by the name of Israel Schwartz was walking along Commercial Road and turned onto Berner Street. As he did so, he saw a man and woman having a disagreement. The woman stood facing the street, with her back towards the gate leading to an area called Dutfield's Yard. As Schwartz proceeded up the road, the dispute became increasingly heated. The man grabbed the woman, turned her around and threw her onto the footway.

The woman screamed three times, though not especially loudly. At this point, Schwartz, who was keen not to interfere in what he believed to be a domestic dispute, crossed the road. Just then, a man who had been standing in the darkness beside a pub lit a pipe and moved in Schwartz's direction. Uncertain if the man was attempting to chase him off, Schwartz now began to panic and broke into a run. As he fled he believed he heard the woman's attacker cry out the word 'Lipski', a reference to Moses Lipski, a notorious murderer and a term of abuse often levelled at Jews.

Fifteen minutes later, Louis Diemschutz, a seller of costume jewellery, was on his way home when he discovered Elizabeth's body lying in Dutfield's Yard. When he found her, she was on her side, facing a wall, in what looked like a foetal position. She held in her fingers a paper wrap of cachous. Diemschutz thought she appeared as if she had fallen asleep.

At the time of the coroner's inquest, both the police and the press believed the woman Schwartz had seen was likely to have been Elizabeth, due to the narrow window of time in which the sequence of events occurred. However, whether the assailant that Schwartz saw was the same man who would eventually murder her with a single cut across her throat will never be confirmed. Indeed, the question as to whether Elizabeth Stride was truly a victim of the malefactor known as Jack the Ripper, or the subject of another man's violence, is as likely to remain as much of an enigma as will she.[27]

Over the course of her life, Elizabeth had been a variety of things to many people; she had been both dark and light, a menace and a comfort. She had been a daughter, a wife, a sister, a mistress, a fraudstress, a cleaner, a coffee-house owner, a servant, a foreigner, and a woman who had at various times sold sex. However, the police and newspapers saw only another victim: an 'unfortunate' who resided in a Whitechapel lodging house, a drunk, degenerate, broken-down woman far beyond the blush of youth. They depicted her passing as sad and unnecessary, but as no great loss. These impressions, when set in typeface, would become fixed and for the most part unchallenged. There were no dissenting voices to object to this portrait and no attempt made to paint a fuller one. No one cared to find her Swedish family and tell their story. No journalist sought out her in-laws, or possessed any true curiosity about her past, about the gentleman in Hyde Park, Mrs Bond on Gower Street, or the customers in Poplar who had sat on the benches of her coffee house. Eventually, the opportunity to truly know Elizabeth Stride would slip away with her killer into the shadows.

Sven Olsson would have read about the murder of two women in the early hours of 30 September long before he suspected that he knew one of them. As the clerk at the Swedish Church and the keeper of the reading room, he had seen Elizabeth Stride pass through their doors on a number of occasions. She was like many of their other impoverished parishioners: far from home, isolated and in distress. Johannes Palmér, the church's priest, found his posting to this degraded part of London dispiriting and, at times, infuriating. He had grown weary of thieves invading his church and contending with what he called the 'parasitic' beggars, among which Elizabeth Stride would have numbered.

Olsson did not find the poor as tiresome as did his priest, and so when the police approached him to identify someone who they believed was part of the Swedish community in the East End, he did not hesitate to lend his assistance.

A hymn book that he had given Elizabeth Stride had been found among her possessions. After the trials she had undergone in her life, Elizabeth was unlikely to have felt the stirrings of devotion that the book was intended to arouse when she took it from his hands. Nevertheless, she had kept it. She did not pawn it, as she had everything else. It held something of significance to her, perhaps some shadowed memory of a farmhouse in Torslanda.

Sven Olsson must have understood that Elizabeth had no blood relations in England. There was no mother or brother to claim her, to mourn for her, to speak for her at the inquest, or even to provide her true name: Elisabeth Gustafsdotter. It fell to him, a stranger, to be all of this for her.

After he said his piece at the inquest, after all his accented words were scrutinized by the coroner and the jury, Olsson felt he owed Elizabeth Stride one final duty.

There was no one to pay for a hearse and ponies to parade her casket around the East End. The newspapers described her funeral as 'sparse'. She was lowered, without any fanfare, into a pauper's grave on 6 October at the East London Cemetery in Plaistow. Sven Olsson stood by to bid her farewell and utter a prayer for her in Swedish.

Kate

14 April 1842 – 30 September 1888

13

Seven Sisters

O N A MILD MORNING in June 1843, George and Catherine Eddowes, burdened with baskets and bundles and whimpering children, boarded a canal boat in Wolverhampton. A journey by train to London would have been far quicker, but such a convenience was considerably beyond the means of the family of eight. Walking the distance, tramping along the country lanes from dawn until dusk for the better part of a week, would have proven near impossible for six children under the age of ten. Travelling by barge, alongside what few possessions the Eddoweses may have owned, was the only sensible option.

For roughly two days, the family crowded themselves onto the broad, flat vessel which they would have shared with fellow passengers, as well as the bargeman and a heap of awkward cargo: boxes, trunks, pieces of furniture and barrels. If it rained, there was no more than a small, enclosed cabin space, partially occupied by a coal stove, to offer shelter. However, the sights along the Grand Union Canal would have kept the children occupied as they wound through the industrial landscape from Birmingham to the capital. Leaving behind the familiar slag heaps and furnaces, the Eddoweses travelled through the strange new scenery of southern England, bisecting villages, weaving between farms, passing through green and yellow fields bright with wildflowers, spying ancient churches and country estates as they progressed. The intricate system of locks, which caused the boat to rise and fall with the water levels, as well as the sturdy workhorse that pulled them along, would have fascinated the nine-year-old Alfred and his sisters: Harriet (eight), Emma (seven), Eliza (six) and Elizabeth (four). However, the youngest, Catherine, born the year before on 14 April, would not be old enough to recall any part of their journey, or even the circumstances that forced her family to leave Wolverhampton in the first place.

Kate, or 'Chick' as her family called her, was scarcely nine months old when the shape of her father's life began to change. For two generations, the Eddowes family had given their sons to the tin-working trade, one of Wolverhampton's principal industries. As described in the 1820 *Book of Trades*, a tinplate man was expected to not only forge 'kettles, saucepans, canisters of all sorts and sizes, milk pails, lanterns, etc.' from sheets of tin but also to have a proficiency in coating ironware with a protective, rust-resistant layer of the molten material. As this was a skilled profession, tinplate men would have been expected to enter their line of work at the age of fourteen and complete a seven-year apprenticeship, though by the early nineteenth century, with the introduction of machinery, such traditional practices were on the wane. George Eddowes, who would have been among the last to have received this form of intensive training, began his in 1822 at the Old Hall Works. Here, George and his younger brothers, William and John, toiled beneath the same roof as their father Thomas, who in later years would be celebrated as the factory's most senior worker. Under the sharp eye of his apprentice master, George would have learned how to wield 'a large pair of shears to cut the tin into a proper shape and size', and 'how to apply heat so as to solder the joints of his work'. For six days a week, from six o'clock in the morning until six at night in the summer, and from eight until eight in the winter months, he would have laboured with his fellow apprentices at their work bench, learning the difference between the hammers for planishing, hollowing and creasing, and when to use 'the large or small anvils, the beak irons, chisels, gouges, knippers, plyers, squares and rules'. Only at the end of this rigorous period of instruction, which concluded with the apprentice presenting a piece of tinware of his own creation to his examiners, would he be granted the right to officially practise the trade. By the end of that period of seven years, he would have acquired not only an essential set of skills, but a keen sense of identity within a community of fellow craftsmen.

Since 1767, the Old Hall Works, a decaying Elizabethan manor house encircled by fields on the outskirts of Wolverhampton, had sat at the heart of tin-working life. The streets that radiated from it – Dudley Street, Bilston Street, and further west into the more rural surrounds off Merridale Road – became the traditional quarter of the tinplate man and the 'japanner': those who decorated and shellacked the tinware with elaborate painted designs. Men who had trained together as apprentices and worked together in the factories also lived side by side in the weathered cottages and back-to-back houses that lined the streets. Families mingled and intermarried. Gossip and rumours spread quickly, especially in the local tin workers' public houses: the Merridale Tavern, the Swan and the Red Cow.

It was at the Red Cow that the Friendly Society of the United Operative Tin Plate Workers of Wolverhampton, or the 'Tin Man's Society', had been meeting regularly since 1834.

Concerns over the introduction of machinery had led to labour unrest in the 1820s; sensing that future conflict with the factory owners was inevitable, the organization began to draw up a strategy to protect the workers' interests. All members were expected to contribute no less than 5 pence and no more than 6 shillings per week to a strike fund. Additionally, they compiled a 'book of rates', standardizing pay for their work, and by 1842 requested that all six of Wolverhampton's tin factories sign up to it. Most employers followed suit, including William Ryton, the owner of the Old Hall Works, who was often celebrated among his peers as 'a well-known friend to the working classes'.[1] Unfortunately, not all of the city's tin-factory owners had a similar reputation or regarded standardized pay to be in their interests – especially not Edward Perry, the man who had only recently employed George Eddowes and his brother William. The response of the Tin Man's Society was to call a strike, and by January 1843, Perry had 'no less than thirty-five men ... out of his employment'.[2]

Edward Perry was no friend of the working man, and he would not abide industrial action under any circumstances. Throughout his career as a factory owner, he would use foreign labour, death threats, spies and imprisonment to break strikes. Perry prided himself on possessing 'a good knowledge of the rights of ... labour, and especially of the laws relating to conspiracy'. Most importantly, 'he felt sure the ignorance and the enthusiasm of ... working men would give him an advantage.'[3] On this occasion, he was determined to pursue, personally and with force, each employee who was in breach of contract. When Perry learned his men were being enticed away to London under the protection of the union he set out after them. With the assistance of informants and detectives, he tracked his errant employees to the metal workers' pubs of Clerkenwell and hauled them back under warrant. Once arrested for contravening the terms of their employment, he had them tried and sentenced to two months of hard labour at Stafford Prison.

Much as he had hoped, Perry's decision to make no concessions began to divide the community of tinplate workers and japanners. Angry, hissing crowds of tin men began gathering outside the court building whenever Perry took the stand to prosecute his employees, and it was not long before the dispute degenerated into violence.

As dedicated members of the Tin Man's Society, the Eddowes brothers were among the thirty-five men who had unlawfully walked out of Edward Perry's factory. It was the brothers, along with a handful of other society members, who sought to pressure their colleagues into joining the protest, promising that the organization would pay them '15 shillings a week as long as the calamity [the strike] lasted'. On 9 January, Richard Fenton, 'one of Perry's men' who had refused to strike, was enjoying his ale at the Merridale Tavern when it is alleged that William Eddowes and two other tin workers pushed through the door and began accosting him. Later, witnesses at the trial believed that he 'and his party had come in for a row'.

'You have a brother out on strike, you shabby devil!' Eddowes was reported to have shouted. He then 'up with his fist and struck Fenton, and kicked him'. Within moments, a group of at least nine tin workers, including William Eddowes's wife, Elizabeth, set upon Fenton, kicking and beating him and crying, 'We'll murder him, murder the bastard! as Fenton attempted to flee upstairs.'[4]

According to the Magistrate who presided at the trial,

Fenton was fortunate to have escaped with his life. It was perhaps upon reflection of the severity of his actions that William
began to fear imprisonment and went into hiding, leaving his
wife to appear at the trial.

Unfortunately, this incident was but the first of the Eddowes
family's misfortunes. On 15 February, Edward Perry ordered a
notice to be printed in the *Wolverhampton Chronicle*. Perry
stated that he and two other factory owners were aware that
'daily secret meetings' were being held for the purpose of
'inducing our men to leave our employment' and 30 pounds
was offered . . .

> . . . to any person who shall give such information as may
> enable us successfully to prosecute any parties conspiring, by
> payments of money or otherwise, to prevent us carrying on
> our respective trades, to withdrawing our men or to compel
> us to alter our methods of carrying on our businesses, or to
> submit to their terms.

By 24 March, the newspaper ad had come up trumps. Whoever the informant was, he had pointed his finger at George
Eddowes.

At the trial that followed, Perry took the stand and directed
his fire at his former employee. 'The defendant', he said, 'had
been a ringleader' and 'was a complete firebrand'. Perry
wanted Eddowes gone and went on to claim that 'he had
coerced the others and had it not been for him, no strike would
have taken place'.[5] The judge had great sympathy for the be-
leaguered factory owner and immediately sentenced George
to two months' hard labour. According to the *Wolverhampton
Chronicle*, Eddowes demonstrated no remorse for his crimes,
nor indeed any concern that he was leaving behind his wife

and six young children. Instead 'he retired ... with something like an air of bravado and a readiness to undergo ... punishment'.[6]

While Catherine Eddowes's father may have hidden his anxiety at the prospect of spending the next two months plodding the prison treadmills, he would not display it openly. As a committed union man, George Eddowes would have known the risks he faced when he became an agitator and would have expected the union to compensate him and his family for their sacrifice. Equally, he would have recognized that his days of finding work alongside his friends and family in Wolverhampton were now at an end.

The Eddowes family made their entrance into London along the grey, effluent-tainted waters of the Thames, through an archway of dangling cranes that framed the docks of Bermondsey. The small house in which they settled at 4 Baden Place was set a safe distance from the polluted waterfront that had greeted them off the boat. George Eddowes would have paid extra to situate his family nearer to the area's open green spaces and the market gardens that flourished between the factories and warehouses. Although the housing stock was not of the highest calibre, plagued by poor drainage and ventilation as well as a lack of running water, the family would not have been subjected directly to the eye-watering stink of chemicals spewn forth from the local tanneries, dyers and breweries. A lungful of relatively fresh air would have been one of the few privileges the expanding family would come to enjoy.

Had George been a single man or even one with a modest collection of children, his move from Wolverhampton might have been the making of the family. The union was likely to have been responsible for his new job at Perkins and Sharpus, a large tin- and copperware manufacturer on the opposite side of London Bridge. As a 'skilled mechanic', George was entitled to a better rate of pay than a general labourer – one of the many porters, 'carmen' (delivery men) or dock workers who populated the neighbourhoods of Bermondsey. According to *The English Book of Trades*, in the 1820s a tinplate man, 'if sober and industrious', could 'with ease earn from 35 shillings to 2 guineas in a week'. However, it is likely that by the mid-century George would have expected to receive a wage of approximately £3 0s. 9d. from his new employer.[7] Such an income would have offered a family with two or three children a degree of certainty that the rent would be paid, the hearth fires lit, and that they might afford a choicer cut of meat for their table. As C. S. Peel describes, in London a man could 'rent a neat little house of six rooms', one of which he would probably let out to a lodger and receive 20 pounds per year. The children would 'probably go to an Endowed school or a British Day [school]. There will be occasional jaunts to Gravesend or Margate: sound boots, Sunday best.' With a reliable working-man's income behind them, George's two or three children could rise in society. If they had an education, his boys might become clerks or shopkeepers; his daughters, schoolmistresses or the wives of clerks and shopkeepers. However, the burden of six children soon eliminated that route to improvement. Indeed, it is unlikely that such a hopeful scenario so much as crossed the minds of George and Catherine Eddowes, both of whom came from large families whose needs far exceeded the stretch of their fathers' wages.[8]

As the social reformer Seebohm Rowntree found, phases of 'want and plenty' marked the life cycle of the working classes. Household income ebbed and flowed according to the number

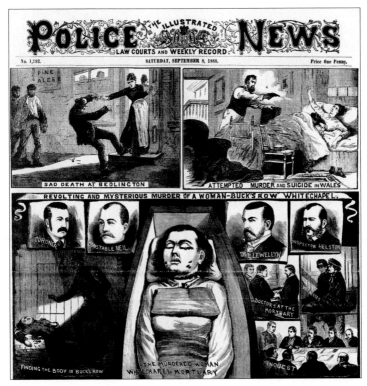

Front page of the *Illustrated Police News*, Saturday, 8 September 1888, depicting the murder of Polly Nichols.

Peabody Buildings, Stamford Street, Lambeth. The Nichols were among some of the first families to be approved as tenants for the charity-operated Peabody Buildings, which boasted of many 'mod cons'. They moved into number 3, D-block on 31 July 1876.

A family portrait, probably taken around the time that William Nichols married Rosetta Walls in April 1894. *Back standing, left to right*: George Percy Nichols (Polly's second surviving son) and William Nichols. *Front sitting, left to right*: Rosetta Walls and Mary Ann Cushway (George's wife).

LEFT: The Smith family home, Montpelier Place, Knightsbridge, London. The Smith family are recorded as having first lived at 29 Montpelier Place in 1851. The house then became the family's permanent address around 1863–4, after the death of George Smith.

BELOW: John and Annie Chapman, photographed at a studio on the Brompton Road, Knightsbridge, around the time of their wedding in May 1869.

Annie Georgina Chapman, Annie and John's second daughter, c. 1881, wearing her sister's dress. Annie Georgina displays a number of the facial features associated with Foetal Alcohol Syndrome.

Emily Ruth Chapman, the eldest daughter of Annie and John, c. 1878. Emily is about eight years old.

Sir Francis Tress Barry employed John Chapman as his head coachman from the late 1870s. A wealthy businessman who made his fortune in the mining industry, Barry purchased the St Leonard's Hill estate in Clewer, near Windsor, where the Chapman family lived. He was later granted a baronetcy and became an MP for Windsor.

St Leonard's Hill House. Francis Tress Barry purchased the St Leonard's Hill estate in 1872 and hired Charles Henry Howell to build him a 'modern' Victorian manor house in the French-chateau style.

Front page of the *Illustrated Police News*, Saturday, 22 September 1888, depicting the events of Annie Chapman's murder.

The farmhouse where Elizabeth Stride was born, Stora Tumlehed, in Sweden.

Portrait illustration of Elizabeth Stride from *Illustrated Police News*, 6 October 1888. Although Elizabeth Stride is recognized as being among the 'canonical five' victims, many continue to question whether she was truly a victim of Jack the Ripper.

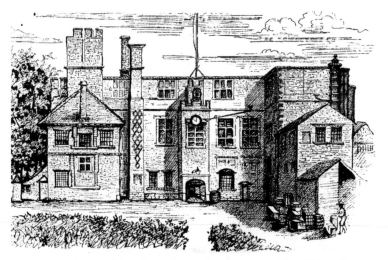

Engraving of The Old Hall Works, Wolverhampton. The Old Hall, or Turton's Hall, had been built by the Leveson family in the sixteenth century. By the eighteenth century it had fallen into disrepair, and by the end of that century it had been turned into a tin factory.

Drawing of Kate Eddowes from *The Penny Illustrated Paper*, 13 October 1888. It is unknown if this image was copied from a photograph of Kate or is an artistic interpretation of her appearance.

A LOST WOMAN
MARY KELLY
IN MILLER'S COURT

Mary Kelly, 'A Lost Woman'. In the wake of her death, Mary Jane Kelly's enigmatic life was subject to much speculation and romanticizing. As the youngest, most beautiful and most overtly sexual of the five women, her life remains the most investigated.

13 Miller's Court was the last address shared by Mary Jane Kelly and her partner, Joseph Barnett. Kelly was murdered in her bed in the early hours of 9 November 1888. It is believed that the killer may have gained access by reaching through a broken window pane to unlatch the door.

of mature earners under a roof. While a young man lived with his parents and had employment, he might enjoy 'comparative prosperity', a situation that would 'continue after marriage until he has two or three children, when poverty will again overtake him'. Most working men were then resigned to 'a period of poverty that will last perhaps for ten years, ie; until the first child is fourteen and can earn wages'. But Rowntree also noted that 'if there are more than three children, it may last longer'. For a working-class woman, this pattern was the same, though she typically contributed less before her earning potential was further crippled by the onset of childbearing and domestic obligation.

The experience of Kate Eddowes's mother, Catherine Evans, mirrored this. As the second of seven children born to an impoverished Wolverhampton latch-maker, little care was taken over her schooling before she was sent to work. By the time she had entered her teens she had acquired experience as a kitchen maid and eventually worked her way up to become a cook at the Peacock Inn, one of the premier hostelries in Wolverhampton. However, it was here in 1832, at roughly eighteen, when her short career was curtailed. Matrimony in the nineteenth century spelt the beginning of a woman's true calling: that of motherhood, and in this regard Catherine proved exceptionally accomplished. In the first five years of her marriage she produced four children, the eldest of whom, Alfred, was mentally disabled and suffered from epileptic fits. While many women from the labouring class continued to work after becoming mothers, whether by taking in washing or mending or by going out to factories or laundries, it is possible that Alfred's condition and the rapid succession of births that followed prevented her from contributing to the family's income. Whatever the case, if either she or George had possessed access to reliable information about contraception, their lives, and those of their children, might have been entirely different.

It is often erroneously thought that the inhabitants of the nineteenth century, those who are charged with inventing the covered table leg, were too strait-laced to contemplate, let alone write about, the reproductive lives of married couples. Nothing could be further from the truth. In the first part of the century, Francis Place, Robert Dale Owen and George Drysdale had each published works on methods by which men and women could 'restrict family size'. Suggestions varied from coitus interruptus, to (reusable) 'French letters' constructed from sheep's gut, to spermicidal douches and 'contraceptive wads' placed inside the vagina. However, while this information was discreetly conveyed to the literate middle classes who could afford books, the dissemination of such material to the working classes was not as successful. Neither George nor Catherine Eddowes could read, nor is it likely they would have even known that such books existed or where to get them. The acquisition of 'French letters' would have proven equally baffling, if not totally beyond the means of a family scarcely able to make ends meet. At any rate, conception and the prevention of it was widely believed to be a woman's responsibility. Like her mother and grandmother and most of the women in her community, Catherine would have been conditioned to accept perpetual childbearing as part of the lot of being a wife. Contraception, when it was used, all too frequently came in the form of her husband's exhaustion or illness. In times of desperation, there were herbal tisanes and douches with spermicidal or abortifacient properties that could be concocted, if a woman possessed either the time, money or the moral courage to acquire the ingredients. In many cases, she had none of these.

The result of all of these factors – lack of information, poverty and a sense of obligation to perform the role of a dutiful wife – gave rise to what the nineteenth-century maternal rights campaigner Margaret Llewelyn Davies called 'a life of excessive childbearing'. Its tolls on the physical as well as the emotional and material well-being of women like Catherine were enormous. In large families like the Eddoweses', where the addition of another mouth became almost an annual occurrence, resources grew increasingly limited. In real terms it meant less food on the table: thinner soup, a forkful of offal, a slice of bread in watered-down milk. In such cases, it was the mother who was expected to go without. Regardless of whether she was pregnant or breast-feeding 'at a time when she ought to be well-fed', she would 'stint herself, in order to save; for in a working-class home, if there is saving to be done, it is not the husband and children, but the mother who makes her meal off the scraps which remain over, or plays with the meat-less bones'.[9] Contemporary experts frequently remarked on the malnourished state of such mothers and the resulting high incidence of miscarriage, stillbirth and infants who failed to thrive in their first year of life.

Nevertheless, women in Catherine's position, forced to contend with the demands of an infant and young children while simultaneously maintaining the home for her husband on ever-diminishing pay, could not permit themselves the luxury of their own pregnancies, or even their deliveries, keeping them from their duties. Even with occasional help from female relations and neighbours, a woman was expected to be on her feet engaged in 'the incessant drudgery of domestic labour' up until the moment of birth. If she didn't possess the means of paying for assistance during her period of recovery, she had no choice but to be 'back at the stove, at scrubbing and cleaning, at the washtub . . . lifting and carrying heavy weights' within days of her delivery. Such strains did not come without serious health repercussions, including haemorrhages, severe varicose veins and crippling back problems.

None of these factors impeded the expansion of the Eddowes family, which continued at a steady pace in the wake of their move to London. The following year saw the birth of a seventh child, Thomas, who was soon joined by George in 1846 and John in 1849. Two further girls, Sarah Ann and Mary, were born in 1850 and 1852. By the arrival of William in 1854, Catherine had given birth twelve times, though only ten of her children survived beyond their teenage years.[10] It must have seemed that whenever an older child flew the nest to go and earn a wage, a new, crying, demanding sibling replaced them. In order to accommodate alterations to their size and amendments to their household budget, the Eddoweses moved house at least four times between 1843 and 1857, though they generally strayed little further than a street or so from where they had originally settled on Baden Place.[11] This in itself is an interesting indicator of how the family would have been perceived in the community. It is likely that no matter how difficult their financial circumstances became, the Eddoweses would have made good on their rent and on whatever debts they owed to the local shopkeepers. Unlike less fortunate families, such as unskilled labourers in irregular work, it was never necessary for George, Catherine and their children to 'do a flit' in the night, disappearing to some other insalubrious neighbourhood, leaving their unpaid bills behind them. This would have been a matter of great pride to the family, who above all would want to maintain a semblance of respectability among their neighbours. Catherine, like other wives of her status, would have attempted where possible to put aside money for lace curtains, a sideboard for crockery, or a carpet that might have been laid down on Sundays. Ideally, all of the children of a skilled labourer would have owned a pair of shoes, and it is unlikely that the 'seven sisters' of the Eddowes clan (as they came to be known) were permitted to mix with those boys and girls who ran barefoot through the streets.

As much as it was possible, given the practical hardships of managing an army of children, it seemed that at least George, if not Catherine, wished their offspring to benefit from some sort of education. While they were under no legal obligation to send their children to school, Elizabeth, aged twelve, Kate, aged ten, Thomas, aged eight, and George, aged six, are all cited on the 1851 census as being scholars.[12] However, in many cases, parents would have claimed their progeny were receiving an education in order to maintain appearances. How much instruction Kate's four elder sisters received is questionable, as none but Emma could write, let alone read, as evidenced by the crosses they marked in place of signatures on their marriage certificates.

Illiteracy, and a poor level of education generally, would have hardly been unusual among the daughters of the working class at a time when 48.9 per cent of English women could not even sign their names.[13] Regular school attendance was not deemed essential when a girl was of more use to her mother at home, or assisting the family by earning money. As the educational reformer James Bryce commented in the 1860s, 'They can help in the house-work and mind the baby . . . Hence it often happens that girls are not sent to school till long after the age when systematic instruction ought to have begun, and . . . they are frequently kept away upon slight grounds.' Those 'slight grounds' amounted to a range of excuses but usually corresponded with the birth of a sibling or a family illness, which could result in the removal of a girl from school for several months at a time, if not permanently. In larger families, where the eldest children were expected to assist in the rearing of their younger brothers and sisters, birth order determined how much schooling a girl was likely to receive. While Catherine's attention was occupied by her infants, it would have been Harriet, Emma and Eliza who took turns minding Alfred, as well as the smaller children, in addition to cooking meals, undertaking the shopping, the laundry and the cleaning. These obligations would have been juggled each time a daughter entered employment, when the next eldest in the queue was called upon to lend assistance at home. While the constant juggling of wage earners with mother's helpers would have placed many obstacles in the four elder sisters' paths to an education, it had the effect of leaving Kate's open.

It is unknown who alerted George Eddowes to the availability of places at the Bridge, Candlewick and Dowgate Schools, little more than a few minutes' walk from the gates of Perkins and Sharpus. The charity, which had been established to provide education for the wards' poor children, had recently extended their admissions policy to accept the sons and daughters of those who also worked in the area. Upon learning this, Eddowes sought to enrol Kate at the Dowgate School.

In the 1840s, Dowgate School accommodated 'not less than 70 boys and 50 girls', for which, at times, a waiting list existed. Although the education that was offered adhered to the religious-based National System, its teaching was much more focused and rigorous. Boys and girls were taught separately, though both were instructed in reading, writing and arithmetic, as well as Bible studies and music. Girls were given additional lessons in needlework. To have been granted a place at such a school would have been an honour for any working-class family. Although Dowgate was not a boarding school, its pupils were subject to a full day of structured learning, seven days a week, from 8 a.m. to 12 noon and 2 p.m.to 4 p.m. in the spring and summer months, and from 9 a.m. during the autumn and winter months. On Sundays they were required to attend no less than two services, usually at St Paul's Cathedral, in whose shadow the school had been built. Cleanliness and respectability were enforced absolutely. Each child was to wear a uniform, laundered and provided by the school and made by the female pupils. Boys as well as girls were responsible for mending their clothing and no child would be admitted into the schoolroom in the morning without a clean face and hands. A special sink was installed for ensuring this, and a sum was budgeted each year for the purchase of soap. Among the schoolmaster and mistress's duties was also 'to attend and see the children's hair is cut every six weeks'.[14]

The intention of the Dowgate School and others like it was to create a better sort of working-class person: one who valued themselves and the principles of Christianity and who would go forth into the labouring force dignified, clean, thoughtful and obedient. When a student approached the age of fourteen and completed their schooling, Dowgate strove to place them in a respectable industry. Boys were offered placements with architects and engineers, or as clerks in banks and businesses, while girls were prepared for roles in domestic service. Successful pupils who persevered at their new trade and were commended by their masters or mistresses became eligible to receive prizes from the school, amounting to as much as 5 pounds, and Dowgate's minute books are filled with such stories.

Ultimately, one of Dowgate's objectives seems to have been

to separate the child as much as possible from the demeaning circumstances of his or her daily life, where they were viewed simply as another pair of hands, rather than as a scholar. The demands of a full day of schooling seven days a week would have meant that children would have rarely seen their families but for dinner and bed, and would have been at least partially removed from exposure to vices present in their home. Any parent who put their child forward for such an opportunity would have recognized that the Dowgate School offered a stepladder out of the cycle of poverty.

How it came about that George and Catherine selected Kate from among their children to benefit from an education at the school is unknown. Her order of birth would have certainly played a role, but it is likely that Kate also demonstrated a particular spark or an aptitude for learning, which set her apart from her brothers and sisters. In later years, Emma recalled her sister's youthful personality as being 'lively . . . warm hearted and entertaining',[15] while other acquaintances remarked that Kate 'possessed an unusual degree of intelligence'.[16] As the school admitted children as young as six, it is probable that she began her education there in 1848, possibly alongside Emma. Every morning and every evening, Kate would have crossed back and forth along London Bridge, just like her father. Dressed in the blue and white uniform she had stitched herself, she would weave her way between the leather market and Guy's Hospital, between factories and tanneries, squinting against the sun in summer and wrapped in a woollen cape in winter.

It is impossible to know what exactly were Kate's experiences at the Dowgate School; her name does not appear in any of the minutes that record exceptional or poorly behaved pupils. It might therefore be assumed that she was an average and obedient student. As a charity, Dowgate attracted the interest of a number of benefactors who wished to see the children excel, but who also believed that education should be imparted with kindness. The trustees instructed the master and mistress to 'abstain as much as it is possible from inflicting severe chastisement' on pupils. Instead, during the period that Kate would have attended the school, prizes were made available by wealthy subscribers to encourage good behaviour. 'A book was to be awarded to the boy who had best conducted himself and a work box to the girl in a like manner.' The master and mistress decided to 'leave the award of the prizes to the children themselves . . . so that they had selected the boy and girl who were really the most worthy'.[17]

The school's eminent donors were also eager to offer the children opportunities. On 26 June 1851, Edmund Calvert, the owner of the nearby Calvert and Co. Brewery, hosted a day's outing for the 124 pupils at the Bridge, Candlewick and Dowgate Schools to the recently opened Crystal Palace in Hyde Park. The spectacle of the Great Exhibition, one of the first world fairs, housed within an equally magnificent plate-glass structure, was unlike anything seen before in Britain. Resembling an enormous greenhouse, its 990,000-square-foot interior towered to a height of 128 feet and housed more than 15,000 exhibitors from around the world. The array of objects on display was staggering. Masterpieces of technological advancement – printing presses, steam hammers and locomotive engines – shared space with vast porcelain vases from China, furs from Canada, a 50-kilogram lump of gold from Chile and the Koh-i-Noor diamond in a cage-like safe illuminated by gas jets. International exhibitors paraded in their native dress; men in turbans, embroidered robes and gold-threaded textiles with foreign faces chaperoned their country's treasures.

'Whatever human industry has created you find there,' wrote the author Charlotte Brontë of her visit. There were . . .

> . . . great compartments filled with railway engines and boilers, with mill machinery in full work, with splendid carriages of all kinds, with harness of every description, to the glass-covered and velvet-spread stands loaded with the most gorgeous work of the goldsmith and silversmith, and the carefully guarded caskets full of real diamonds and pearls worth hundreds of thousands of pounds. It may be called a bazaar or a fair, but it is such a bazaar or fair as Eastern genii might have created. It seems as if magic only could have gathered this mass of wealth from all the ends of the earth – as if none but supernatural hands could have arranged it thus, with such a blaze and contrast of colours and marvellous power of effect.[18]

The experience of the Crystal Palace would have dazzled the nine-year-old Kate Eddowes. That morning, she and her classmates, accompanied by the schoolmaster and -mistress, were conveyed by vans specially laid on by the brewery 'to the great centre of attraction'; 124 little cap-covered heads were counted in and out, guided in rows through the wonders of what would have seemed to them a type of fairyland. Children who had seen little beyond the basic interiors of their homes and schoolroom would have been mesmerized by the circus-like swirl of the exotic. Then, after 'having enjoyed themselves for some hours in the many attractions of the place, they were conveyed back at about six o'clock in the evening to the brewery'. Here 'an excellent dinner was prepared for them', and they dined in the company of the heads of Calvert and Co. Toasts were drunk before the children rose to their feet and sang the national anthem 'in a highly effective manner'.[19] This would have been an exceptional occasion for the children of Dowgate School, and Kate would be unlikely to forget it or the splendours she had briefly glimpsed.

Childhood, for the sons and daughters of the Victorian labouring classes, was a fleeting phase of life, often curtailed abruptly by family circumstances. Kate's fourteenth birthday in April 1856, which would have ordinarily marked the end of her education, also coincided with the dissolution of Perkins and Sharpus, her father's employer. If George was easily able to find further work is unknown, but certainly there would have been an added urgency in seeing his daughter placed swiftly into employment. However, it is possible that the upheaval visited upon the Eddowes family in 1855 brought her days as a schoolgirl to a close earlier than this.

For the better part of 1855, Catherine Eddowes would have been suffering from a terrible cough. Her family would have watched her grow weak, thin and feverish. It is likely they knew what she was suffering from, even before she received the diagnosis of consumption. One of the elder daughters would have been called upon to nurse her, and George, because he had little choice in a house of three or so rooms now occupied by eight family members, continued to sleep beside his ailing wife as she sweated and spluttered up blood. By November, as the chill and damp set in, she worsened. Kate was only thirteen when she lost her mother on the 17th of that month. Catherine, whose body had been ravaged by childbearing, physical labour and poor nutrition, had, at forty-two, lived an average number of years for a woman of her class.

A reorganization of household responsibilities followed in the wake of Catherine Eddowes's illness and death. In an account written in 1888, Emma claimed that, as the second eldest daughter, it was left to her to manage the home and to look after Alfred and the four youngest siblings, all still under the age of twelve. However, these arrangements were only to prove temporary. In 1857, less than two years after tuberculosis claimed the life of his wife, George too began to sicken.[20] The family knew the inevitable would come and by September of that year, the elder Eddowes daughters had begun to consider their futures. On the 27th, Elizabeth, at the age of nineteen, agreed to marry her beau, Thomas Fisher, a neighbour, then only eighteen and calling himself a labourer. Under other circumstances, George might have hoped for a husband with better prospects, but at least one of his girls would have been legally married and settled in a home of her own when he departed this life. While deathly ill, George, with the assistance of his daughters, attended the wedding at St Paul's, Bermondsey, on Kipling Street, a short but difficult walk from their home on King's Place. Here, he gave away Elizabeth and came forward as a witness, to put his cross upon the register beside his name. The occasion during that gloomy autumn would have been a bittersweet one, and would have marked out the final weeks in which the Eddowes would ever live together as a family.

As the leaves reddened and dropped and October became November, the problem of what was to be done with Alfred and the younger children following their father's death loomed ever larger for the two eldest sisters. In Emma's account of events, which appeared in the *Manchester Weekly Times*, she suggests that Harriet was already settled with (though not married to) Robert Carter Garrett, a carman.[21] Eliza had acquired a place in service and the newly wedded Mrs Fisher and her husband had taken over the running of a bird shop in Locks Fields.[22] Emma too recognized that she would have to return to full-time employment in order to support herself, and when an opportunity arose in a good household on Lower Craven Place in Kentish Town, north of the river, she left the care of the children and the nursing of their father to Harriet.

It may have initially been their plan, between them, to assume responsibility for their siblings, but as the family was so large, this would be no simple undertaking. The issue of who would look after Alfred became 'a constant source of trouble' for the elder sisters, but for some unspecified reason, Emma claimed they were most concerned about Kate. 'We wished especially to get her away,' she recalled. At fifteen, it is likely that Kate was profoundly affected by the loss of her mother, and the impending death of her father would surely have only worsened her grief. It is possible that Emma and Harriet believed their sister required more guidance and stability than they could provide, or perhaps they felt Kate, bright and with an education, was capable of further improvement under the watchful eye of the family. Whatever the case, Harriet had a letter sent to her uncle and aunt, William and Elizabeth Eddowes, in Wolverhampton, 'to see if she could get Kate a situation away from London'. Her relations agreed, but were unable to provide the train fare. With time running short, Emma, who never failed to paint herself as the most resourceful among her sisters, took matters into her own hands and approached her employer. 'My mistress,' she recalled thirty-one years later, 'upon learning our unfortunate position, paid Kate's fare to Wolverhampton.' And that was that. Whether Kate had any say in the matter, which would ultimately come to determine the course of her life, is doubtful.

Given the family's limited resources, the fate of the other Eddowes children was a sad inevitability. Neither Elizabeth and Thomas Fisher nor Harriet and Robert Garrett had the means of supporting 13-year-old Thomas, 11-year-old George, 7-year-old Sarah Ann, 5-year-old Mary, or 23-year-old Alfred. On 9 December, a week after the death of their father, perhaps even on the day of his funeral, Alfred and the three youngest were sent to Bermondsey Union Workhouse as orphans. Thomas joined them there on the following day. It cannot be imagined that George went to his grave easily in the knowledge that the seams that held his family together would be torn apart upon his death.

As for Kate, alone on a Wolverhampton-bound train, December 1857 marked the end of her childhood. She would leave behind all she had ever known for a place she did not remember, to live among strangers with whom she shared nothing but a surname.

14

The Ballad of Kate and Tom

A STRANGER TO WOLVERHAMPTON COULD never have guessed that the romantic sixteenth-century moated manor house surrounded by the fields off Bilston Street housed one of the city's hives of industry. Like virtually everything around it, the once proud home of a family of wealthy wool merchants had given itself to the advances of commerce and progress. Notwithstanding the carefully laid-out flower beds and ornamental goldfish ponds, the Old Hall Works was no different inside than any of the other factories that lined the streets and filled the courtyards of the soot-choked town. Its former kitchens were 'utilised for tinning . . . goods'; its large open fireplace contained 'vats of molten metal and grease', while 'the kitchen floor was strewn with pans and dish covers in the process of tinning'. The grand oak staircase which sat at the house's centre, 'instead of leading to the state ballroom, now led to warehouses where women and girls were employed in wrapping up goods'.

Onto the south part of the mansion, a functional modern brick extension had been built which was filled with the constant thump and hiss of steam presses in the stamping room. In the polishing shop adjacent to it, women stood for as many as twelve hours a day, repeatedly rubbing shellacked japanware into a high finish. Nearby in what were called 'the lions' cages' the red-hot japanning stoves were stoked, while two powerful engines rattled and chugged beside a boiler and a burnishing mill.

Amid these furnaces and machinery was a room filled with vats of acid over which a collection of women, known as 'scourers', wielded what were called 'pickling forks'. With their hair tightly bound inside their caps, and their clothing protected by heavy aprons, they used their long-handled tongs to dip a piece of recently forged tinware into an oxide bath in order to prepare it for the japanning process. Once the debris had been stripped off, the piece would be dried in sawdust. This entire process would then be repeated, again and again, from 7 a.m. to 7 p.m. in the summer and 8 a.m. until 8 p.m. in the winter, six days a week. Burning eyes, raw throats and the occasional industrial accident were all to be expected.

Work as a scourer was a good position, William and Elizabeth Eddowes would have lectured their niece, and they had done her proud by securing it for her. Three generations of Eddoweses had toiled at the fires and work benches of the Old Hall Works, including her father, and after the industrial disputes of the 1840s and 50s, the owner, Benjamin Walton, welcomed the family back into his workforce and offered them a fair wage. However, this was unlikely to have been the 'situation' that Emma or Harriet or even Dowgate School had envisioned for a pupil who had been educated for a life in domestic service.[1]

A new chapter of Kate's life had begun as her train from London had passed through the deadened, scorched landscape of the region which had only recently come to be called 'the Black Country'. An industry of chain making, brick baking, and steel forging had risen from the land, fed by a 30-foot deep vein of coal which ran through the countryside. Those who did not graft in factories or before furnaces hammered at the seam itself, drawing forth the life-blood that sustained the engines. By day the chimneys rained soot; by night the forges glowed demonically through the darkness. Even for those accustomed to horrific scenes of misery, the spectacle presented by a journey through the Black Country could come as a shock. Dickens described a hellish vision that seemed to appear:

> On every side, and far as the eye could see into the heavy distance, tall chimneys, crowding on each other, and presenting that endless repetition of the same dull, ugly form, which is the horror of oppressive dreams, poured out their plague of smoke, obscured the light, and made foul the melancholy air.

The approach to Wolverhampton was crowded with 'mounds of ashes', beside 'strange engines that spun and writhed like tortured creatures clanking their iron chains, shrieking in their rapid whirl from time to time as though in torment unendurable, and making the ground tremble with their agonies'.[2] Although Kate had grown up in the shadow of London's tanneries and factories, this new environment shaped by heavy industry would have seemed as foreign and strange to her as did her family in Wolverhampton.

It is likely that the first time Kate had ever met her father's brother William and his wife Elizabeth was when she, with her small collection of childhood possessions, came to live at their house at 50 Bilston Street. Her cousins – William, aged thirteen, George, seven, and five-year-old Lizzie – would have stared at her with hesitant and curious eyes. Sarah, the eldest at fourteen, would have made a perfect companion, someone with whom Kate would have shared her bed and her thoughts. Gradually, she would have been introduced to her grandparents, Thomas and Mary, who lived around the corner, and her uncle John and his four young children. How willing the Eddowes clan were to embrace their London relation is unknown. Another mouth to feed could never have been an entirely welcomed prospect, though at fifteen Kate was certain to earn her own keep and contribute to the household income. Although sad, the loss of parents was too much of a commonplace occurrence to be considered an excuse for not pulling one's weight, and Kate would have been put out to work without delay.

By the time Kate had entered her late teens, her cousin Sarah had left the family home to become a servant, but her position within the family was soon filled by the birth of Aunt Elizabeth's final child, Harriet. After working long hours, Kate would have been called upon to assist with domestic duties as well: cooking, cleaning and looking after her cousin Lizzie as well as bringing in the extra shillings. It was probably at about this period in her life that she began to acquire what her uncle described as 'a jolly disposition'; a fondness for drinking and keeping what he called 'late hours'.[3] The tin workers' public house, the Red Cow, stood only a few doors down the road from her home, and would have offered an escape from the close quarters beneath her uncle's roof.

As an outsider, the extent to which Kate ever felt she entirely belonged with the Wolverhampton Eddoweses is questionable, and by the summer of 1861 she had grown both restless and reckless. According to members of her family, the turning point came when Kate was caught stealing from the Old Hall Works.

While passing through the drying rooms or packaging

areas, it would not have proven too difficult to slip a tin card case, a small box or a pen tray into a pocket or beneath her garments. Not every pawn shop was scrupulous about the objects it accepted, and for someone who had grown weary of labouring over an acid bath day upon day, such a risk might have seemed worth it. Unfortunately, the Old Hall Works was full of eyes, and at least one pair fell upon Kate.

It was probably down to the Eddoweses' long-standing relationship with the factory owners that Kate was scolded and dismissed from her position but not brought before the magistrate. The mortification she had caused her family was extreme and the shock of her actions reverberated from Wolverhampton to London as Emma and Harriet, the architects of her new life, received word of her disgrace. Back at 50 Bilston Street, the words and recriminations would have been thunderous.

In later years, it was Sarah Eddowes, now known as Mrs Jesse Croote, the wife of a Wolverhampton saddler and horse dealer, who recounted the family drama to a newspaper reporter.[4] According to Sarah, this incident would come to define Kate's future life and the Eddoweses would neither forget it nor forgive her for it. At nineteen, she once again packed her belongings to start her life afresh, and on this occasion, it was she who determined her destination. She set out for Birmingham, a 14-mile walk to the south of Wolverhampton, where she hoped to find refuge with a more sympathetic member of the family.

For many years, Wolverhampton's renowned Peacock Inn, the establishment at which Kate's mother once stirred sauces and made puddings, had also been a venue for bare-knuckle boxing matches. Throughout the 1850s, the inn yard was regularly cleared, sod laid and a ring pitched for prize fights. Among those to appear was the English heavyweight champion and local hero William Perry, also known as the 'Tipton Slasher', as well as Joe Goss, who went on to make his pugilistic fortune in the United States. It is likely that here, too, Tom Eddowes, aka the 'Snob', fought his way into his niece's heart.

Bare-knuckle boxing had been big business in England since the eighteenth century. Jack Broughton had attempted to formalize the sport and attach to it a sense of gentlemanly and patriotic merit. With the patronage of the Prince of Wales, boxing schools that purported to 'impart the art of pugilism' appeared in London. A burgeoning sporting press helped to create a buzz around prize matches by publishing pre-fight taunts between participants. British men of all classes were hooked, and matches governed by Broughton's rules, where contestants stripped to their waists and wrapped wadding around their fists before slugging it out for cash sums, became nationwide events.

Fighters generally came from working-class backgrounds and the Midlands contributed a number to their rank. While a few pugilists carved out full-time careers from the sport, many more were amateurs, who occasionally put aside their leather aprons and tools to step into the ring. Tom Eddowes was one of these. A shoemaker or 'snob' by trade, Eddowes supplemented his income through the exercise of his brute strength.

Born in 1810, Uncle Tom's best fighting years would have been behind him by the time Kate had watched him raise his fists. However, with prize money of up to 25 pounds a side at stake, Thomas Eddowes did not go eagerly into retirement. As late as 1866, the country's foremost sporting newspaper, *Bell's Life in London*, was advertising a match between 'Ned Wilson and Tom Eddows [sic] (alias The Snob)', two 'old Birmingham men' who had spent years cultivating their pugilistic talents.[5]

Just as it is today, the early-nineteenth-century boxing match was as much a piece of theatrical entertainment as it was a sporting competition. Before the introduction of the Marquess of Queensberry Rules in 1867, fighters were permitted to wrestle as well as to throw punches.[6] Poised at the centre of the ring in a bare-chested display of their physical prowess, competitors would have appeared as heroic actors on a stage, while the prospect of a large prize fight, announced in bills plastered about town, would have seemed as thrilling as the arrival of the circus.

On the designated day, the event would have begun slowly. A crowd of men in top hats and flat caps would have gathered, eagerly checking the time, fiddling with their watch chains or tucking their hands into their waistcoat pockets. Eventually, the combatants would have appeared, one after the other, accompanied by a second, and a bottle-holder responsible for refreshing and sponging down the fighter between rounds. The pugilists would shake hands and a coin would be tossed to decide who would choose their corner. Once these formalities were concluded, the men would strip down, and 'have their drawers examined' to ensure that there was no 'insertion of improper substances'. Only then could the fight officially commence.

While it would not have been expected for 'respectable' ladies to be present at such matches, the attendance of working-class women would have been neither encouraged nor entirely frowned upon. It is likely that Kate watched her uncle from amidst the crowds, slightly star-struck. Whatever relationship they formed, whether it was one based on a niece's admiration of an older family member, or common interests, Kate came to believe that her Uncle Tom would offer her the sort of home and sympathy she did not find in Wolverhampton.

In 1861, Tom Eddowes and his wife Rosannah were living at

the heart of Birmingham's industrial centre. Across the way, Eldridge & Merrett's pin works, an imposing brick mill with thrusting smokestacks, pounded out tiny steel pins and needles. At Brooks & Street, a few doors down, brass wire was woven into sieves and spark guards, while at Thomas Felton's manufactory, carriage lamps and chandeliers were melted and smelted into shape. Wedged between these larger concerns, along Bagot Street were assorted workshops occupied mostly by toy-makers and gun-makers, the trade that lent its name to the quarter. The hard, functional face of Birmingham differed little in appearance from that of her sister, Wolverhampton. Brick had been built upon brick, and all of it smudged with thick black coal dust.

The Eddowes residence, in a courtyard off Moland Street, was situated adjacent to the incessant thud and chug of heavy industry. There would scarcely have been a quiet hour in the day unbroken by the sound of a cranking engine or when a cloud of smoke did not hang over them. The presence of the manufactories with their metals and mercury had rendered the neighbourhood's water unfit to drink, and residents relied on deliveries from a cart. Their courtyard house, constructed of late-eighteenth-century brick, would have seen its share of wear after nearly a hundred years. With a room on both the first and second floors, as well as a ground-floor kitchen and a cellar, the house would have provided sufficient enough space for the couple and their two youngest children: sixteen-year-old John, who made brass tubing at a local factory, and twelve-year-old Mary, who remained at home to assist her mother. When Uncle Tom was not throwing punches in the ring, he was driving nails into shoes, either in a room partially converted for that purpose, or in a nearby workshop.

In nineteenth-century working-class families, distant relations would have received a welcome that was proportionate to their ability to contribute practical or financial support to a household. Whatever Kate's plan had been in plotting her flight to Birmingham, work would have been inescapable, and if she had hoped to avoid returning to a life of factory drudgery, she would have been sorely disappointed. Kate knew tin work, and in Birmingham there were plenty of places to be had for young women. It wasn't long before Uncle Tom had found her a position much like the one she had left behind in Wolverhampton. No longer a scourer, Kate now sat at a long table with polishing cloths, rubbing round and round the faces of newly shellacked japanware trays, working their surfaces into a high sheen so that somewhere in a house with a parlour, a serving maid could deliver tea to her mistress on an object pretty enough to make her visitors envious. Kate's hours would have been the same: rising at dawn or in darkness, home for supper and then into a bed shared with Mary, in a room divided by a curtain from the snoring John or her uncle and aunt. It did not matter where she fled – Wolverhampton or Birmingham; to the household of a pugilist or a tinplate worker – the routine of Kate's life would be this until she married. Then it would be her mother's life: the pain of childbearing, the weariness of child-rearing, worry, hunger and exhaustion, and, eventually, sickness and death.

The wet Indian heat smothered the soldiers of the 18th Royal Irish Regiment into listlessness. As they rested in the shade of Asirgarh Fort's ruined mosque, they played cards, polished their boots and listened to stories. There were always stories to be told: stories from back home in Ireland; stories from the jungles; battle stories; stories of willing women with wanton smiles and dark skin, or twinkling eyes and fair faces.

The man his commanding officers called Thomas Quinn would have listened to such tales with a keen interest. Quinn, or Thomas Conway as he had been born on 21 November 1836 in County Mayo,[7] was a collector and, later, a pedlar of stories, though one that he never offered up was the reason for his change of name. Men who wished to escape their past, whether a broken marriage or a situation far worse, frequently assumed another identity when they 'took the Queen's shilling' and enlisted. In October of 1857, Thomas Conway had done just this.

When he marked a cross by his name on the enlistment roll it is likely that Conway knew he would be destined for India. Word had reached Britain in September of the rebellion of British East India troops near Delhi, which had grown and threatened to spread through the north of the country. News of the Sepoy Mutiny supplanted that of the Crimean War in the headlines, as British troops, who had scarcely recovered from the sieges of the Black Sea, shifted their number to the dust of the subcontinent. The call for reinforcements became an urgent one, and Thomas had received barely a month of training before he, along with the rest of the second brigade of the 18th Royal Irish, boarded the steam ship *Princess Charlotte* bound for Bombay. For a young man on the eve of his twenty-first birthday, who had seen little beyond rural life and sod houses, this decision would prove the greatest adventure of his life. India would become a harvest of stories for him.

The journey by sea took three months, but not one of the sights he glimpsed along the way – not the flying fish or the sharks or swells of the Cape of Good Hope – could have prepared him for the alien exoticism of India. When they landed at Bombay, many Irish and English recruits were completely bewildered by the hectic, colourful scenes. They gawped at women wrapped in bright silk saris, jingling with bangles and nose rings. They were baffled by the bold scents of ginger and garlic, and the dozy buffaloes shuffling through the market-places. The extreme cultural and climatic differences in some cases proved too difficult an adjustment, and many found themselves succumbing not only to 'the rigours of the wea-ther' but to 'the melancholy of homesickness'.

It was the former rather than the latter that ultimately felled Conway during his Indian adventure. The humidity entered his chest. He coughed and wheezed so much during the marches that he was eventually sent to the army hospital in Madras, where the cool breezes were expected to revive him. Unfortunately, the mutiny had been put down before he man-aged to recover. Upon his return to Dublin in 1861, the senior medical officer examined him and soon determined that he would never recover. Conway's 'physical disability and con-tinual infirmity' was diagnosed to have been 'the result of former illness, principally rheumatism and chronic bronchitis'. To make matters worse, the doctor had also detected that Con-way, at twenty-four, suffered 'from a disease of the heart'. As a consequence, he was recommended for discharge; however, it was noted rather favourably that the soldier's disorder was 'par-tially, if not entirely attributable to military service and climate and not intemperance or other vice'.[8]

With a bad heart and a weak chest, Conway could neither soldier nor return to the life of casual labouring that had sus-tained him prior to joining the army.[9] While this news would have been disquieting for a young man without formal train-ing in a trade, his consolation would come in the form of a pension, to be paid twice yearly. Generally, privates' pensions, especially for those like Conway who had served only four years and six days, were menial sums, enough to supplement a worker's income, but not to replace it. According to his records, he was eligible to receive sixpence per day, a sum that over the years was reassessed and adjusted upward or downward by one penny to take into account any improvement of his medical condition.[10] Conway would be forced to find some way of subsisting that did not involve swinging a hammer, mowing hay or lifting burdensome loads.

As a child in rural Ireland, Conway would have come to know the chapmen who plodded the roads through County Mayo visiting farms, taverns and turf-roofed houses. Chased by dogs and followed by curious children along his route, the chapman with his linen pack ferried an assortment of useful goods and materials to those who might otherwise not have had access to a nearby shop. Part vagabond, part towncrier, part wily salesman, the chapbook man was viewed with a mix of suspicion and welcome. He moved from village to settlement to town, collecting and depositing local knowledge, news and gossip wherever he landed, which was for some villagers his most essential role. However, a good hawker knew his business well and understood how to make the most out of every stop. Farmers' wives and daughters were enticed by the assortment of scissors, combs, thimbles, knives, ribbon, thread, buttons, even brooches and small toys that he spread over their kitchen tables. He also carried on him an array of printed material: in particular chapbooks – or short pamphlets – decorated with wood-cut engravings, which recounted everything from fairy tales to biographies, poems and short stories. At the taverns and pubs, he might pull out his collection of broadside ballads: songs printed on a single large sheet, which told of the loss of love, or recounted the story of a bloody crime. As these lyrics were usually set to a well-known tune, the purchasers could throw down their penny, grab the broadside and launch into a new song over a pint of ale.

The chapbook seller's life was an entirely peripatetic existence. Each day began with an empty stomach and no promise of a bed. *The History of John Cheap the Chapman*, a chapbook usually found in the packs of most chapbook pedlars during the first half of the nineteenth century, offers some insight into the daily lives of those who took to roads with their wares. The narrator of the tale makes it plain that the hazards and discomforts frequently more than outweighed the adventures. Falling into a ditch or a sewage-filled midden, escaping the wrath of a farmer's dog or the horns of a bull were ever-present dangers. He grumbles equally over the inconvenience of sleeping on wheat sacks, in a field of kale or beside a cow on a cold winter's night. He barters with farmers' wives for a bowl of soup or cabbage, and often complains of 'travelling all day and getting neither meat nor bread nor ale, going from house to house'. But irrespective of this, the peddling life offered a degree of freedom that couldn't otherwise be achieved. There was a certain romanticism in slipping the ties that held a nineteenth-century existence together. In wandering, living by one's wits, encountering different sorts of characters and visiting new places, a chapman was beholden to no one, not family, community, church or employer, and for some that liberation was thrilling.

Not surprisingly, life as a chapman appealed to single men without families, though, much like modern travelling salesmen, marriage was certainly seen as no impediment to pursuing this profession. Those thought most suited to it were former soldiers who, it was believed, were already accustomed to long marches and hardships.

Becoming a chapman must have seemed a logical choice for Thomas Conway, who since his teens had been no stranger to a nomadic existence. The Great Famine that devastated the Irish countryside from 1845 to 1852 fell hardest upon County Mayo. By 1851, nearly 30 per cent of the population of the region had died or emigrated. Conway was no exception. At the time he enlisted in 1857, it appears he had already moved across the Irish Sea to Yorkshire where he had been working as a casual labourer near Beverley. Upon his discharge on 14 October 1861, he claimed his pension, paid a visit to relations in Kilkerry and returned to England, this time to Newcastle, where he stood a better chance of making a living. With the money he'd been paid, the young Irishman purchased the necessary goods to fill his pack and set out on a pedlar's path, which took him south to Coventry and then to London, before he arrived in Birmingham by the summer of 1862.[11]

The stories differ as to how Kate and Thomas Conway met. According to one account, at twenty years old, she was 'a nice-looking girl with a very warm heart'. He was a grey-eyed Irishman with light brown hair and a talent for telling tales. Both Sarah Croote and Emma claim that Kate met him in Birmingham, but Uncle Tom Eddowes insisted to the contrary. It was not under his watch that 'she formed the acquaintance of this man Conway'. Whatever the case, nine months into her life in Birmingham, at about the time she would have met him, Kate declared a sudden desire to return to Wolverhampton, the direction in which Conway was headed.

Thomas Conway would certainly have cut a romantic figure, with his tales of tigers and fragrant jungles, with his songs and sack of stories. His engaging patter would have enchanted strangers in every pub and marketplace. He was footloose and went where the wind blew him. It was understandable that

Kate – jolly, outgoing and open – would find him and his life an attractive alternative to the drudgery of her situation.

The Eddoweses were not pleased by this turn of events and Kate discovered as much when she appeared back at Bilston Street. Thomas Conway was never well liked by Kate's family: not by William and Elizabeth, by her cousin Sarah, her Uncle Tom, or even by her sisters in London. It is no mystery why. Judged medically unfit by the army and with no real occupation, as well as no home, no family and no reliable income beyond a paltry pension of 6 or 7 pence per day, this Irish drifter was like a figure in a Victorian cautionary tale about whom young women were warned. Any liaison with his kind was seen as a ticket to poverty, starvation and the workhouse. Worse still, if Conway had offered Kate marriage, he demonstrated no obvious intention of entering into it immediately.

Still, this did not discourage Kate's attachment: she was, according to an account of events in the *Black Country Bugle*, completely 'infatuated with the handsome, poetical Irishman'. Aunt Elizabeth eventually gave her an ultimatum: either she finished the affair with the penny-ballad salesman, or she left the house.[12] Kate chose the latter and moved with Conway into a lodging house. The timing of this rupture was key; by July of that year, 1862, she was pregnant.

While the Eddoweses would have been ashamed and embarrassed by their niece's behaviour, unmarried pregnancy was not unusual. Where female chastity among the privileged classes was taken as a measure of a young woman's character and her worth as an unsullied commodity, virginity did not hold the same significance for the working classes whose lives were governed by practicalities. The innocent femininity cultivated in middle- and upper-class girls was not expected of her working-class sister. Commentators expressed concern that sexualization of the labouring classes occurred at a very young age on account of cramped domestic arrangements. With living space in short supply, and family members, extended relations and even visitors sharing bedrooms and beds, the notion of bodily privacy and modesty were luxuries they simply could not afford. The sight and sounds of sex were normal; temptation and experimentation were a consequence of exposure. Equally, lack of room at home pushed young teenagers outside, beyond the watchful gaze of their parents. As a young woman told the pornographic writer 'Walter': 'There are lots of girls about . . . their mothers don't care what they do . . . when they's about thirteen or fourteen years old they won't be kept in, they is about the dark streets at night . . .' She then went on to explain that 'the girls went with the coster boys who are their sweethearts' and that 'a virginity was a rarity at fourteen years old'. Mayhew made similar discoveries when interviewing teenage girls employed in 'slop work', or the manufacture of cheap clothing. One confessed to him: 'I am satisfied that there is not one young girl that works at slop work that is virtuous, and there are some thousands in the trade.'

At a time when sexual relationships tended to result in pregnancy, many couples waited until conception or even birth to marry. However, others among the labouring class chose instead to cohabit. Certain professions, such as ballad sellers and costermongers, whose work required mobility, were more inclined to this arrangement. In theory, a certain fluidity in relationships could suit both the man and the woman. The need for a man to follow work, sometimes quite far afield, left the woman free to form another relationship with a potential partner closer to hand. Because of this, many couples did not feel the need to legitimize their union in a church, although a significant number regarded their bond as if it were a legal one, and remained together for life, or for extended periods. As nineteenth-century journalists and social reformers were apt to discover, working-class communities tended to refrain from probing the circumstances of their friends' and neighbours' relationships and lived by a simple rule: if a couple said they were married and behaved accordingly, then they were. 'Ask if the men and women living together . . . are married, and your simplicity will cause a smile,' Andrew Mearns wrote. 'Nobody knows. Nobody cares.'[13] However, this is not to suggest that attitudes towards cohabiting couples were not full of contradiction and nuance. Landlords and employers, who were in many cases of the same class, could be quick to turf out or dismiss those whom they discovered not to be legally wed, and women naturally bore the brunt of any social persecution, especially if illegitimate children were involved. While a man might walk away from cohabitation and suffer no ill consequences, a dependent woman, with reduced earning potential and additional mouths to feed, might find herself instantly plunged into penury.

When Kate threw in her lot with Thomas Conway, she would have been fully aware of the risks she took – yet this seemed preferable to the life she already knew. Sarah Croote intimates that the couple did not remain long in Wolverhampton, and soon after set out on their life together, back towards Birmingham.

Joining forces with Kate would have had its advantages for Conway too. Not only was it convenient to have a woman at his side to tend to cooking and laundry, but Kate would have proved herself to be a useful if not masterful business partner. While in rural areas, selling chapbooks and assorted small items door to door was easily accomplished on his own; in larger villages, market towns and cities, he required a more visible method of turning trade.

Conway and Kate belonged to a class of pedlars that Henry Mayhew described as 'flying stationers' or 'general paper sellers'. These could be broken into further categories depending on how they set about selling their wares. The 'running patterer' walked through the streets and squares shouting out titles and giving summaries of their broadsides and chapbooks. The 'standing patterer' sought out a patch on the corner of a street or outside a pub and seduced buyers from across the road with his tales of accidents, scandal, battles, horrors and executions. Both the standing patterer and the running patterer were often accompanied by a female 'chaunter', who would assist by singing or reciting passages of a ballad as her male companion flogged them to passers-by. Together the couple might also perform duets or engage in a theatrical repartee. As an extrovert who had been taught music at school and who loved singing, street performance would have suited Kate's inclinations far better than factory work.[14]

When Thomas Conway set out to make his living as a chapbook seller, he may have aspired to write his own material but had no means of achieving this aim by himself. As the cross he marked on his army discharge papers demonstrates, Conway was illiterate. Kate was not. Whatever inspiration he had gathered from his adventures in India (and such stories made for highly popular ballads in the 1850s and 60s) would have had to be dictated and transcribed before he had met Kate. Allowing her to take on this role made the entire endeavour more economical. One can imagine the couple hunched over a pub table, Kate with inky fingers acting the scribe to Conway's poet, furiously scratching out lines, arguing, recomposing, singing the verses to themselves. Under such circumstances, it would be difficult to conceive that Kate did not have a hand in the composition of these works.[15]

Yet, while Kate had made her escape from a conventional life, the one she had chosen was not necessarily as happy or carefree as she might have imagined. Pattering in towns and selling chapbooks door to door in rural areas did not pay especially well. Mayhew writes that the average earnings of these sorts of vendors were roughly 10 to 12 shillings a week. In order to earn 12 shillings, one had to be willing to write or sell anything: ballads, chapbooks, poems and pamphlets. Illness, drunkenness or any other unforeseen circumstance would have made this impossible. The miseries of itinerant life, of sodden, frozen, filthy clothing and a rumbling belly with no shelter in sight, could not be underestimated. The occasions on which Kate would have enjoyed a bath or laundered her clothes would have been limited. While the couple may have successfully begged beds in rural areas, in cities they would have been dependent upon crowded, unpleasant lodging houses and casual wards, if they didn't sleep rough. What little they possessed they carried with them, which made them prey to robbers and tricksters. To have braved all the hazards of a gypsy existence whilst pregnant would have rendered this experience all the more wretched. It is hardly a wonder then that in April 1863, in her ninth month of pregnancy, Kate found herself knocking on the workhouse infirmary doors at Great Yarmouth, in Norfolk.

For one who had no guarantee of a bed, a workhouse infirmary where she might go to bear a child would have seemed a welcome respite. By the 1860s, all workhouses accommodated expectant destitute mothers, though in many cases the Guardians sought to distinguish between 'deserving married women' and 'the fallen' who had arrived to bear children out of wedlock. When Kate appeared at the gates, she gave her name as Catherine Conway and claimed she was married to 'a labourer'. Thomas may have accompanied her there or, more likely, placed her in the care of the workhouse while he set out in search of work.

Although Conway could rest assured that his 'wife' had a roof over her head, the workhouse infirmary was by no means a safe haven for childbirth. Dedicated maternity wards were exceptional; instead women in the throes of labour were often integrated into the general ward alongside patients with a variety of ailments and contagious diseases, from tuberculosis to smallpox and syphilis. Sanitation was universally appalling. Poor Law reformer Louisa Twinning reported that during her visit to a women's ward she discovered that a broken lavatory had been left to degenerate into an open sewer, cleaning was performed without disinfectant and infants were delivered without the use of soap and water. At the infirmary at Yarmouth Workhouse, where Kate gave birth to her daughter, Catherine 'Annie' Conway, on 18 April 1863, it was noted that the gas jets were regularly left on to deter the infirmary's rats. However unpleasant this must have seemed, to Kate it would have been far preferable to delivering her first child in the mud by the side of a road.

The arrival of tiny Annie Conway would have only slightly slowed the couple's progress through town and country. In fact, at the sight of an infant strapped to Kate's back or nestled against her breast, the offers of an extra loaf of bread or a comfortable place to rest would have been more forthcoming. In the years that followed her birth, the couple continued to roam. They had been as far north as Newcastle, and by late summer were in Hull, before returning to Coventry, and then briefly, in June of 1864, stopping in London, which may well have been Kate's first visit since her departure from the city. In the course of this wandering, Kate would have laid Annie down to sleep in stable stalls, churchyards, against walls, or under trees as the rain thrashed against them. Such a mode of life could have never felt entirely satisfying, though she must have found something that sustained her: the joy of performance; the singing and the storytelling and the composing of the tales, perhaps. And drink would have helped, too, when money allowed for it.

If it was at Conway's insistence that they tramp the country from end to end in search of success, then, ironically enough, he was to find it back in Staffordshire, directly under the noses of the Eddowes family.

In the early hours of the morning of 9 January 1866, spectators bundled in scarves and shawls began to gather in the yard at Stafford Gaol. There had not been a hanging for a 'crimson crime' for some time, and so they had risen especially early and come from the surrounding towns and villages to watch this murderer, Charles Christopher Robinson, twitch and wiggle like a fish on a line. The vendors of tea and coffee and hot milk had set up their stalls. The crowd filled their stomachs with currant buns, boiled eggs, sheep's trotters and cakes. Although the popular enthusiasm for public executions had begun to wane by the 1860s, hangings could still compare with the excitement of a fair or a market day. Factory and mill-workers would have stopped by on their way to work, neighbours met and chatted and hawkers came to sell their wares. Among those elbowing and jostling for a good view of the drop, Kate and Thomas Conway had set out their pitch.

Hanging days were big business for ballad and chapbook sellers, who belted out the rhyming lamentations of the murderer. Nothing sold as well as criminal tales, and as soon as an execution was announced every penny bard and printer in the county scrambled to get their version in ink. In many cases, 'true' last confessions, some purported to be spoken on the gallows, were being sold in the prison yard before they were even uttered. Executions would have been Kate and Thomas's bread and butter. Much of the traversing that they did would have been in order to reach the county towns in which these events were scheduled to take place. However, this hanging would have been of particular importance to the couple, as Charles Christopher Robinson was Kate's distant cousin.

Like Kate, Charles had been left an orphan and was raised in the home of Josiah Fisher, a relation who worked as a house agent in Wolverhampton. As a man of some standing and wealth, Fisher acted as the guardian to another family member in distress, Harriet Seager, the sister of his son's wife. As Seager was close in age to Charles Robinson, a romantic attachment developed and eventually the couple became engaged, though Harriet remained wary of her fiancé's quick temper and jealous tendencies. On 26 August 1865, Robinson was spotted wandering about the garden in a fury, unwashed, unshaven and wearing no more than his shirt. After finding his sweetheart, an argument ensued where Robinson attempted to grab and kiss Harriet. She ducked his advances, and he slapped her. The couple parted angrily, and Robinson was not prepared to forgive her for quarrelling with him. A short time afterwards, a servant spotted him striding downstairs to the scullery with his razor. Frantic noises and a gunshot alerted the household to the crime. When they discovered him, howling and screaming, Robinson had unsuccessfully attempted to shoot himself and was in the midst of drawing a razor across his neck. At his feet, in a pool of blood, lay Harriet Seager, 'with a gash in the throat that had laid the spine bare'.[16]

How well Kate actually knew her cousin is unknown, but she and Conway would have been determined to make something of this connection. Wolverhampton Archives possesses a copy of one of the only publications believed to be linked to the pens of Thomas Conway and Kate Eddowes: *A Copy of Verses on the Awful Execution of Charles Christopher Robinson, For the Murder of his Sweetheart, Harriet Segar, of Ablow Street, Wolverhampton, August 26th*, written to be sold at the hanging in 1866.[17] The perspective of the ballad is interesting. While many authors would have written a dramatic account of the killing, or shaped the events into a tale of murderous love, the lyrics instead paint Robinson as a remorseful figure, worthy of pity.

> Come all you feeling Christians,
> Give ear unto my tale,
> It's for a cruel murder
> I was hung at Stafford Gaol.
> The horrid crime that I have done
> Is shocking for to hear,
> I murdered one I once did love,
> Harriet Segar dear.
>
> Charles Robinson is my name,
> With sorrow was oppressed,
> The very thought of what I've done
> Deprived me of my rest:
> Within the walls of Stafford Gaol,
> In bitter grief did cry,
> And every moment seemed to say
> 'Poor soul prepare to die!'
>
> I well deserve my wretched fate,
> No one can pity me,
> To think that I in my cold blood,

Could take her life away,
She no harm to me had done,
How could I, serve her so?
No one my feelings now can tell,
My heart was full of woe.

O while within my dungeon dark,
Sad thoughts came on apace,
The cruel deed that I had done
Appeared before my face,
While lying in my prison cell
Those horrid visions rise,
The gentle form of her I killed
Appeared before my eyes.

O Satan, Thou Demon strong,
Why didst thou on me bind?
O why did I allow thy chains
To enwrap my feeble mind?
Before my eyes she did appear
All others to excell,
And it was through jealousy,
I poor Harriet Segar killed.

May my end a warning be
Unto all mankind,
Think on my unhappy fate
And bear me in your mind.
Whether you be rich or poor
Your friends and sweethearts love,
And God will crown your fleeting days,
With blessings from above.

While Kate would have watched nooses tighten around the necks of many villains, to have witnessed the execution of a blood relation would surely have proven a different experience. Whether or not Kate was affected by the sight of her kin clad in mourning will never be known. Neither will it be known if they recognized her, the impertinent chaunter bellowing her verses into the chilled air.

If the *Black Country Bugle* is to be believed, Kate and Tom's ballad turned an exceptional profit that day. The couple fared so well that they were able to 'return from Stafford in style, booking inside seats on Ward's coach with the proceeds'. The takings allowed Conway to invest in a donkey and cart and order another four hundred copies from his printer in Bilston, which they then sold 'at their regular pitch on the following Monday'. Conway is even said to have rewarded Kate 'with the price of a flowered-hat'. 'Such was their lifestyle', continues the piece, 'that they lived for a spell in lodgings at Moxley', a village outside Wednesbury. This stroke of good fortune was what Conway had been hunting for over the years. Rather than resting on his laurels, it is suggested that he set his sights on a permanent move to London, 'where his rhyming talents . . . would be even more fully appreciated'.[18]

The veracity of the *Black Country Bugle*'s account of the couple's lives has always been questionable, but Conway's pension records do support the suggestion that the pair began to spend more time in London from this period. Their decision to settle in the capital may have been driven in part by Conway's ambitions, but also by other factors. If Kate had learned anything since the death of her parents, surely it was that her true family were not those who lived in Wolverhampton. London was the home of her youth and the home of her sisters, and, after years of roving, it was now time for the prodigal daughter to make her return.

15

Her Sister's Keeper

Emma had always attempted to do what was correct. As the second eldest girl of a large brood, she had been handed bawling infant after bawling infant. She had been taught to stir the soup, to change the baby's filthy napkins, to keep the toddlers from the hot coals and the carriage wheels. She had kept an eye on her brother Alfred, helping him when he had seizures, offering protection to an older sibling who could not return the favour. It was Emma who helped to nurse her dying mother, Emma who sought to comfort her sick father. It was Emma who learned to read and write, who went out to service in order to support her brothers and sisters, and Emma who agonized over how these orphaned children were to live when they no longer had a home. Emma sent Kate to Wolverhampton, hoping for the best outcome, while she continued in her post, dutifully scrubbing, washing and serving a middle-class family, quietly saving what she earned. Around 1860, at the age of twenty-five, she met James Jones, a neighbour of her sister Harriet, who lived in Clerkenwell. James and his family were tallow chandlers – those who made and sold candles – once an esteemed profession with its own guild in the time before gas lamps and domestic gas jets began to extinguish the trade. Emma did what was expected of a woman of her era;

she married the man who had paid his addresses to her on 11 November. Only after that did the children begin to arrive: six in total.

In Kate's absence, her four elder sisters' lives continued to grow and twist closer together like the roots of trees. Throughout the 1860s, the women who had guided and mothered her had all managed to relocate from Bermondsey, south of the river, to Clerkenwell, a working-class district set around Smithfield meat market. They had each married in the same church, St Barnabas, and lived no more than a few streets apart. Eliza had wed a local butcher, James Gold, in 1859, while Harriet and Robert Garrett solemnized their union in 1867, after a period of cohabitation that produced no children. Only Elizabeth lived on the opposite side of the Thames, in Greenwich where she had settled with her husband, Thomas Fisher. In spite of the cares that accompanied a constantly growing family of children and the responsibilities of housekeeping, the sisters remained in regular contact, sharing gossip and news. One day, the news was that Kate had returned to London.

The fifteen-year-old motherless girl whom Emma had dispatched like a package to unknown recipients had come back a fully fledged woman, with a child of her own and a man she called her husband. However, Kate was careful about revealing too many details of her life to her sisters. Initially, she told Emma that she and Conway had been settled in Birmingham, choosing to omit the stories of her vagrant's existence. Her marital status and the lack of a wedding ring was likely to have raised questions as well, as would have the tattoo of Thomas Conway's initials that were inked crudely onto her forearm.

Although they would become fashionable briefly in the late nineteenth century, in the middle of the Victorian era few symbols were more associated with society's lowest element than the tattoo. Traditionally, body art had been the preserve of sailors who had travelled to parts of Asia and Oceania where decorating oneself in ink was common. The practice of tattooing followed them back to Britain, as did the seafarer's reputation for poverty, vice and criminality. Soldiers too were known for having initials, regimental insignias and other designs permanently drawn onto their limbs and torsos. Thomas Conway would have been no stranger to the sight of inky snakes, hearts, crosses and sweethearts' names etched into his army companions' biceps. However, while men might be forgiven for defacing their bodies as a mark of their manliness and spirit of adventure, tattooing amongst women was not regarded with such lenience: a tattoo on a woman's body not only flouted conventions of feminine purity and beauty, but also rendered her masculine. Tattooing was dirty and painful; in the nineteenth century it involved a needle, a pot of ink and a sustained succession of pricks. Any woman who sought out such an experience was seeking to challenge her 'natural delicacy' and to permanently alter her God-given appearance. Like many of the decisions Kate had made – not to marry, to bear a child out of wedlock, and to lead a nomadic existence – acquiring a tattoo was deeply subversive. It is likely that the suggestion had come from Thomas Conway, who may have also had her initials marked onto his arm. Perhaps by these means the couple solemnized their commitment to one another on their own terms, without wedding bands and a church service.

Whatever Harriet, Emma, Eliza and Elizabeth whispered among themselves about their sister, Kate's appearance in London seems to have signified a desire to make alterations to her life. By 1868 she and Conway were settled in what was described as a 'clean and comfortable' small house at 13 Cottage Place. The area, off Bell Street in Westminster, was a significant distance from Clerkenwell, a choice that may have reflected an unstable relationship with her family, which regularly swung between intimacy and antagonism. Whether her siblings were present that same year to assist her with the birth of her second child, Thomas Lawrence Conway, is unknown, but by March of 1869, she was content enough to name a newborn daughter after her eldest sister, Harriet.

If Conway had brought his wife and child to London in order to further his ambitions, within three years his hopes had stalled. While the capital offered a wider market for the sale of ballads and chapbooks, it was not a patch on which Thomas ever seemed to entirely establish himself. By the late nineteenth century, London was home to hundreds, if not thousands, of individuals singing and selling their songs on the street. Worse still, Westminster was cited as one of the primary haunts of such pedlars, who had earned themselves a reputation for doing as much begging as they did singing.[1] In the past, such a setback would not have hindered Conway and Kate, who simply would have cut their moorings and drifted north or south in the direction of prospective work; however, the anchor of young children now fixed them in place. In spite of his heart condition, Thomas returned once more to physical labour in order to make ends meet. For a time, he worked as an assistant to a bricklayer, which succeeded for a while in making the rent and paying for meagre meals, but these comforts were to be short-lived. The money and sustenance soon ran thin and the infant Harriet Conway, suckling at her mother's empty breast, began to wither. Within three weeks, Kate was reporting the child's death from malnutrition, the final convulsions of which she had felt in her arms.

It may have been this incident that, by the end of the year, prompted Conway to consider leaving London in search of work. That winter he headed north, towards Yorkshire, to look for employment. In his absence, Kate took seven-year-old Annie and two-year-old Thomas to Abbey Wood, near Greenwich, possibly to live with her sister Elizabeth and her family. As the Fishers were eight in number by 1870, this arrangement could only have been a temporary one and inevitably, by 20 January, Kate, Annie and little Thomas found themselves standing before the gates of Greenwich Union Workhouse.

What had begun as an expedient method of dealing with a problem rapidly evolved into a way of life for Kate. Over the next ten years, whenever faced with misfortune, she placed herself in the care of a Board of Guardians. On 15 August 1873 she gave birth to another son, George Alfred Conway, in the maternity ward of Southwark Workhouse. Records suggest that on these occasions the length of her sojourns varied, in some instances lasting for weeks and others for several months. On each occasion, Kate was accompanied by at least one, if not all, of her children.

For a destitute woman, entering the workhouse with her children presented a number of complications. According to the Poor Law, single mothers with illegitimate children were not entitled to receive 'outdoor relief', or parish handouts designed to assist poor families who were resident in their own lodgings. Authorities were concerned that providing financial support to immoral women in their own homes would be tantamount to a state subsidy of prostitution. Although they were aware that many poorer women like Kate cohabited with monogamous common-law partners, no real distinction was made between these 'fallen women' and acknowledged prostitutes. As far as 'respectable society' was concerned, a mother had either borne her child as a result of a legal union or as a result of a sinful coupling. Once inside the doors of the workhouse, the Board of Guardians was at liberty to discriminate between the decent and the damned; to separate out fallen women from impressionable young girls, or to feed mothers who had given birth to illegitimates on a punishment diet of watered skilly.

After they had passed through what was known as 'the archway of tears', the admission routine for families would have been the same for all, regardless of the mother's marital status. Everyone was separated by gender and by age, stripped of their clothes and possessions, ordered into the bath and handed their workhouse uniforms. According to the stipulations of the Poor Law, children under the age of seven were allowed to remain with their mother, sleeping in her filthy, hard bed and playing beside her on the bench as she picked oakum. Children between seven and fourteen were removed from their parents and taken to live in separate school facilities. Parental 'interviews' were permitted with their children in the dining hall once a week, so long as their sons and daughters remained on-site. In November 1876, when Kate arrived at Greenwich Union in anticipation of the birth of her fourth child, Frederick, three-year-old George Alfred was allowed to remain at her side, but Annie, who was then thirteen, and Thomas, at the age of eight, were dispatched to the Industrial School in Sutton.[2]

In spite of its terrifying reputation, the workhouse was often able to effect good, especially in the lives of destitute children. The Poor Law Union's insistence that workhouses provide lessons in literacy and numeracy for a minimum of three hours daily meant that many boys and girls were able to acquire at least a semblance of an education. By these means, it was believed that children had an opportunity to step out of the poverty trap in which their parents and grandparents had been caught. In order to further these aims, the government made provisions in 1857 for the expansion of what were called Industrial Schools, which strove to remove young paupers not only from the corrupting influence of the workhouse but also from the unwholesome environment of urban centres, and provide them with a practical education. This amounted to occupational training as well as formal schooling, to provide them with the means of earning a respectable income. Boys were taught trades such as shoemaking, tailoring, carpentry and music; girls were educated in the domestic arts, such as needlework and knitting, in order to prepare them for lives in service.

The school that Annie and her brother Thomas Conway attended at Sutton absorbed most of the workhouse children from the south-eastern London parishes and boasted of a capacity of up to a thousand pauper scholars. In the 1870s, its facilities were considered state-of-the-art and included expansive kitchens, a laundry, washrooms, a boiler room and a steam engine to pump fresh water into the school's tanks. In addition to open, spacious stairwells, dormitories and class-rooms, there were workshops for learning trades, as well as a farm where students were educated in agriculture. By comparison to Dowgate, the small charity school that Kate attended, the facilities provided by the Poor Law Union offered far greater scope for a child to improve their prospects. According to the memoirs of the otherwise anonymous 'W.H.R.', a former pupil at Sutton, his experiences at the school were coloured as much by the compassionate encouragement of some of his teachers as they were by the brutal violence of others. However, on the whole, Sutton offered cleaner beds, more plentiful food and a cheerier environment than Greenwich Union Workhouse, with opportunities for song and musical performances on the harmonium. The regime had an overwhelmingly positive impact on him. 'At Sutton', he concluded, 'I was thoroughly de-pauperised, for come what would in a fair way, I was determined never again to enter the workhouse as a pauper.'[3]

Its success can also be measured in terms of the impact it had on the lives of Kate's younger brothers and sister, Thomas, George and Mary, who were sent there from Bermondsey Workhouse after the death of their father. Within several years, George Eddowes had been trained as a shoemaker, while Thomas Eddowes had been taught music and was sent to join the band of the 45th Nottinghamshire Regiment of Infantry in Preston. Mary too had been successful enough in her 'domestic studies' to warrant placement as a servant.[4] Had Kate been a year or so younger in 1857, she too may have benefited from Sutton's educational scheme and the course of her life may have taken a very different turn.

By the late 1870s, Kate's problems appear to have become twofold. Like many working-class women, she was caught in a vicious circle: Conway had to leave London to find work, but in doing so, he abandoned his common-law partner and their children without any support. No amount of women's labour in a factory, sweat shop or laundry, selling items on the street or doing piecework from home would ever bring in an amount adequate to cover a family's needs and keep them from the workhouse. Worse still, when Conway did return, he was violent.

Conway's absences and the extreme hardship the family faced had begun to lead to physical arguments. Kate's sisters and her daughter had all noticed a dark pattern emerging.

Although Emma claimed that 'on the whole, they lived happily together', the 'quarrels between them' had become difficult to ignore. According to Annie, as well as to Emma, the couple's disagreements were exacerbated by Kate's 'habit of excessive drinking', while Conway was committed to abstinence. It appears that the pair 'could never agree' on this point, and both Annie and her aunts eventually came to the belief that in this regard, Kate was the author of her own misfortunes.

Such an attitude was not out of step with Victorian working-class sentiments about domestic violence, which frequently placed the onus for a beating on the woman herself. A certain degree of violence within the home was thought to serve a disciplinary function. Husbands felt no remorse for administering a chastising slap, while wives were often made to feel that they had 'asked for it'.[5] The displeasure of one's husband might be incurred for a lengthy catalogue of offences which included the use of foul language, the rejection of his sexual advances, disobedience, impertinence or simply offering a challenge to his superior role within the family. However, nothing appears to have factored more prominently in these cases than alcohol. A drunken man was just as likely to beat his wife as was a sober husband who disapproved of his wife's intoxication. A wife's perpetual drunkenness was often used successfully by a spouse as a defence in trials against a claim of assault.[6] In 1877, the very year that Kate and Thomas Conway's union began to fracture under similar circumstances, a legal textbook, *Principles of Punishment*, described wife-beating as a crime that 'varies infinitely in degree of criminality'. While some serious cases might warrant imprisonment, the author concluded that most incidents of physical abuse were deemed so 'trifling as almost to permit of justification'.

There were, however, limits to this attitude and not everyone in a community or a family was prepared to turn a blind eye. While neighbours and friends might tactfully avoid direct physical intervention during a domestic dispute, communities closely monitored warring couples by checking up on the woman, or by reminding the man that they could hear what he was doing. Most action was taken indirectly, usually by offering the woman shelter on occasions when she found it necessary to avoid her husband's wrath. It was in this manner that the Eddowes sisters chose to deal with Kate's deteriorating domestic situation.

In a one-year period between November 1876 and December 1877, Kate was in and out of workhouses and casual wards on at least seven separate occasions. On 6 August 1877, she was arrested for drunk and disorderly behaviour and sent to Wandsworth Prison for fourteen days.[7] In every instance, including that of her incarceration, she brought some or all of her children with her. As Kate's life fell to pieces, Emma was there to help her gather them. According to an interview with the *London Daily News*, in the worst of times Kate had fallen into the habit of appearing at her sister's door and begging her for help. Emma recalled that her sibling's face appeared 'frightfully disfigured' from Conway's beatings. Kate, with her emotions further loosened by drink, would give way to sobs: 'I wish I was like you,' she would cry.[8] Although Emma's life, contained in a few shabby rooms in Bridgewater Gardens, might not have appeared worthy of envy, to her younger sister it would have represented everything Kate had failed to become.

The situation would only worsen. In December of that year, she was arguing furiously with Conway again. Shortly before Christmas, she had left him and taken nine-month-old

Frederick with her to the casual ward for the night.[9] At least some form of temporary reconciliation had been reached by Christmas Day, which was spent with her sisters and their families. Unfortunately, the festive celebrations did not go well. The Eddowes women were shocked by Kate's battered appearance. Emma recalled that 'both her eyes had been blackened' and that she bore 'a dreadful face'. She was equally horrified by Thomas's attitude. 'The man, Conway', she referred to him disdainfully, 'appeared to be attached to her', though Emma found it difficult to fathom how any affection could exist between the two of them, especially when her sister so obviously 'suffered from his brutality'. Much to Emma's disgust, Conway exhibited no shame at his actions and remarked openly and with a sigh of exasperation, 'Kate, I shall be hung for you one of these days.'[10] Whatever occurred during that family gathering, Kate came out of it appearing no better than Thomas Conway in her sisters' eyes. Whether this was on account of excessive drink or something else, Emma indicates that a rift developed between them and that eventually she and Harriet broke off relations with Kate altogether. Unfortunately, this pattern of family estrangement would only continue.

Like many women caught in the cycle of domestic violence, Kate always returned to Conway. The couple experienced periods of stability and discord, harmony and chaos, upon which their children's lives were constantly tossed. Their perpetual financial distress made it necessary for them to move frequently between addresses, from Westminster to Southwark and Deptford, occupying single rooms and resorting to lodging houses as necessity demanded. However, with Annie old enough to look after her younger siblings and mind the home, Kate was able to take whatever work she could gain.

Sometimes this was labouring at a laundry, sometimes a bit of charring for her better-off neighbours, but towards the end of the 1870s, it appears she and Thomas Conway returned to hawking ballads together.

In 1879, their regular patch was Mill Lane, a small commercial street near to the Woolwich army barracks, frequented by an assortment of vendors and pedlars catering to residents and soldiers. On 4 October eleven-year-old Thomas and his six-year-old brother George accompanied their parents as they pattered and sang out their wares. Eventually, both parents wandered off and instructed the boys to wait where they had been left, outside number 8 Mill Lane. When it began to grow dark and no one returned for them, questions were asked and the children were escorted to Greenwich Workhouse, a place they had come to know well over the years. Nearly a week would pass before Kate could be located and made to reclaim her progeny.[11] This incident was followed by a similar one on 11 November. This time, the children were escorted to the workhouse by police officer 251, who had found them 'deserted by their mother' on the street.[12] On this occasion, Kate could not be found. Instead, nearly a month later, their sixteen-year-old sister was called upon to collect her brothers. Where Kate had disappeared in that time is anyone's guess. Certainly, her behaviour begs many questions about her state of mind and her use of alcohol. Earlier that year, Kate had suffered the loss of her infant, Frederick, a circumstance that may have only exacerbated her existing problems.

Kate and Thomas Conway's destructive and abusive relationship limped on into 1881. Although they are recorded on the census of that year as living together with their two sons in Chelsea, in a room at 71 Lower George Street, the couple had split by the autumn. When journalists interviewed Conway and his daughter, neither could recall the precise date when this event occurred; however, Conway was quick to paint himself as the victim. According to his version, he had found it necessary to leave Kate on account of her drinking, and he made certain to take his children with him when he went. The Eddowes sisters disputed this narrative. Elizabeth claimed that her sister had left Conway 'because he treated her badly', though Annie added that 'before they actually left each other she [Kate] was never with him for twelve months at a time'.[13] The split had been a long time in the making, though when it came it offered respite to both parties.

For a time, following the breakdown of her relationship with Conway, Kate appears to have turned to her sister Elizabeth for assistance, though this arrangement did not last for long. Much like Emma and Harriet before her, Elizabeth soon found her sister's behaviour unsupportable. In September of that year, Kate was once again charged with drunken disorderliness and dragged off the streets as she spewed obscenities at passers-by. On this occasion, the magistrate spared her a prison sentence. However, where the law was forgiving, her family was not, and by the end of that year, Elizabeth too had broken off relations with her younger sister.

Now without Elizabeth, without Conway and her sons, without Emma or Harriet, Kate sought out the company of the only remaining sister with whom she still maintained a bond: Eliza.

At some time prior to 1881, Eliza Gold had become a widow. Although she had been the wife of a butcher, a skilled and respected trade, the family struggled financially. No provision appears to have been made for Eliza's widowhood and, consequently, as was the case for so many women of her station in life, Eliza's circumstances were significantly compromised by the death of her spouse. With no savings or pension and a son who would not yet be old enough to earn a proper wage, it was essential that Eliza attach herself to another partner as quickly as possible.[14] Little is known about Charles Frost, the man whom she came to call her second husband. Both had been widowed and, in the tradition of many working-class men and women who formed attachments following bereavement, they chose not to officially solemnize their vows. In an interview, Eliza claims that her 'husband' 'worked at the waterside unloading cargoes of fruit', and occasionally sold penny-farthing books at Liverpool Street Station.[15]

Until the death of James Gold, Eliza had always lived near to her sisters, either in Clerkenwell or Hoxton, but widowhood and Charles Frost brought her to Whitechapel. At least since 1881, the Frosts inhabited a garret room at 6 Thrawl Street, with her son and a daughter from Frost's previous relationship. Eliza's new address was far from desirable. Whereas in Hoxton she had lived in a mixed area comprised of the poor and the comfortably-off, Thrawl Street was one of the most notorious sinks of poverty in Spitalfields.[16] It was here where Kate came to visit her sister, almost certainly to beg a coin or two off her, if not a meal or a narrow space in one of their beds.

That year, whenever she had the 4 pence to do so, Kate rented a bed at 55 Flower and Dean Street, a lodging house around the corner from her sister. 'Cooney's', as it later came to be called, was also the doss house of choice for John Kelly, the man who would come to fill Thomas Conway's empty boots. In Kelly's words, which bear all the hallmarks of journalistic embellishment, he 'first laid eyes' on Kate while she was staying at 55 Flower and Dean Street. After 'being throwed together a good bit', the two took a liking to one another 'and decided to make it a regular bargain'.[17]

If the Eddowes women had taken a disliking to Thomas Conway, their disdain for John Kelly seems to have been even greater. As far as Emma was concerned, Kate's life 'went from bad to worse' when she left Conway; at least when she was with her abuser 'her home was clean and comfortable'.[18] While with Kelly, she had no home, only a vile, impermanent bed at a doss house. Although Kelly was described as 'quiet and inoffensive', which was more than could be said for Thomas Conway, in the eyes of Kate's family he possessed one major failing that Conway did not: he drank, heavily. Annie, who blamed her mother for tearing apart their family, was unequivocal in her feelings about Kelly: 'I've never spoken to him and I don't like him.'[19]

Irrespective of her family's sentiments, once free of her abuser, Kate's life settled into a happier, though no less erratic, pattern. She and Kelly shared a common love of the bottle and their conviviality made them popular with their fellow lodgers at Cooney's.[20] According to newspaper interviews with those at 55 Flower and Dean Street, Kate was always ready with a song and didn't hesitate to spare her last 4 pence for someone who hadn't made their doss money. For a time, both she and John worked; Kate, like Elizabeth Stride, took on charring for Jewish families in the area, while John laboured at the market, though this income was always disappointing and never reliable.

Although they came to regard 55 Flower and Dean Street as their home, they, like the majority of those who inhabited Whitechapel's lodging houses, could not afford to spend every night there. Kelly makes it clear in his inquest statements that he and Kate might pass the night at Cooney's or at number 52 Flower and Dean Street, in the casual wards or on the streets. Kate, who had spent much of her life slumbering with the night sky as her blanket, was well-known among the rough sleepers in Spitalfields. In the wake of her murder, a handful of homeless women were some of the first to come forward and identify her. She was cited as being one of '10 to 20 houseless creatures who are without the means of paying for their beds' who were regularly to be found curled up in a shed off Dorset Street.[21]

Kate and Kelly's hand-to-mouth existence did not permit them to linger for too long in any one place. Casual-ward records indicate that, from 1883, the couple appear to have made regular excursions to Kent in order to find work, roaming between London, Dartford, Sevenoaks and Chatham. Kate never abandoned hawking, which must have become to her as much of a way of life as it was a means of earning an income. After twenty or more years of wandering, this existence may have seemed to her more comfortable than a settled life ever could. A pedlar's experience, as Conway would have taught her, was one beholden to no one – not even family.

After Kate took up with John Kelly, even her sister Eliza and her daughter Annie attempted to distance themselves from her. Annie had left home in her teens, choosing to cohabit with and later marry a lamp-black packer called Louis Philips. According to Annie's statements at her mother's inquest, Kate hounded the couple, frequently appearing at their door, intoxicated and begging for handouts. The situation became intolerable, and the Philipses were forced to move in order to avoid her. Annie complained that so long as her mother drank, it was impossible to maintain a normal relationship with her. In August 1886, the situation came to a head. Annie had been preparing to give birth to her third child and, on this occasion, appealed to her mother for assistance. Kate agreed to be present with her daughter in her period of 'confinement', but insisted on receiving pay for it. Annie grudgingly obliged, only to later discover that her mother had taken the money and gone out 'to get too much to drink'. 'The result,' Annie commented, 'caused unpleasantness . . . we did not part on very good terms.'[22] Little more than a week after giving birth, Annie had thrown Kate out and decided she would have no more to do with her. The Philipses moved from their home on 22 King Street in Bermondsey, and did not leave a forwarding address.

Perhaps what most suited Kate about her association with John Kelly, as opposed to any of her other relationships, was that Kelly appeared to make very few demands of her. Although everyone who knew them, from Kate's sisters to their friends at Cooney's lodging house, attested that the couple 'had a sincere attachment for each other', and that Kate 'never went with any other man', their connection appears to have been one based more on practicality than emotional intimacy.[23] Kelly called Kate his wife, but she preferred to bear the name of Conway, to whom she insisted she was legally married. Kate only used Kelly's name when it proved convenient. John never seemed to ask too many questions of Kate. He kept his distance from her family, never enquiring about her relationship with Annie, never speaking to her about Thomas Conway, apparently never venturing to intrude on Kate's inner thoughts. For one who lived as her partner for seven years, he knew surprisingly little about her, not even that she had been born in Wolverhampton. As he and others attested at her inquest, they rarely argued; Kelly recalled only one occasion where 'they had words' before Kate returned to him a few hours later.[24] First and foremost, Kate and Kelly appear to have been committed to each other's daily survival. By the time Kate had found John Kelly, she had lost the goodwill of most of her family, she had suffered domestic violence and bereavement, and had experienced the degradation of the workhouse, near-starvation and illness.[25] Under such circumstances, what mattered most was the here and the now: acquiring the drink that dulled the pain and the food that stopped the hunger. Kelly's company, his protection on the street and his occasional income made survival simpler. For a woman who had so little, this in itself would have proven comfort enough.

16

'Nothing'

FOR THOSE LIVING IN the poorer parts of London, the end of the summer meant one thing: the opportunity to earn some money and to enjoy themselves in the Kentish country-side bringing in the hop harvest. Hop picking was for many the closest they would ever experience to a holiday: a chance to enjoy the fresh air, campfire camaraderie and free barrels of beer and cider laid on by the farmers. Each September, thousands of city dwellers poured into the area; the marginally better-off arrived by train, while many more walked the roads from London. In a good year, like 1890, it is estimated that between fifty and sixty thousand men, women and children arrived for the hop harvest, where they were paid twopence a bushel for their labour and housed in huts, sheds or barns near to the hop gardens.

With free accommodation and drink on offer, Kate and John Kelly were not likely to have missed an opportunity to fill their pockets and bellies. They had been regulars among the hop pickers in past years, and in the summer of 1888 joined the procession of Londoners heading south to Kent. Unfortunately, they and others were met by an especially poor harvest. *The Echo* remarked that workers found 'the hops were not considered worth picking' in many parts of Kent. 'After trying many quarters for work' labourers were then forced 'to walk back to London, having earned nothing'.[1]

Kate and Kelly had set out towards the end of August, while the orchards and berry fields were seeking hands to bring in the fruit harvests. This was part of their usual circuit through Kent, and the two would have been hawking as well as seeking to pick up odd labouring jobs until the hops were ready for picking. Gradually the couple worked their way towards Maidstone, where they would have heard the hop crop was slightly better than in other areas. As a county town, Maidstone offered Kate and John an opportunity to acquire some necessities for the work ahead; Kelly was in need of a new pair of boots, along with a jacket, which were purchased from a pawn shop. They then headed towards Hunton, a village about 5 miles away, where, like other prospective pickers, they soon discovered that the crop was so sparse that 'outsiders could get nothing to do'.[2] Disappointed, they decided to 'hoof it back' to London.[3]

The pair arrived in town on the evening of Thursday 27 September. Having eaten and drunk everything they had earned in the countryside, they were forced to seek lodgings that night at the casual ward at Thavies Inn, on Shoe Lane. After years on the tramp, Kate and John had become experts at selecting the best spikes, and Thavies Inn was a particular favourite among vagrants. In spite of the rules set forth in the 1882 Casual Poor Act, which required all inmates to be detained for a minimum of two nights, thereby allowing for a full day's labour picking oakum and breaking stones prior to release, Shoe Lane was more liberal in its approach and was cited as a place to which 'paupers flocked' because 'detention and work are not enforced'.[4] This would concur with Kelly's account of events; he and Kate were released early on Friday morning, which then allowed him to find some work at Spitalfields Market. By that afternoon, he had earned sixpence, which would have covered the expense of a night's lodgings for one of them, but not both. John, not wishing to look like a negligent husband in the wake of his partner's murder, claimed in his official statement that he offered to tramp to Mile End Casual Ward while Kate took the 4 pence for a bed at Cooney's. 'No, you go and have a bed and I will go to the casual ward,' Kate was said to have protested. However, what was agreed and what actually transpired is a bit more 'muddled', as John Kelly himself admitted to the coroner.

Much of what is known about Kate and Kelly's movements in September comes from John's confused account, several versions of which appear in the newspapers.[5] Initially, Kelly states that Kate went off to Mile End around 3 or 4 p.m. on Friday afternoon to join the queue for a bed, but under questioning he revealed that this was not in fact true. The coroner produced a pawn ticket for a pair of boots Kelly said he had put in hock, dated Friday the 28th. John was taken aback by this, as he had originally claimed he pawned the boots the next day, on Saturday morning, and bought food and drink with the 2s. 6d. it provided. 'It was either Friday night or Saturday morning. I am all muddled up,' he stated, as the lie began to unravel. He further revealed that it was in fact Kate who had pawned the boots that Friday night, while Kelly had stood in the doorway in his bare feet.[6] 'Had you been drinking when the pawning took place?' the coroner asked him. 'Yes,' Kelly admitted sheepishly. His confession made it plain to the jury why his memory of the events was poor.[7]

In fact, neither Kate nor Kelly would have eaten since leaving Thavies Inn that morning, and filling their rumbling stomachs with food and drink would have been foremost on their minds. The sixpence that John had earned had evidently been spent buying alcohol, which accounted for the state he was in while he and Kate pawned his boots. According to John's testimony, 'the greater part' of the 2s. 6d. they received was then used in purchasing provisions that were to last them through the next morning.[8] The couple bought tea and sugar, which Kate loaded into her skirt pockets, and probably a few more drinks. By the end of the evening it would have become apparent that they had run through most of the pawn money too and it was decided that John should have the 4 pence for a single lodging-house bed. That night Kelly stayed not at number 55 Flower and Dean Street, but at number 52, while Kate was almost certainly not among the casuals at Mile End. Not only is there no record of her admission, but Mile End did not share Thavies Inn's lax reputation for the enforcement of regulations. Had Kate taken a bed there, she would have been detained for two nights in order to pick oakum. Instead she appeared to meet Kelly the following morning at the unfeasibly early hour of 8 a.m. What John would have been loath to mention was that Kate almost certainly slept rough that night, perhaps even in the shed off Dorset Street.[9] However, in light of the recent murders in Whitechapel, he knew that an admission of this would not have reflected well on him.

The coroner and the jury were obviously sceptical of Kelly's narrative; not simply because many of his statements did not add up, but because they, like the police and the press, were convinced that the killer was targeting prostitutes. Neither the testimony of John Kelly, nor that of Kate's sister, Eliza Gold, her daughter, or even Frederick William Wilkinson, the deputy lodging-house keeper at Cooney's, provides any evidence in support of this. Wilkinson, who claimed to have been acquainted with the couple for seven years, cited with certainty that he 'never knew or heard of [Kate] being intimate with anyone but Kelly'.[10] The coroner pressed John on this point too. In all of the time he had been with her, Kelly claimed that he never knew of her 'going out for immoral purposes at night'; nor had she ever 'brought [him] money in the morning after being out'. He stated categorically that he would never have suffered such a situation.[11]

Unfortunately, in the course of defending Kate's honour, Kelly made the mistake of using a turn of phrase with a double meaning. When he stated his concern over their lack of doss money, he claimed that he didn't want to 'have to see her walk about the streets at night'. The coroner picked up on this immediately.

'What do you mean by "walking the streets"?' he asked.

'Well Sir, many a time we have not had the money to pay for our shelter, and have had to tramp about,' John clarified.[12]

'Walking the streets', as explained by William Booth in his book *Darkest England*, was part of the experience for rough sleepers; it described the never-ending nocturnal quest for somewhere quiet to rest before a patrolling constable moved them on. According to Howard Goldsmid, this was a common way of life for those who frequented the lodging houses on Thrawl Street, Dorset Street and Flower and Dean Street. When not lying 'on the kerbstone, in the gutters, on heaps of rubbish, anywhere', they could be seen walking 'up and down with their hands in their pockets, and their dull sleepy eyes almost closed'.[13] Regrettably, the clarification of this term did little to dissuade many journalists from persisting in their identification of Kate as a prostitute. According to the *Daily Telegraph*, which was echoing the prejudices of its era while also attempting to tell a more salacious story, homeless women and women who sold sex were one and the same. The newspaper reported that Kate regularly bedded down on the street, or in a shed alongside what they called 'houseless waifs, penniless prostitutes, like herself . . .'[14]

Wherever Kate had spent Friday night, she and Kelly were back at Cooney's on Saturday morning, making themselves comfortable in the communal kitchen and turning their minds once again to how they would find their doss money. Eventually, it was this question that compelled them out of the door and onto the streets. They walked south, in the direction of Bishopsgate, though probably with no particular destination in mind.

By early afternoon they were in the vicinity of Houndsditch, the centre of the Jewish rag-selling trade, a street whose shop fronts were usually draped with stained calico petticoats and frayed woollen trousers. As John had pawned his boots the night before, it is possible that Kate had contemplated selling one of the many layers she wore beneath her chintz skirt and black cloth jacket. However, as it was Saturday, the Jewish Sabbath, the couple would have only met with closed shutters.

According to Kelly, Kate then suggested that she would go to Bermondsey and attempt to get money from her daughter. This could not have been a serious proposal. It had been over two years since Kate had last spoken with Annie. She didn't even know her address. Like so much of John's story, the details of what happened here are 'muddled' as well.

It's unclear where the couple had spent the afternoon until this point. Houndsditch was only a short walk from Flower and Dean Street, but the doors of many drinking establishments would have been passed along the route. As residents of Whitechapel for seven years, Kate and Kelly would have had no shortage of acquaintances and convivial companions, many of whom would have been ready to 'stand them a drink' or several, in exchange for those the couple had 'stood' them on earlier occasions. After a round or so, Kate may have thought that attempting to find Annie somewhere among the streets of south London no longer seemed impossible.

When John and Kate parted, she assured him she would return by four o'clock. According to Kelly, they hadn't a penny between them as he watched her bob down Houndsditch towards Aldgate.

Kate didn't get very far. In fact, she did little more than turn the corner, once or even twice, onto Aldgate High Street, before she encountered someone who undoubtedly owed her a drink or two. Kate was not the sort to refuse and her resolve, as it often did, disappeared with the contents of her first glass.

At eight thirty that night a woman sat in a heap against a wall at 29 Aldgate High Street, paralytic from drink. She babbled and sang and cursed, which inevitably drew a gathering of people. This was hardly an unusual sight for Whitechapel, but nevertheless, the onlookers would have stared, some with amusement, others with genuine concern for this unfortunate soul. A passing police constable, Louis Frederick Robinson, decided to investigate what was captivating the crowd. He looked down to see at the centre of it a pitiful figure whose unsteady head was tied into a black velvet and straw bonnet. She reeked of alcohol. Robinson asked the spectators if any of them knew the woman or where she lived. No one answered, although there were some present who knew precisely who she was and even ran off to tell John Kelly that his 'wife' had been collared for drunkenness.

Robinson tried to lift her off the street, but Kate's legs in her men's lace-up boots were as shambling as those of a marionette's and she soon slipped sideways out of his hold. It was only with the assistance of a colleague, PC George Simmons, that he was able to lead the inebriated woman to Bishopsgate Police Station. As was routine, before they put her in a cell, they needed to record her name in the ledger.

'What's your name?' Robinson demanded.

'Nothing,' Kate slurred.

They placed 'Nothing' in a cell in the hope she would soon sober up. Instead, she slid into a drunken slumber.

At around 9.55 p.m. and then several times after that, George Henry Hutt, the gaoler at Bishopsgate Station, looked in on her. At about a quarter past twelve, Kate woke up and began to sing to herself. This continued for around fifteen minutes before Hutt came to see her in the cell.

'When are you going to let me out?' she asked him in a tired, dry voice.

'When you are capable of taking care of yourself.'

'I'm capable of taking care of myself now.'

This was not the case. If Kate was entirely incapacitated at 8.30 p.m., then it was improbable she would have been sober by 1 a.m., the time Hutt decided to release her. She may have seemed steadier on her feet when she was led from the cell to the station office, but their prisoner was still intoxicated.

'What time is it?' Kate asked the gaoler drowsily.

'Too late for you to get any more drink,' answered Hutt.

'Well, what time is it?'

'Just on one.'

'I shall get a Damned fine hiding when I get home,' she muttered, knowing this was all for show.[15] When she lived with Thomas Conway, that would have been the truth.

'And serve you right, you have no right to get drunk,' taunted Hutt, who, like Kate's sisters and her daughter, would have held with the era's thoughts on such a matter: an errant wife deserved a beating.

Before discharging her, James Byfield, who was manning the desk, once more quizzed her about her name and address. Kate, who had spent the better part of her life attempting to decoy casual ward and workhouse staff by inventing and swapping around names and addresses, knew exactly how to play this game. By this stage in her life, her contempt for authority was second nature.

'Mary Ann Kelly,' she lied. She gave her address as '6 Fashion Street', and claimed she had just returned from hop picking, which was not so much of an exaggeration.[16]

The police officers then handed her back the contents of her pockets, an assortment of necessities that Kate would have always kept on her person: six pieces of soap and a small-toothed comb, a white-handled table knife and metal teaspoon, her tin boxes of tea and sugar, an empty tin matchbox, a piece of red flannel in which were kept pins and needles, a thimble and a collection of menstrual rags. She refilled her skirts with her other possessions, a few hawkable items: an empty red-leather cigarette case, two short black clay pipes, and a ball of hemp.

Once she had assembled herself, Hutt moved to show her out. 'This way, Misses,' he said, pushing open the swing door leading to the passage. Kate followed the passageway to the outer door. Hutt then politely reminded her to 'pull the door to' when she left.

'Alright,' Kate replied. 'Good night, Old Cock.'

To Hutt's irritation, she had only pulled the door partially closed. He watched as she turned left out of the station, towards Houndsditch.[17]

At 1 a.m., Kate's first thought would have been to locate John. As he had been penniless when they parted, she had no reason to believe he would have been able to pay for a bed at

Cooney's. At any rate, by that hour the deputy keeper would have been ejecting the lodgers who had failed to produce their doss money. She had last seen him around Houndsditch, and her hazy-headed instinct would have been to return there to ask those still about in the drinking dens if they knew of his whereabouts.[18]

The streets, with their handful of hissing gaslights, would have been as black as pitch in the earliest hours of 30 September. Kate was accustomed to being abroad in the dark and she knew the byways and passages of Whitechapel as well as she did the bottom of a bottle. Here and there, lights would still be burning, guiding her as she circled Houndsditch and wended her way along Duke Street, searching for a familiar face. Although it was late, Whitechapel's streets were never still or empty. There would always be people about: those like her, the drunk, the dispossessed, the homeless, the criminal. Some were in search of dark corners, others wandered towards their beds. After a spell of about twenty minutes, Kate must have concluded that her search was not likely to yield the answers she was seeking. She was tired and would have reconciled herself to spending another night sleeping rough.

By now, for this forty-six-year-old woman, this routine would have been familiar. Kate knew how to sleep beneath the stars, how to find a less painful way of lying her head against a hard wall, how to ignore the muck that gathered in her skirts or the trickle of waste water that rolled over her feet.

She found a spot in the far corner of Mitre Square, away from the lamps dropping pools of light. Here, she lowered herself down, her back against the wall as if it were a chair supporting her. As she did so, the assorted objects in her pedlar's pockets must have moved against one another. Amongst them were several small tin boxes filled with sugar and tea and pawn tickets. For one who carried no mementos of her family, who seemed determined to outrun a painful past and sever all ties, did these little items taunt her? Would the unexpected scent of tin remind her of Wolverhampton or the Old Hall Works, or her father? For all of her good humour, her singing and jolliness, Kate's heart must have been sodden with injury.

Kate closed her eyes against the night and reached for whatever respite she could find. Like all of those without moorings, who drifted or 'walked the streets', she understood that it was only a matter of time before someone came along and moved her on.

On the morning of 30 September, a little girl came racing up the stairs to the top floor of number 7 Thrawl Street. She banged on the door and called out to her neighbour, 'Mrs Frost'. There was a gentleman to see her on the street and a police inspector was with him. Mrs Frost, who was also known as the widow Eliza Gold, and prior to that Eliza Eddowes, moaned from her bed. She was very ill and could not get up. She promptly sent the child away.

The girl returned to the men below and reported the message. As this was urgent business, the police inspector sent her back up the stairs again to implore Mrs Frost to come down immediately. This time, he charged the little girl with a far more potent message: You must tell her that her sister is dead and she is required to identify the body.

Shaken to the core, Eliza, fully dressed but weak and sick, came down to the street supported by a neighbour and her son, George. Together with the police inspector and John Kelly they proceeded to the mortuary on Golden Lane.

When the coffin lid was drawn back, Eliza let forth a stream of anguished wails. The intensity of her distress was such that it was necessary to lead her from the room.

It was some time before she could compose herself enough to speak. Although Kate's face had been disfigured, Eliza claimed that she could recognize her sister's features perfectly well. The killer had not stripped her of that which distinguished her as an Eddowes. She burst into violent sobs once more, as she related this to a journalist at the mortuary. 'Oh my poor sister,' she cried, 'that she should come to such an end as this!'[19]

In spite of their financial circumstances, the Eddowes family would not have their sister dropped into a pauper's grave; neither would the residents of Whitechapel permit Kate to be laid to rest without a resounding send-off. Hundreds filled the streets on 8 October; in some places the crowds were so thick that it slowed the progress of the glass hearse and the mourning carriage that followed behind it. At Ilford Cemetery where she was interred, nearly five hundred people gathered to pay their respects. Among them were members of the Eddowes clan who had not seen one another in years. In removing a family member, sisters, daughters, cousins and aunts were pulled more tightly together: an act of reunion that closed the now empty space at their centre.

Mary Jane

c. 1863 – 9 November 1888

17

Marie Janette

IN THE EARLY 1880s a gentleman in search of the carnal pleasures on offer in London's West End might find them rather
more difficult to come by than in previous years. The Haymarket, once London's whirling circus of vice, had been
silenced in the previous decade. The doors to the decadent
gilt- and crimson-lined Argyll Rooms, where wealthy 'swells'
swallowed champagne and danced until midnight with
silk-clad prostitutes, had been shut. The lights had been
extinguished on Piccadilly's 'night houses', the after-hours
venues to where the 'fast set' and their 'frail companions'
repaired for cigars, food and refreshment. Gone were the
accommodation houses, where they might seek a convenient
room afterwards. Even the damask-hung, mirrored brothels
were shuttered. As a result, vice was forced to become fashionably discreet.

Wealthy gentlemen, especially those favoured by the well-
dressed prostitutes living in St John's Wood, Brompton or
Pimlico, might be fortunate enough to receive an invitation to
a private ball. A set of function rooms would be hired at a
venue somewhere between Oxford Street and Marylebone for
a group of about eighty guests, forty men and forty women.
Each male guest would pay for a woman's admission, which

then covered the cost of the room hire, the band and the supper. To the casual observer, this gathering of gentlemen in top hats and evening dress, and beautiful young women in ball gowns and jewels, hinted at nothing untoward. As the sexual adventurer known only as 'Walter' records in his memoirs, there was little that could be described as 'immodest' or irregular about the occasion, with the exception that 'no introductions were needed, and men asked any woman to dance . . . and women did not hesitate to ask men to dance . . .' However, following supper, the tone changed: 'the dancing became romping, and concupiscence asserted itself . . . Suggestive talk was now the order of the night, bawdy words escaped, the men kissed the women's shoulders as they waltzed, one or two couples danced polkas with their bellies jogging against each other, suggestive of fucking.'[1] Eventually the evening came to an end; couples peeled off and departed in their carriages, only to continue their revels in private, at the women's lodgings in the leafy suburbs.

It was into scenes like this that a woman calling herself Mary Jane Kelly arrived at some point between 1883 and 1884. The stories she told about herself contained some truth and some fiction, but no one has ever been able to ascertain which parts were which. She may have borrowed components of her identity from someone she knew, or even reinvented herself altogether, a phenomenon which was fairly common for women of her profession.

According to one version of her tale, Mary Jane was born in Limerick around 1863. Her father, a man thought to have been called John Kelly, took the family across the Irish Sea to Wales when she was very young and settled for a time either in Caernarvonshire or Carmarthen, where he was employed as the foreman of an ironworks. She claimed to have been one of nine children: six brothers who appear to have been younger and still living at home in 1888, and one named Henry who, strangely, was called John or 'Johnto' and served in the 2nd Battalion of the Scots Guards. Mary Jane also had a sister, who she said was 'very fond of her' and led a respectable life travelling 'from marketplace to marketplace' with her aunt. At the age of sixteen, Mary Jane claims that she married a coal miner (or collier) named Davis or Davies who died in an explosion a year or two later. Following his death, she went to Cardiff where she had family. While there, she spent 'eight or nine months in the infirmary' and then fell in with a female cousin 'who followed a bad life'. Without admitting to it directly, she implied that it was this relationship that drew her into a life of prostitution. At some time around 1884, if not slightly earlier, she came to London 'and lived in a gay house in the West End of the town'.[2]

Mary Jane's story, as she presented it to her erstwhile lover, Joseph Barnett, amounts to nothing more than a collection of disconnected snapshots. To others who knew her, she offered slightly different versions of this tale. To one she claimed that 'she was Welsh, and that her parents, who had discarded her, still resided at Cardiff'. She stated that it was from there that she came directly to London. 'There is every reason to believe that she is Welsh, and that her parents or relatives reside in Cardiff,' reported another. Intriguingly, this source went on to say that Mary Jane arrived in London as early as 1882 or 1883 and hailed from a 'well-to-do' set of people in Cardiff. She was described as having been 'an excellent scholar and an artist of no mean degree'.[3] Two other individuals, her landlord and a City missionary, claimed that Mary Jane had told them she was Irish and that she received letters from her mother who still resided in Ireland.[4] To confuse matters further, a neighbour stated that Mary Jane frequently spoke to her about her family and friends, and that 'she had a female relation in London who was on the stage', while also telling other people that she had a two-year-old child, who would have been born around 1883.[5]

Not a single statement made by Mary Jane about her life prior to her arrival in London has ever been verified. In 1888, enquiries were made both in Limerick and in Wales to no avail. The search for a brother in the Scots Guards also yielded nothing. As news of her murder spread across the UK and around the globe, not one friend or relation from the past appears to have recognized Mary Jane Kelly's name or any part of her story enough to have come forward. In subsequent decades attempts to research her history have proven equally fruitless; no Kellys or Davieses or Mary Janes match up in censuses or parish records in Wales or in Ireland. The only conclusion that can be drawn is that the tale of Mary Jane Kelly's life and even her name was a work of fabrication.

In the nineteenth century creating a new identity for oneself was relatively straightforward. A move to another town or even to another district and a change of moniker was easy enough. Inventing a new persona based on a manufactured history, an alteration in dress and manners allowed many to pass successfully through different social strata, either above or below them. However, a higher quality of education and the indelible mark that it left on a person was far more difficult to either falsify or hide. An individual's schooling came across not only in their ability to read or write, but in their speech, their bearing, their interests, and often in their artistic or musical accomplishments. While the poor had access only to the most basic instruction, the rising middle classes sought to distinguish themselves socially by investing in the education of their children so that their progeny might bear the stamp of respectability.

According to those who knew her, this distinction seems to have made itself apparent in Mary Jane, who it was said came 'from a well-to-do family'. One of her landladies remarked on her high level of 'scholarship' while also commenting that she was a capable artist. This statement was made at a time when training in drawing was given to girls at fashionable young ladies' schools, and did not feature on the average school curriculum.[6] A girl from a large, impoverished rural family would have had no access to instruction in such skills, or the money to purchase the materials, nor would she have been likely to receive the encouragement necessary for becoming an artist. More interesting still, no one who knew Mary Jane noted any regional accent and those who enquired about her origins had to be told she was Welsh or Irish. If Wales or Ireland flavoured her speech, the traces of this were almost indiscernible, possibly as a result of elocution lessons. 'You would not have supposed if you had met her on the street that she belonged to the miserable class as she did,' remarked a missionary who knew her in Whitechapel, 'she was always neatly and decently dressed, and looked quite nice and respectable.'[7] Kelly may have been telling the truth when she claimed to Joe Barnett that her father was a 'gaffer', one in a position of authority at the ironworks. It is possible that Barnett mistook her meaning and that Mary Jane's father was in fact the owner of the business or played some role in its management. This certainly would have placed her in an altogether different social class.

Although Kelly insisted that she was legally married at sixteen to a miner named Davies or Davis, no record has ever been found attesting to this. If Kelly had indeed become romantically entangled with a man, it is more likely to have been as his mistress or common-law wife. This, too, may accord with the suggestion that Mary Jane bore a child around 1883, at roughly the time she is said to have spent eight to nine months 'in an infirmary' in Cardiff. Like everything else that features in Mary Jane's narrative, no trace has been found of the birth of a child, nor is there any indication as to its fate. As such an extended stay at a publicly funded general hospital in the 1880s was highly unlikely; it is more probable that this sojourn was at a private institution, perhaps a reformatory for fallen women or an asylum. Either of these two options would have been an appropriate recourse for a middle-class family whose daughter had transgressed the social norms by engaging in sex outside of marriage. At the time, Cardiff had at least two refuges for fallen women: the Protestant House of Mercy and the Catholic Convent of the Good Shepherd. Both took in young women in their teens and twenties from the lower classes. On occasion, middle-class girls participated in their rehabilitation schemes, which mainly consisted of religious instruction and training in domestic skills and needlework. However, for some middle-class families, female sexual desire expressed outside of marriage was regarded as evidence of mental instability and was to be dealt with by trained doctors. At this period Cardiff did not have its own mental asylum, but instead sent its patients to the United Counties Lunatic Asylum in Camarthen, where Mary Jane also claims to have spent part of her life.

Although the precise chronology of this period is cloudy, Kelly appears to have told Joseph Barnett that it was following her stay in the 'infirmary' when she fell in with her badly behaved cousin. As the rehabilitation offered at both asylums and at refuges for fallen women was often unsuccessful, this order of events is not improbable. Unfortunately Joe Barnett never elaborated upon what Mary Jane meant when she referred to her cousin's 'bad life'. Was she part of a sporty 'fast set'? Was she a prostitute or a man's mistress? Was she a madam? And was she the connection that facilitated Mary Jane's move to London?

Of all of the holes in Mary Jane's account none is so gaping as that which explains how or why she left Cardiff for a 'gay house' in the West End of London. Travel or a change of residence to another city or town was not something a single woman embarked upon haphazardly in the nineteenth century. London, though linked by rail to Cardiff, was still a considerable distance from Wales, both physically and culturally. Generally, unmarried young women came alone to London for two reasons: because a job had been arranged for them or because there was a social or familial connection who lived in the city. Either or both of these possibilities must have guided Mary Jane to the capital, otherwise as a newcomer it would have proven difficult to negotiate an immediate entry into the mid to upper ranks of the sex trade. Personal contacts in a new and confusing city would have been just as essential to women in the higher end of the sex trade as they would be to anyone in 'respectable' society wishing to be introduced to the right circle. An acquaintance may have given Kelly the name of a 'landlady' who offered women introductions to gentlemen. Alternatively, she may have arrived in London with a lover from Cardiff or with the intention of joining one there.

By the last quarter of the nineteenth century, it was no longer common for prostitutes to live where they practised their trade. Those who walked the pavements of Piccadilly, the Haymarket and Regent Street tended to make their homes in the outlying parts of the capital. For poorer women this was frequently the East End, while those who catered to the middle classes and above often opted for locations such as Chelsea, Pimlico, St John's Wood and certain streets in Knightsbridge and Brompton, where Mary Jane Kelly took lodgings.

Since the middle of the century, the little streets that extended from Knightsbridge Barracks to Brompton Road, as far west as Brompton Square, had acquired a reputation as being a haven for army officers' mistresses, actresses and the artistic set, those who indulged in sin discreetly behind shutters and dark velvet drapery. In 1881, the oblong Brompton Square, with its green centre, appears to have been the favoured address of a number of female heads of households describing themselves as 'lodging house-keepers'.[8] Number 15, inhabited by two 'actresses', was a house owned by Mary Jefferies, one of the most formidable madams of the Victorian age, who catered to aristocrats, politicians, wealthy capitalists and at least one member of the royal family. This was only one of the procuress's many properties in Brompton and Chelsea; her network of residences and women extended across west and north London. Jefferies operated her business from a safe distance, like a puppet mistress, arranging for her 'girls' to meet clients by appointment at various locations, thereby keeping her hands as clean as possible. While the 'French woman' with whom Mary Jane came to reside was unlikely to have possessed such an empire, her concern was probably run in a similar manner, whereby her 'boarders' were offered opportunities to make the acquaintance of gentlemen.

While procuresses who ran middling to upmarket businesses would have facilitated introductions to men, by the later part of the century, clients did not necessarily come to their premises in search of women. In some cases assignations were arranged through an exchange of letters or a conversation, while others occurred by chance meeting. On one occasion 'Walter' gained an introduction to a discreet Marylebone brothel disguised as a shop by exchanging glances with its madam while on a train. After he struck up conversation she informed him that she was a dressmaker and employed only the prettiest girls at her place of business. Before disembarking she handed him a card and invited him 'to call and try on her gloves'. Walter was certain that she drummed up a good amount of trade by approaching men in railway carriages and on public transport.[9] One of Mrs Jefferies' methods of exciting interest in her latest recruits was to drive to the Guards Club in her landau and distribute personal invitations to meet her young ladies. Officers in the most elite regiments, from wealthy and titled families who had money to spend and time to kill while in barracks, were notably good customers. Considering Mary Jane's proximity to the Knightsbridge Barracks and the area's association with regimental mistresses, a number of such men may have been among her clientele, including, perhaps, the Henry or 'Johnto' she mentioned in the 2nd Battalion of the Scots Guards. 'Johnto' may not have been her brother at all, but rather an officer and a former lover with whom she maintained a correspondence when his postings took him abroad.[10]

The men who sought the company of women like Mary Jane through a procuress would have expected to commit to an evening of entertainment in addition to receiving sex. Walter's dressmaker-madam introduced him to a young woman working in her shop called Sophy, whom he met formally in an adjoining house. The madam instructed him that he would not be having sex with her on the premises but that he was to pay her 5 pounds up front and was then to take Sophy to dinner the following night. Five or six years earlier, men like Walter might have met Sophy or Mary Jane at the Argyll Rooms before taking them to an accommodation house, but now, evenings often began at venues like St James's Restaurant, known as 'Jimmy's', at 69 Regent Street, or at the Café de l'Europe on the Haymarket.

Here, women and their male companions sat down to dine in smoke-filled, mirrored and palm-fronded rooms and were tended by French and Italian waiters known for their discretion. After gorging on oysters, devilled kidneys and roast beef and washing it all down with bottomless glasses of champagne, Moselle and hock, the couple would travel by hackney cab or in the gentleman's carriage to an equally discreet hotel, or back to the woman's lodgings. Such assignations might not necessarily end the next morning, nor did they have to begin at a restaurant. A trip to the theatre, the music hall, the races, or any number of other activities might be involved, until the gentleman exhausted himself sexually, grew tired of the woman's company or found that duty called him elsewhere. In exchange for the pleasure of her company, he would expect to be billed accordingly. The 'price' generally involved the purchase of 'trinkets' as well as cash. In addition to the 'five pounds upfront' demanded by Walter's dressmaker-madam, Sophy also managed to negotiate 'three sovereigns and a new dress' from him for a night's activities.

Arranged meetings were only one method by which those in the sex trade expected to do business. Women of all ranks made themselves accessible to potential clients through public display. This included appearing in the promenades and galleries of certain music halls and theatres, as well as street walking. In the years that followed the closure of the Argyll Rooms, the West End's smartly dressed prostitutes and their louche companions decamped to the Alhambra Theatre in Leicester Square. One social explorer, Daniel Joseph Kirwan, described the scene on a night in 1878 as he moved beyond a group of 'young ladies smoking cigarettes' and entered the promenade. This he found 'choked with men and women, walking past each other, looking at the stage, drinking at the bars, chafing each other in a rough way, and laughing loudly'.[11] He was surprised to discover that the men seemed 'of a good class', while the women were 'cheerful, pleasant-looking girls, of quite fair breeding, and of a far better taste in their dress than the honest wives and sweethearts of the mechanics and shopkeepers, who sit in the place of virtue, within the painted railing'.[12] However, the Alhambra catered to every rank of prostitute, and on that night, a police sergeant estimated there to be 'at least 1,200 women of the town' present. Upon ascending into the gallery Kirwan noticed that the mood changed, 'the clamour and the smoke made the place unbearable' and that there was 'not the slightest disguise in the conduct of the females'. Worse still was the gallery above it where 'the riffraff collected', the sight of which prompted him to remark, 'When a woman goes to the sixpenny gallery in the Alhambra she is indeed lost beyond all hope of rescue.'[13]

When not passing an evening in the Alhambra or venues like it, West End prostitutes of the middle ranks also sought custom through street solicitation. The Haymarket, Regent Street, Piccadilly and the smaller streets that flowed from them into Leicester Square and Soho formed the parade ground along which women devised their individual circuits. A slow, meandering progress might begin at Piccadilly Circus and proceed up Regent Street, where she would take her time gazing at the shop windows, seeming to admire the hats, china or the toys on display, while cautiously glancing at either side to note if the male passer-by who slowed his gait and joined her was a genuine shopper, a potential John or a police constable. If she had no luck, she might cross over the road and proceed southward, perhaps stopping at the Café de l'Europe where she hoped to meet the eye of a gentleman and his friends. Failing this, her route would perhaps take her eastward down Coventry Street to Leicester Square where she might stop in at the Alhambra. Somewhere along this route, at least once that night, a man would likely place himself next to her and tip his hat. He may have noticed that she raised the hem of her skirt an inch or so too high as she crossed the road and stepped onto the kerb; however, as the busy West End was also filled with respectable shop girls leaving their places of employment for home, and maids out on errands for their mistresses, he had to be careful not to make an offensive remark. Even the seasoned philanderer Walter commented that he often found it difficult to differentiate between a prostitute and 'a virtuous girl'. One he followed all the way from Bond Street to Piccadilly, uncertain of whether to approach her, because 'she was so neatly dressed like a superior servant, that I couldn't conclude if she were gay or not . . . she seemed to look at no one when stopping and looking at shops. When she did, I also stopped and looked, standing by the side of her.'

In this quarter of London, it was obligatory for a potential client to make the first approach and for the woman to respond, either with flirtatious feigned horror or acceptance. Eventually, Walter leaned toward the young woman and asked:

May I go home with you?
   She looked at me as if half astonished, then after hesitation,
   Yes, but I live three miles off –
   Let us get into a cab –
   Oh no, I can't take you home.

The situation was remedied by Walter hailing a cab and finding them 'a snug accommodation house' ten minutes away.[14]

While the area around Piccadilly and Leicester Square formed the semi-respectable, high-class heart of the city's sex trade, prostitution was present in most parts of the metropolis, and in other corners of the West End. In the early 1880s, the area between the Strand and Charing Cross Station was still a haunt for street walkers, as it had been for well over a century, while other West End streets, such as Brewer Street and Lisle Street, just to the north of Leicester Square, became noted for their older and cheaper women.[15] Prostitution had also begun to move nearer to train stations, into areas with transient populations, hotels and lodging houses, such as Euston and Victoria. However, Mary Jane, a young woman in her early twenties and at the height of her career, would have found no obstacle to making a good living in the centre of town, at the top end of the sex trade. With a fashionably stout, 5-foot-7-inch figure, blue eyes and long luxuriant hair, her physical attractions allowed her 'to drive about in a carriage' and 'lead the life of a lady'. She referred to herself as Marie Janette and accumulated 'numerous dresses of a costly description'. Those at the Alhambra, Café de l'Europe and Jimmy's would have undoubtedly known her well.

Mary Jane would have also been accustomed to well-dressed gentlemen making her offers and promises: offers to entertain her at the races, to buy her gloves and jewellery, promises to spoil her with fine food and drink. The savviest women in the sex trade understood that their youthful allure was fleeting and that in order to capitalize on their worth it was essential to seize every opportunity put before them. So when 'a gentleman' offered to take Mary Jane to Paris, she agreed.

Like everything Kelly recounted to Joseph Barnett about her past, the circumstances surrounding this particular proposal, the name of the gentleman involved or any other detail concerning the trip were not revealed. How she came to know this man – if he was a client, a serious romantic prospect, an acquaintance or one who came to her with a business offer – is unknown. However, what is certain is that this visit to Paris was not what it appeared to be on the surface. Mary Jane's French landlady-procuress may also have had a role to play in what transpired. At a time when international travellers sent their luggage separately to their intended destination, Kelly packed most of her expensive wardrobe in a trunk which she evidently expected her madam to forward to her address in Paris. The box was never sent, and perhaps it was its absence that first alerted Mary Jane to the possibility that she had been deceived.

By the last quarter of the nineteenth century, the trafficking of women between Britain and Continental Europe had become a lucrative enterprise. The expansion of rail networks and shipping enabled cheaper and easier travel for people and goods. It also allowed those 'goods' to reach a wider range of marketplaces and fulfil more particular tastes. Just as London became a receiving hub for young women from France, Belgium and Germany, so English girls were procured and shipped out to brothels in these and other countries. A former trafficker, in an interview with W. T. Stead, estimated that in 1884 at least 250 British women were sent to Belgium and northern France alone. Of those, two-thirds were abducted after accepting a position in service abroad or a sham proposal of marriage.[16] Often, they were plied with drink or doped, given false travel documents and bundled onto a train.

In 1879, Adelene Tanner, a recently unemployed domestic, was horrified to find herself in this position. It had all begun innocently enough, when John Sallecartes, a 'respectably dressed man' with a foreign accent, struck up a conversation with her in a railway waiting room.[17] By chance, Adelene encountered 'Sullie' again and on this occasion agreed to join him for a drink at a hotel in Soho. A more experienced young woman – one like Mary Jane, who knew the sex trade – would have immediately sensed the direction of travel, but nineteen-year-old Adelene was a virgin, and a sheltered one. Sullie saw to it that the girl's glass of wine was regularly refilled and soon 'she could scarcely remember what [she] said'. He also took the opportunity to introduce her to his business partner, a handsome Belgian called Frederick Schultz, who, like Sallecartes, was a *placeur*, or a recruiter for continental brothels. With the room spinning, Adelene was then presented to the man who would be her pimp. This was Edouard Roger, a Frenchman, who, after a short conversation, told her that he had 'taken a great fancy to [her]; that he would like to take [her] to Paris, and if after seeing his grand house, carriages &c. [she] would like to be his wife, he would marry [her]'.[18] The intoxicated, dazzled servant enthusiastically agreed. Of course, the problem was that Adelene, along with two other young women who had been tricked by Sullie and Schultz, was not destined for Paris, but for Brussels and the locked rooms of a *maison close*, a state-sanctioned brothel. Before departing England, all three were issued with false identities. Upon their arrival in Belgium they were warned that this was in fact illegal and would lead to their immediate arrest if they ever attempted to flee Roger's house.

Although some were duped into foreign prostitution, it was suggested that at least one in three women who agreed to go abroad was already working in the sex trade and 'anxious for a change'. In his 1885 series of articles, 'The Maiden Tribute of Modern Babylon', exploring the murky world of the trade in women and underage girls, W. T. Stead recounts the story of 'Amelia Powell', who found herself transported from London into a brothel in Bordeaux. While never openly admitting to it,

Amelia insinuates that she practised as a prostitute after leaving her husband placed her 'on the verge of destitution'. She claimed that 'a friend in an honest position' was eager to introduce her 'to a certain Greek' who ran a cigar shop on Regent Street. This man promised that he could get Amelia and three other women 'excellent situations' in Bordeaux. It did not take much persuading for her to agree to go. Amelia admitted, 'I grasped the suggestion . . . as affording the means of escaping from the associations and sufferings with which I was so painfully familiar in London.'[19] However, they were not long in Bordeaux before the realities of their 'excellent situations' were made clear to them. Once inside the *maison close*, Amelia states that 'our clothes were taken away, and we were tricked out with silk dresses and other finery' as a way of forcing a debt on them and making it impossible for them to leave without being accused of theft. Amelia was told that she owed her madam 1,800 francs, which not only included the clothing she was compelled to wear but 'the cost of the commission for being brought over'. She was instructed that once she had paid down the outstanding sum by entertaining gentlemen, she might be free to leave, but she soon learned that this too was impossible: 'When the account shows that you have only four or five hundred francs against you, the mistress sets to work to induce you, by cozening, cajoling, or absolute fraud, to accept other articles of clothing. Thus you go on month after month.'[20]

Such ruses had been common practice in brothels for centuries and were just as likely to catch seasoned sex labourers off guard as they were to entrap the novice. Those involved in international sex trafficking worked discreetly and in advance, plotting out their manoeuvres, so that a woman destined for overseas trade would not guess what awaited her. It is probable that Mary Jane's French landlady had some role in sending her to Paris and colluded with 'the gentleman' to place her in a brothel there. Whatever the scenario, she seemed certain enough that Marie Janette would have no need for her trunk of pretty gowns when she arrived at the *maison close*.

Once inside, life within these houses was extremely tightly regulated. In order to keep the streets free of the nuisance of visible prostitution, the law restricted women's movements in and out of a *maison close*. Women were only permitted in public during certain hours and even then were not allowed to congregate in groups, loiter near their doors or even make themselves visible through their windows, which were to remain shuttered. Additionally, all new recruits were expected to register with the Police de Moeurs (the regulating authority) and submit to twice-weekly examinations for venereal disease. If indebtedness to a brothel was not enough to break a trafficked woman's will, the strict code of legislation governing her personal freedom would have done that on its own. Once caught within the rigid jaws of a foreign *maison close*, a woman with no friends and unable to communicate in French had little hope of escape.

Mary Jane must have sensed this. She explained the situation to Joe Barnett by telling him that she had gone to Paris but as she 'did not like the part' she did not stay. Barnett seemed to indicate that by 'part', she had implied 'the purpose' of her journey there. She returned after no more than a fortnight. How she managed to wriggle free from the snare that had been laid for her is another mystery altogether. As Salle-cartes mentioned in his interview with Stead, it was not unusual for girls to 'have their suspicions aroused' and 'take alarm' after they arrived abroad. If Kelly had been as well educated as it was suggested, she would have possessed at least a basic grasp of French, which may have assisted her. If the 'human parcels', as they were called, were able to communicate with the police, this could pose a real threat. However, even after the captive had been delivered to her destination, dangers for the traders and the brothel keepers remained. According to statute, anyone (and often it was an amenable customer of the *maison close*) who suspected illegal trafficking might make an appeal to the Police de Moeurs who were 'bound by law to release any English girl detained in a brothel against her will, even if she has not paid her debt'.[21] Setbacks such as these were not taken lightly by the traffickers or the brothel, both of whom would have found themselves out of pocket. Perhaps more troubling for them still, there would be a young woman at large who could attest to their crimes.

As Stead was keen to point out, international slave traders were not people with whom to trifle. These rings were managed by extremely dangerous men, mostly 'ex-convicts, who know too well the discomforts of the *maison correctionelle*' and who would feel no compunction at 'removing an inconvenient witness' if it helped them escape another conviction.[22] Although Mary Jane had not intended it, by fleeing her captors she had made some fearsome enemies. Although she managed to outrun them in Paris, she would never again find life easy in London.

18

The Gay Life

D URING THE SUMMER MONTHS, ships from the northern French port of Boulogne carrying travellers from Paris landed at St Katharine's Docks, beside the Tower of London. Disembarking passengers were more likely to come down the gangway and turn west towards the centre of the city than they were to cross the road and turn east. Just beyond the confusion of the docks, piles of luggage and cargo, the blasts of steam and smell of tar, rattled the continuous traffic of a roadway known as the Ratcliff Highway. At first appearance, the mouth of the road offered an innocent mercantile impression: an emporium for maritime crew, stuffed with ship-utensil marts, lamp depots, seamen's outfitters and a few dingy gin palaces; however, a progress further along the thoroughfare revealed the area's true character. Cheap lodging houses replaced the ship chandlers, beer houses nestled beside pubs and music halls, and the thrumming sound of sin grew steadily audible.

The Ratcliff Highway was as much a neighbourhood as it was a road, bearing its own identity and an economy driven largely by the steady influx of ships and sailors who stalked its streets in search of drink and sex. At the end of the century it still retained the reputation for violence it had acquired in 1811 when seven people were murdered in their beds in one of England's first serial killings. In spite of the blazing gas lights and bouncy polka melodies, the Ratcliff Highway was a dark and miserable place. The smashing of glass and jaws, the spilling of drink and blood was a regular occurrence among the multilingual customers who filled the music halls and drinking cellars. Late into the night, as merry-makers stumbled in search of unlicensed pubs and opium dens, the riotousness rolled out onto the surrounding streets, which echoed with shrieking and arguing, singing and copulating.

Mary Jane Kelly certainly did not intend that her life should take her to the Ratcliff Highway, but the situation in which she had found herself left her little choice. Had it been safe for her to return to the West End she might have simply continued in her previous existence. Prostitutes at the middle to upper end of the trade did not work in isolation; they would have acquired networks of friends and knowledge of other landlady-procuresses upon whose door they could knock if in need of another position. It was also not uncommon for such women to call upon the assistance of good clients or former lovers when in a pinch. Mary Jane would have had a number of people to whom she might have turned and easily resumed her place in the promenade of the Alhambra and the dining room of the Café de l'Europe had she believed there was no risk of being discovered. Instead, she chose to turn eastward from St Katharine's Docks, down the Ratcliff Highway.

Number 79 Pennington Street, on the corner of Breezer's Hill, was little more than a ten-minute walk from the dock. Until 1874, the soot-covered brick building which faced onto warehouses had been the Red Lion public house. It had only recently been converted into a home, which in 1885 was inhabited by the Millers – a German family of tailors – and a

Dutch couple, Eliesabeth Boekü and Johannes Morgenstern and their twin infant daughters. Mrs Boekü, as she called herself, had been born in the Netherlands as Eliesabeth Bluma, the daughter of a sugar-baking family who appear to have immigrated and settled on Pennington Street during her youth. Eventually, Eliesabeth married a man from the Dutch community, Louis Boekü, who claimed to be a gas fitter. However, rather mysteriously for one earning a labourer's wage, Mr Boekü began to acquire property. By 1880, if not earlier, 79 Pennington Street came into his possession.

Boekü appears to have let the former Red Lion to the Millers, who, under his authority, took to subletting rooms to prostitutes. This was not an uncommon practice in an area where the rents could be easily made by simply turning a blind eye to the activities of one's tenants. While the Millers tended to his dirty work, Louis Boekü was content to live elsewhere with his wife and family. However, following his death in 1882, Eliesabeth decided to take control of her husband's investment. Along with her new common-law partner, Johannes Morgenstern, she moved into 79 Pennington Street, upstairs from the Millers, with a view to making a career from the sex trade.

Number 79 Pennington Street was likely to have been only one of several similar properties in Louis Boekü's portfolio. Interestingly, at about the same time that Eliesabeth and Johannes moved to Pennington Street, Johannes' brother, Adrianus Morgenstern, moved to a property in Poplar with a woman named Elizabeth Felix. According to Adrianus's descendant, this house was also used as a brothel.[1] While Mrs Boekü appears to have been a determined entrepreneur, it was only with the assistance of the Morgensterns that this endeavour truly became a family enterprise.

While the Boekü-Morgensterns occupied at least one of the upstairs rooms at number 79, as a former pub, there were still several more to let. In 1881, three young women – Mary Beemer and Ada King, both twenty-one, and twenty-year-old Emily Challis – were living there. According to the census, they were engaged in entertaining two visiting sailors at the time the enumerator called. When Mary Jane, a pretty 22-year-old 'gay girl', turned up at the door, she was just the sort of lodger that Mrs Boekü would have been seeking. It is unknown how much of her past she revealed to her new madam, but if the name Kelly was not her real one, then it is likely she adopted it at this point. Upon her return from France, Mary Jane did not wish to be found and if her pursuers were hunting for a Welshwoman, then it would have been sensible for her to become Irish by assuming one of the country's most ubiquitous surnames and slipping into anonymity.

If Mary Jane had arrived at 79 Pennington Street penniless, Mrs Boekü could be assured that she would soon earn the price of her rent, though the establishments, the clientele and even the practices along the Ratcliff Highway would prove to be somewhat different to those to which she had been accustomed in Piccadilly. 'Ratcliff and Wapping have ways of their own,' wrote the social reformer Edward W. Thomas, 'and in no particular could this be better illustrated than in the conduct of the sailors and the women . . .'[2] During a visit to the area, Thomas observed that there existed a certain protocol among prostitutes when it came to recruiting their customers. The women and their pimps and procuresses kept abreast of when the vessels were due into port and 'when a ship arrives in the docks, so many of the women as are disengaged go down to the entrance, and there and then endeavour to inveigle the seamen . . .' These attachments then became binding for the duration of the time that the sailor was ashore. According to Thomas, mariners had a custom of selecting their 'particular girl', a situation that the Ratcliff sex trade used fully to its advantage. A sailor's chosen 'girl' would then 'accompany him hither and thither, always in the neighbourhood, carousing by night . . . and sleeping by day' with her in her bed. During this time, should his interest wane, 'he is fought for by his paramour, as long as his money remains unexhausted'.[3] When his purse was empty or his shore leave had ended, there was always the next shipload of seamen or the usual methods of attracting trade on which to fall back; street walking and plying in one of the many public houses, gin palaces or music halls.

As moralists noted, women from the Ratcliff Highway appeared to tout for trade more brazenly than those in the West End and other parts of the city. Given that the demand for commercial sex quite literally swelled with the tide, even the police found it difficult to regulate prostitution and restrain the proliferation of brothels. 'Gay women' walked the streets openly without much fear of the authorities. Thomas observed that 'not a bonnet or head-dress of any kind . . . nor indeed any superfluous clothing', even on the coolest of nights, was to be seen on those out for an evening stroll.[4] He further commented that 'many of them were remarkably well-clothed', though their low-necked gowns, which 'were equally limited in length', and their 'jewellery of a cheap and flashy kind' made them 'very conspicuous'.

The better sort of 'gay woman', those who were young, or at least bore a youthful appearance, were to be found in the public singing-rooms. In order to draw in seafaring custom, most of these smoke-filled drinking dens were decorated with a nautical theme, their walls daubed with crude seascapes, anchors and mermaids. Dancers with rouged faces, dressed in diaphanous material, performed amid wooden waves, while singers melodramatically reminisced about lovely lasses left onshore. With the exception of the women and a few locals, most of the audience spoke Swedish, Danish, German, Portuguese, Spanish or French, and didn't understand a word of what was being sung. Still, they were happy to slump on the wooden benches, quaff the bar dry and fondle their girls until a fight broke out.

Not unlike the more expensive West End, an evening's entertainment along the Ratcliff Highway revolved around drink; however, the most savvy women in the sex trade would tipple with care. Unfamiliar customers, whether sailors or swells, could be dangerous. To fill one with a bottle of champagne or several glasses of gin was like placing a bullet in one of the chambers of a gun and spinning it. A woman could never predict what sort of john he would be once intoxicated (or even while sober). If she was fortunate, he might slip into a stupor; if she was less so, he might beat her senseless. Her best defence was to remain clear-headed, which could prove difficult if her customer constantly refilled her glass. One of the era's ladies of pleasure wrote that when she was with a client 'it was seldom necessary to drink'. She need only touch the glass to the lips before the contents were discreetly deposited elsewhere.[5] However, drink also offered a convenient escape from a miserable existence. It dulled the fear of unwanted pregnancy and disease, a very real possibility in every penetrative encounter. It obliterated the horrors of intimacy with a man who was physically repellent, and it quieted, even for a short time, feelings of self-loathing, guilt, pain, and traumatic memories of violence. Mary Jane Kelly was likely to have drunk throughout her career in the sex trade, but after her return from France, this habit seems to have grown into a bad one. Mrs Boekü's 'sister-in-law', Elizabeth Felix (or Mrs Phoenix, as she is erroneously called in the papers) had observed Kelly's behaviour first hand. She was 'one of the most decent and nicest girls [you could meet] when sober', Felix stated, but became 'very quarrelsome and abusive when intoxicated'.[6] Even for a family like the Boekü-Morgensterns, who would have been accustomed to such conduct from many of their soul-dead, disillusioned boarders, Mary Jane's 'indulgence in intoxicants' had started to make her 'an unwelcome friend'.[7] Eventually, either Kelly or her landlords decided it was time for her to leave. However, when she did go, it wasn't very far.

Next door to the former Red Lion was 1 Breezer's Hill, a boarding house that belonged to Mrs Rose Mary (or Mary Rose) McCarthy and her husband John. The McCarthys' establishment was almost identical to that of 79 Pennington Street in that they provided beds for women like Mary Jane and their guests.[8] They were also running an unlicensed public house on the premises, which not only sold alcohol unlawfully, but used prostitutes to inveigle 'sailors and other unwary persons into these places' where they were then robbed.[9] Whether or not Mary Jane was involved in these activities is unknown, but presumably the McCarthys were not as concerned about her angry drunken antics, so long as she was capable of paying her rent.

Whether Mary Jane was able to comfortably discharge her debts to landlords and landladies is questionable, particularly where the Boekü-Morgensterns were concerned. Mrs Felix recalled an incident that she claimed occurred shortly after Mary Jane arrived at 79 Pennington Street. Either because Mary Jane was in desperate need of funds, or because Mrs

Boekü had convinced her she had nothing to fear, the two women decided they would attempt to reclaim Kelly's missing trunk of expensive dresses from her former landlady in Knightsbridge. Although she was undoubtedly eager to have her possessions once again, Mary Jane could not have felt easy about returning to a part of London where she was known. In an attempt to reassure her boarder and perhaps to demonstrate to her former French madam that Mary Jane was now under the protection of the Morgensterns, Mrs Boekü travelled with her across town on this errand. It was likely to have been the first time since her return from Paris that Kelly had seen these familiar streets, and a sense of trepidation must have gnawed at her as she sat beside her East End procuress.

In the end, there is nothing to suggest that their mission was successful. If 'the French Lady' was as sharp as Mrs Boekü and other women in her position, it is probable that she had sold on Mary Jane's valuable belongings long before her former girl showed her face again in Knightsbridge. To worsen matters still, this venture into the west of London was perhaps as ill-judged as Mary Jane would have feared.

Apparently at some point after Mary Jane's visit to her former landlady, a man came to the Ratcliff Highway in search of her. According to Joseph Barnett to whom she told the story, a middle-aged man calling himself her father 'tried to find her'. He must have been fairly determined, asking after her in the various pubs and drinking establishments, and making enquiries among the young women who plied the streets. Eventually, she 'heard from her companions that he was looking for her'. Mary Jane knew that this man was trouble and went out of her way to hide from him.[10] Whatever his identity, he was almost certainly not Mary Jane Kelly's father. Mrs Felix insisted that Kelly had no contact with her family, 'who had discarded her', and Barnett too stated that 'she saw none of her relations'. At the inquest in 1888, Barnett claimed that Mary Jane did harbour fears for her safety, though she never articulated who or what may have caused this anxiety. Even if Kelly was concerned about being found, the more pressing worry about a killer on the loose in the autumn of that year invariably supplanted this.

If Mary Jane was beginning to weary of her existence on the Ratcliff Highway and her arguments with her landladies, then this alarming visit may have compelled her to begin considering her future. Then, at some time between late 1886 and early 1887, what must have seemed a solution to her problems appeared: someone fell in love with her.

Kelly – young, pretty and sexually alluring – would have had no shortage of admirers and, in spite of the area's constantly shifting population, a number of regular clients. One of them was a 27-year-old plasterer from nearby Bethnal Green called Joseph Fleming (or Flemming). As a labourer in the building trade, Fleming was not financially secure, and certainly far less comfortably off than any of the men whose hearts she might have captured in the West End. However, according to Mrs McCarthy, whose house she left to live with Fleming, he was smitten and 'would have married her'. Mary Jane appears to have reciprocated his feelings and confided her fondness for him to her female acquaintances.[11] For a handful of months at most, the couple inhabited what was probably no more than a single furnished room on Bethnal Green Road, or Old Bethnal Green Road, before the relationship fell apart.[12] The reason for this is unclear, though Mary Jane's friend, Julia Venturney, suggests that Fleming may have been violent towards Kelly and 'ill used' her.[13] The first Mrs McCarthy heard of Mary Jane's change in circumstances was when her former lodger appeared at her door at two o'clock in the morning, during the early part of 1887. She had come in search of a bed for herself and a male companion. The landlady seemed somewhat puzzled and asked 'if she was not still living with the man who took her from the neighbourhood'. Kelly replied that the relationship had ended and that she had returned to soliciting. Mary McCarthy said no more, but took 2 shillings off her for the convenience of a room.[14]

When Mary Jane parted with Joe Fleming she did not wish to remain in Bethnal Green, nor did she want to return to the Ratcliff Highway. Instead she moved somewhere entirely new, to Spitalfields. Here she is said to have taken residence at Cooley's lodging house on Thrawl Street and worked a patch around Aldgate. In his shamelessly romanticized memoirs of his tenure in the Metropolitan Police, Detective Chief Inspector Walter Dew claimed that he often caught sight of Mary Jane 'parading along Commercial Street, between Flower and Dean Street and Aldgate, or along Whitechapel Road'. He asserted that she was always 'fairly neatly dressed and invariably wearing a clean white apron, but no hat' as she promenaded down the road 'in the company of two or three of her kind'.[15] Dew's comments about her outward appearance and demeanour seem to be echoed by many who knew her. 'She was one of the smartest, nicest-looking women in the neighbourhood,' commented a missionary who was interviewed by the *Evening News*. She never failed to be 'neatly and decently dressed, and looked quite nice and respectable'. Her neighbours too were charmed by her humour and kindness, claiming she was 'a good, quiet, pleasant girl' and 'well liked'. According to several of them, Mary Jane enjoyed singing and telling stories, especially about her time in the West End, for which, by comparison to the rough, filthy surroundings in which she found herself, she must have longed. She 'made no secret' about her previous adventures, and regaled her companions with tales of how she drove about in carriages, and 'led a life . . . of a lady', and even boasted that she had been to Paris. This seemed to have captured the affection of many, as did her fantasies about Ireland, and 'returning to her people'. However, what these gentle portraits of Mary Jane serve to illustrate is that she had become adept at masking her feelings, an essential accomplishment for a so-called 'gay woman'. In a rare moment of openness, she spoke candidly to her neighbour, twenty-year-old Lizzie Albrook, who seemed enchanted by Kelly's worldliness. Mary Jane warned her off embarking upon a similar career before remarking that in truth 'she was heartily sick of the life she was leading'.[16]

Intriguingly, there is another description of Mary Jane Kelly, which is much at variance with the generous comments of everyone else. Tom Cullen, when researching his book on the murders in 1965, spoke with Dennis Barrett who had been a boy in 1888 and claims to have remembered Kelly. Barrett, who knew her as 'Black Mary', described her as 'a bit of a terror'. When it came to soliciting trade outside the Ten Bells pub, she was as fierce as a bulldog. 'Woe to any woman who tried to poach her territory . . . such a woman was likely to have her hair pulled out in fistfuls,' he remarked.[17] Of course, Barrett's boyhood identification of Mary Jane may be confused, but if this account is to be believed then it presents two very disparate sides to her character. Mary Jane may have been skilled at presenting a sweet facade, disguising an internal life of turmoil and distress.

A street-walking existence in the East End could not have afforded Mary Jane much solace. The brief period of settled domesticity that she experienced with Joseph Fleming, however imperfect, must have come as a relief from the unpredictability and ever-present danger of soliciting. Inevitably, it was not long after she and Fleming parted that she began to search for a similar, more stable arrangement. It soon presented itself as she touted for custom on Commercial Street around March 1887.

Joseph Barnett, the primary narrator of Mary Jane's history, shot into her life like a comet, or so it appears from his one-sided description of their meeting. It occurred on a Thursday night, near to Easter. Barnett was instantly taken with Kelly, whom he 'picked up with', and invited for a drink at a public house. He discreetly omits any mention of paying for sex with her, stating instead that he 'arranged to see her the next day'. Not forty-eight hours into the relationship and Barnett was a man in love. By Saturday he had proposed that they move in together, to which Mary Jane agreed. Barnett immediately went and secured them a room in nearby George Street. 'I lived with her from then, till . . . the other day,' he told the coroner eighteen months later.[18]

In November 1888, as he stood before a judgemental middle-class coroner's jury, Joseph Barnett did not leave the best impression of himself. Having been interviewed by the police for four hours, he was utterly terrified as he took the stand. His testimony was earnest but fraught, and he stammered and repeated his words. This was not the man whom Mary Jane Kelly knew, who was confident and determined when it came to acquiring what he desired.

The Barnett she had met that night on Commercial Street was a 29-year-old, blue-eyed, fair-haired Whitechapel man who had been born into an Irish family and who sported a fashionable moustache. Like many children of his class and era, Joseph had lost both of his parents by the age of thirteen and was raised by his older siblings. It was his brother who introduced him at Billingsgate Fish Market and assisted him in getting a job as a porter, a specialist trade that required a licence to transport goods to the vendors. Such a position was a coveted one and could earn a man a good living, if he was quick and strong. Joseph, who is described as being 5 feet 7 inches tall and of a medium build, certainly seemed physically equipped for the work. Notwithstanding this, the couple still struggled for money. Both of them enjoyed a good drink and this habit may have been the source of their problems. In the roughly eighteen months they were together Barnett and Kelly moved addresses four times. They left their shabby room on George Street for another one on Little Paternoster Row, from which they were evicted for drunkenness and failing to pay their rent.[19] From here they took up residence on Brick Lane, before moving again to a single room in Miller's Court around March 1888.

In the earlier part of the century, Miller's Court had been two adjoining gardens belonging to 26 and 27 Dorset Street. This space had later been developed and turned into a set of cramped workers' cottages in which thirty people lived, sharing three public toilets at one end of the courtyard. As the downstairs back parlour of number 26 faced onto a rather disagreeable view of a squalid yard, it was partitioned off from the rest of the house and rented out as 13 Miller's Court. For the cost of 4s. 6d. a week, Mary Jane and Joe Barnett made this 10-by-12-foot space at the end of a dark alley their home. It was no better or worse than any of the other wretched hovels to be found along Dorset Street and contained only the sparsest of furnishings: a bed, a table, a disused washstand, a chair, and a cupboard. Someone at some stage had attempted to brighten the grimy, bare surroundings by tacking a print entitled *The Fisherman's Widow* to a wall.

Unfortunately, like everything contiguous to it, little could be done to lift the gloom of Miller's Court and the misery of those who inhabited it. Its owner, a slumlord known as John McCarthy (no relation to the McCarthys of Breezer's Hill), described as 'a bully' and one who swindled 'poor people out of small sums', appeared to favour compromised, lone women as his tenants.[20] Elizabeth Prater, who lived upstairs from number 13, had been deserted by her husband. Julia Venturney at number 1 was a widow in her late forties, working as a char-woman, while Mary Ann Cox, who called herself a 'widow and an unfortunate' resided at number 5. Although Mary Jane claimed that Barnett promised he would never 'let her go on the streets' while she lived under his care, Kelly apparently took on the rental of number 13 in her own name.[21] McCarthy must have known that women, especially those who were known prostitutes, would always be able to make good on outstanding sums. The true test of this arrived during the late summer, when Joseph lost his job at Billingsgate. The reasons for this are unknown, but if the couple drank heavily enough to warrant eviction from their previous home, alcohol may have played a role. With Barnett out of work, the debts to McCarthy, who also ran the adjoining chandler's shop where tenants bought groceries, candles and necessities on credit, soon began to mount. By the beginning of November 1888 the couple had fallen six weeks behind in their rent and owed 29 shillings to their landlord.

It may have been McCarthy who had a word with Mary Jane about a return to soliciting. She would hardly have embraced this prospect willingly after more than a year of sharing a bed with only one, familiar partner. For nearly eighteen months she had not needed to inspect a strange man for signs of syphilis. She had not wondered how she would manage if she found herself pregnant. She had not stood hungry on a corner in the rain without a hat or shawl, smiling. She did not have to consider what she might do if the unwashed man she had just pleasured refused to pay her. It was Barnett who had insisted that she need not solicit while they lived together, that he would provide for them, and the anger and resentment she must have felt for him at having failed her would have been palpable. Unfortunately, however Joseph tried, he was unable to find any work beyond odd labouring jobs which did not cover the cost of the rent. The couple began to argue frequently and furiously. On one occasion, while drunk, Mary Jane broke a pane of glass in the window beside their door. She stuffed it full of rags to stop the draught, but, now damaged, it was not to be repaired.

While Mary Jane lived at Miller's Court, she was said to have received letters from Ireland, which she claimed were from her mother, or possibly her 'brother'. Interestingly, from August 1888 the 2nd Battalion of the Scots Guards were based in Dublin, and it is equally probable that she was receiving correspondence and possibly small sums from a former paramour in the regiment.[22] She also remained in contact with Joseph Fleming, who, according to Julia Venturney, visited her on occasion and 'used to give her money'.[23] Joe Barnett was not aware of this and might not have taken kindly to their continued meetings. Apparently, Mary Jane was known to taunt him with mentions of his predecessor, of whom she stated 'she was very fond'. However, what Barnett claimed angered him the most was Kelly's frequent associations with prostitutes, whom she brought into their home. Although he had met

Mary Jane in the course of practising her trade, after he had settled down with her it appears Barnett did not wish to be reminded of her past. His resentment was probably a proxy for his frustration at Mary Jane's proposal that she return to street walking, rather than an annoyance at having his space invaded by women he claimed to dislike. As their disagreements continued to rage, Mary Jane eventually sent Joseph a very clear message that she valued her friendship with 'gay women' more than she did her relationship with him.

By October, Jack the Ripper's killing spree was the talk and terror of everyone in Whitechapel. The residents of Dorset Street and Miller's Court, home to so many vulnerable women, were especially anxious. Barnett claims that during those tense months he and Mary Jane read the newspapers daily, hoping to learn that the murderer had been caught. However, while he remained at large, Kelly decided to offer sanctuary to acquaintances who might otherwise have had to solicit or sleep rough. The first of these women was a prostitute known only as 'Julia'.[24] Shortly after this, she took in Maria Harvey, an unmarried laundress who hadn't enough money for a bed and who left behind a pile of clothing in the room. These nocturnal guests were the final straw for Joe Barnett. Although he recognized that Mary Jane had been moved by compassion, her actions were also obviously designed to push him out. He left her on 30 October, though not without a great deal of remorse.

In spite of their difficulties, Barnett obviously cared for Kelly and hoped that they could be reconciled. He took a bed at Buller's Boarding House on the corner of Bishopsgate Street but made certain to look in on her as he continued to search for work. During the early evening of Thursday 8 November, he rapped on her door. The window that had been shattered was still plugged with rags, and a coat that Maria Harvey had left in the room was hung across it as a makeshift curtain. On that night, Barnett might have pulled out the ragged stopper and unlatched the door from within, as he and Mary Jane had done after losing the key, but perhaps this seemed too forward. A candle was burning inside and he noted that Kelly was not alone. She had been chatting with Lizzie Albrook and when Joe arrived Mary Jane's neighbour excused herself. Kelly had only recently returned from drinking in the Ten Bells with a friend, Elizabeth Foster, but Barnett claimed that she was perfectly sober at the time he came to see her.

The couple were together for about an hour. They may have conversed softly, or quarrelled, or given in to their desires, but whatever occurred failed to shift their impasse. In the end, Barnett rose to leave and apologized to Mary Jane. 'I told her that I had no work, and that I had nothing to give her,' he repeated sadly at the coroner's inquest, 'for which I was very sorry'.[25] Mary Jane, in a worn black velvet bodice and skirt that had once been made of a fine material, watched him go. What she felt about the loss of her relationship with him will never be known.

No one is absolutely certain where Mary Jane went after she bid farewell to Joseph Barnett. Mary Ann Cox, her neighbour at number 5, believed she saw Kelly turn from Dorset Street into Miller's Court with a man at around 11.45 p.m. She thought Mary Jane was very drunk, but none of the area's publicans claimed to have seen or served her that night. According to Cox, Mary Jane and her male guest then disappeared into her room, but before they did, Kelly warned Mary Ann that she was 'going to have song'. The door then banged shut and a glimmer of light began to shine from behind her crudely curtained window. After a moment or so of silence Cox heard

Mary Jane's voice rise into the first verse of 'A Violet Plucked From My Mother's Grave When A Boy':

Scenes of my childhood arise before my gaze,
Bringing recollections of bygone happy days
When down in the meadow in childhood I would roam.
No one's left to cheer me now within that good old home,
Father and Mother, they have pass'd away;
Sister and brother, now lay beneath the clay,
But while life does remain to cheer me, I'll retain,
This small violet I pluck'd from Mother's grave.

Only a violet I pluck'd when but a boy,
And oft'times when I'm sad at heart this flow'r has giv'n me joy;
So while life does remain in memoriam I'll retain,
This small violet I pluck'd from Mother's grave.

Well I remember my dear old Mother's smile,
As she used to greet me when I returned from toil,
Always knitting in the old arm chair.
Father used to sit and read for all us children there,
But now all is silent around the good old home;
They all have left me in sorrow here to roam,
But while life does remain in memoriam I'll retain,
This small violet I pluck'd from Mother's grave.

Cox seemed fairly certain that she heard Kelly singing until at least around 1 a.m., but as with so many of the witness testimonies in all five of the cases, there are omissions, questions and inconsistencies.[26] What precisely had happened to Mary Jane's male customer in the course of this hour-and-fifteen-minute concert is anyone's guess.

Elizabeth Prater, who lived upstairs from Mary Jane, claimed she could hear most sounds clearly through the thin partition wall and floor. At 1.30 a.m. nothing stirred in Kelly's room.

At some point in the very early hours of 9 November, Mary Jane decided to bring an end to the day and retire to sleep. She removed her clothes piece by piece, a few shabby items of a once resplendent wardrobe diminished by wear – the hems had been dragged along the uneven pavements of Dorset Street, and the fabric splashed with beer and gin. In spite of their faded state, she folded each article neatly and placed them on her chair. The flame of her only candle, which she had balanced on a broken wine glass, guttered and bobbed until snuffed. Enveloped in darkness, she slid under her bed sheet and pulled it snugly around her, protecting herself from the night.

Joseph Barnett was the nearest thing Mary Jane Kelly had to a family member, and even he never knew the true identity of the woman who was placed into the casket. Because she called herself Kelly and claimed she had been born in Ireland, she was interred at a Catholic cemetery – St Patrick's in Leytonstone – but if she was as Welsh as everyone else attested, Mary Jane might well have been buried by Methodists.

Mary Jane had been whatever she wished to be, and in the wake of her death, she became whatever Joseph Barnett wished to commemorate. It was he who insisted that the name on her brass coffin plate read 'Marie Jeanette Kelly', a moniker brimming with all the flounce and flamboyance of a Saturday night in the West End.

Following her death, Mary Jane, an otherwise anonymous resident of Spitalfields, also became what Whitechapel imagined her to be: a local heroine who had suffered at the hands of a monster still on the loose. Her open hearse, two mourning carriages and polished oak and elm coffin, decorated with two floral wreaths and a cross of heart-seed, became a show of defiance. It also became an excuse to gawk and drink and exclaim at the carnival of mourning as it passed through the streets, trailed by publicans and their best customers, as well as the sort of females newspapers called 'unfortunates'. Women with infants on their hips watched from the doorsteps; men removed their hats as she passed.

'God forgive her!' they were said to have cried out through their sobs. 'We will not forget her!'

Conclusion

'Just Prostitutes'

'The loss of these five . . . lives is clearly a tragedy . . . You may view
with some distaste the lifestyles of those involved : . . whatever
drugs they took, whatever the work they did, no-one is entitled
to do these women any harm, let alone kill them.'

Mr Justice Gross, *R v. Steven Gerald James Wright*
(the 'Suffolk Strangler'), 2008

SHORTLY AFTER THE DEATH of Annie Chapman, Mr Edward
Fairfield, a senior civil servant at the Colonial Office and a
resident of the upmarket South Eaton Place in London's Belgravia, was moved to pick up his pen and write a letter to *The
Times*. He was particularly concerned about the series of
Whitechapel murders. The actual deaths of 'the vicious inhabitants of Dorset Street and Flower and Dean Street' were not
what was bothering him. Edward Fairfield was far more anxious that in the wake of this disturbance women like Annie
Chapman would be displaced from their hellish hovels in Spitalfields and make their way into his neighbourhood, carrying
their 'taint to the streets hitherto untainted'. 'The horror and
excitement caused by the murder of the four Whitechapel

outcasts imply a universal belief that they had a right to life . . .' continued this representative of the government.

> If they had, then they had the further right to hire shelter from the bitterness of the English night. If they had no such right, then it was, on the whole, a good thing that they fell in with this unknown surgical genius. He, at all events, has made his contribution towards solving 'the problem of clearing the East-end of its vicious inhabitants'.[1]

While today we are likely to shiver at such a comment, Edward Fairfield was simply expressing what would have been if not a widely held sentiment, then one that he did not feel was inappropriate to discuss openly in 1888. Fairfield was a bachelor, a man who spent a good deal of time at his club, where he was noted for his 'slightly flippant, slightly dissipated personality'.[2] When he was not there, he was cared for by a cook and a parlour maid and regularly hosted intimate dinners for his male friends. Fairfield, like most of the literate public, had learned all he needed to know about the 'vicious inhabitants' of the East End from the newspapers. He had been educated about their disgusting, impoverished, drunken lives from the snippets of information he had read. Whatever gaps remained in his understanding of slum-dwelling women would have been filled in by 'common knowledge': they were all desperate, filthy, foul-mouthed prostitutes. Sadly, however, what he and the rest of the readership of *The Times* failed to realize was that there was much more to the story of 'the typical Annie Chapman', as he called women of her ilk, than what appeared in the press. Little did Edward Fairfield know that Annie Chapman had already 'carried her taint' into his part of town, because Annie Chapman had spent a good part of her life there. Annie Chapman's family lived a fifteen-minute walk from Fairfield's front door, and in her final years, ragged, sick, dejected, 'vicious' Annie came to visit her sisters. Edward Fairfield may have even passed her on the Brompton Road, on his way to Harrods.

The truth of these women's lives was not simple and the sensationalist nineteenth-century press was certainly not in the business of telling the whole story to readers like Edward Fairfield. Nor did any of the editors or the journalists covering this story deem it necessary or worthy of interest to delve with any depth into the victims' biographies. Ultimately, no one really cared about who they were or how they ended up in Whitechapel.

The cards were stacked against Polly, Annie, Elizabeth, Kate and Mary Jane from the day of their births. They began their lives in deficit. Not only were most of them born into working-class families, but they were born female. Before they had even spoken their first words they were regarded as less important than their brothers and more of a burden on the world than their wealthier female counterparts. Their worth was compromised before they had even attempted to prove it. They would never earn the income of a man; therefore their education was less important. What work they could secure was designed to help support their families; it was not intended to bring fulfilment or to engender a sense of purpose or personal contentment. The golden ticket for working-class girls was a life in domestic service, where it was possible after a number of years of back-breaking work to rise in station and esteem to become a cook, a housekeeper or a lady's maid. There were no desk jobs for poor girls like Kate Eddowes or Polly Nichols, both of whom were literate, but many which involved twelve-hour days stitching trousers in a sweat shop or glueing together matchboxes for a wage that would barely pay for a bed and sustenance. Poor women's labour was cheap because poor women were expendable and because society did not designate them as a family's breadwinner. Unfortunately, many of them had to be. If a husband, father or partner left or died, a working-class woman with dependants found it almost impossible to survive. Society was designed to ensure that a woman without a man was superfluous.

A woman's entire function was to support men, and if the roles of their male family members were to support the roles and needs of men wealthier than them, then the women at the bottom were driven like piles deeper and harder into the ground in order to bear the weight of everyone else's demands. A woman's role was to produce children and to raise them, but because rudimentary contraception and published information about birth control was made virtually unavailable to the poor, they – like the women of the Eddowes family, like Annie Chapman's mother, and like Polly Nichols – had no real means of managing the size of their families or preventing an inevitable backslide into financial hardship.

Atop this heap of burdens placed on a woman's shoulders was balanced the most cumbersome weight of all: moral and sexual immaculacy. As a woman was the keystone at the centre of family life, her character must be unimpeachable; if it were not, it was she who was responsible for the ruin of others. Her circumspection and self-sacrifice calibrated her children's moral compasses; her dedication to her husband's needs kept him from sin – away from the public houses and other women. The double standard ensured that while it might not be entirely acceptable for a man to seek sexual relations with a number of women, it was completely understandable and normal. A woman, on the other hand, could only have sex with a man if she was legally married to him. The all-pervasiveness of these ideals meant that even in more permissive working-class communities – where couples frequently had sex outside of wedlock, didn't marry, split and recoupled at regular intervals – women still bore the brunt of moral judgement, especially when it came from mainstream, middle-class Victorian society. In the narrow-eyed censorious gaze of this world, Polly and Annie were fallen women the moment they parted with their husbands and threw in their lots with other men. Kate was deemed as much a dissolute woman as Mary Jane for living out of wedlock with two partners, and Elizabeth was ruined twice: once in Gothenburg, when her name went on the register of public women, and a second time after her marriage failed, when she supported herself through soliciting. The double standard rendered life in black and white. If missionaries offered pity and promises of redemption for those who had taken the wrong path, this balm was applied only after years of shame and condemnation. Is it any wonder that Polly fled the comforts of the Cowdrys' home, that Annie could not bear to tell her sisters where she lived, that Elizabeth never let anyone truly know her, that Kate fell out with her children, and that by twenty-five Mary Jane had become an angry drunk?

At the time of the murders, the belief that 'Jack the Ripper was a killer of prostitutes' helped to reinforce these moral codes of right and wrong. However, while it served an agenda in 1888, this often repeated line fails to serve any immediately obvious purpose today. Nevertheless, it is still the one 'fact' about the murders upon which everyone can agree, and yet it does not bear scrutiny.

From the introduction of the Contagious Diseases Acts in the 1860s through the period of the Whitechapel murders, very few authorities, including the Metropolitan Police, could agree as to what exactly constituted a 'prostitute' and how she might be identified.[3] Was a prostitute simply a woman like Mary Jane Kelly who earned her income solely through the sex trade and who self-identified as part of this profession, or could 'a prostitute' be more broadly defined? Was a prostitute a woman who accepted a drink from a man who then accompanied her to a lodging house, paid for a bed, had sex with her and stayed the night? A woman who occasionally masturbated men behind the pub for money but didn't have intercourse with them? A woman who let a man put his hand up her skirt for threepence? A woman who had sex for money twice over the course of a week, before finding work in a laundry and meeting a man whom she decided to live with out of wedlock? A woman who used to work in a brothel but then left to become the kept mistress of one of her clients? A woman who tramped and agreed to have sex with a man because otherwise she felt threatened and alone? A young factory worker who had sex with the boys who courted her and bought her gifts? A woman with a 'free and easy' reputation who stayed out late at night carousing in pubs? A woman with three children by three different fathers who lived with a man simply because he kept a roof over their heads?

Some of these women might be classed as professional or 'common prostitutes', while others might be called 'casual prostitutes' or just women who, in accordance with the social norms of their community, had sex outside of wedlock. But as the Metropolitan Police came to recognize, the lines separating these groups were often so blurred that it was impossible to distinguish between them.

The question of who could or couldn't legitimately be called a prostitute came to a head in July 1887, after Elizabeth Cass, a dressmaker who had gone out on her own one evening to buy a pair of gloves and view the Golden Jubilee illuminations on Regent Street, was erroneously arrested as a street walker. The resulting trial and acquittal of Cass forced the police to re-examine their assumptions about the morals of lone women and to think twice before slapping the label of 'prostitute' onto all of them. Sir Charles Warren's order of 19 July 1887 was issued in an attempt to make an official clarification of how the police were to formally define a prostitute. It was stated that 'a Police Constable should not assume that any particular woman is a common prostitute' and that the police were not 'justified in calling any woman a common prostitute unless she so describes herself, or has been convicted as such . . .' Furthermore, in order to charge a woman with being a prostitute, proof was required in the form of a formal statement by a person who had been 'annoyed or solicited'.[4] A year later, Warren was equally cautious about identifying 'prostitutes' among the Whitechapel lodging-house population and acknowledged that there were 'no means of ascertaining what women are prostitutes and who are not'.[5] After having their fingers burned in 1887, police officials were forced to recognize that the inter-section between working-class women who were not part of the sex trade and those who were was so seamless as to make them impossible to isolate into distinct groups. However, this did not always prevent police constables from ignoring these orders and doing whatever their prejudices dictated.

In the absence of any evidence that Polly, Annie and Kate ever engaged in common prostitution, many have taken to claiming that these women participated in 'casual prostitution': a blanket term cast over the ambiguities of the women's lives that is steeped in moral judgement. It ascribes guilt by associ-ation because a woman was poor and an alcoholic, because she left her children, because she became an adulteress, because she had children out of wedlock, because she lived in a lodging house, because she was out late at night, because she was no longer attractive, because she didn't have a settled home, because she begged, because she slept rough, because she broke all the rules of what it meant to be feminine. This line of reasoning also explains why Polly, Annie and Kate's homelessness was entirely overlooked as a unifying factor in their murders; a 'houseless creature' and a 'prostitute' by their moral failings were one and the same. There were many reasons why an impoverished working-class woman may have been outdoors during the hours of darkness, and not all of them were as obvious as street soliciting. Those without homes or families, those who drank heavily and those who were dispossessed did not lead lives that adhered to conventional rules. No one knew or cared what they did or where they went, and for this reason, rather than for a sexual motive, they would have appealed to a killer.

If the official criteria established by the Commissioner of the Metropolitan Police for defining the term 'prostitute' is applied to Polly, Annie and Kate, it immediately becomes obvious that they cannot be identified as such. Even when relying on inquest testimony, there exists no proof to support these assertions. Similarly, there is no absolute confirmation that Elizabeth Stride had returned to prostitution in the period prior to her murder. Quite simply, there is no evidence that any of these four women self-identified as prostitutes or that anyone among their community regarded them as part of the sex trade. Furthermore, on the nights they were killed, no one came forward to state that they had been solicited by Polly, Annie, Kate or Elizabeth. After the coroners had heard the evidence provided by all of the witnesses they made their absolute conclusions as to the victims' identities. These were recorded as 'occupation or profession' on the women's death certificates. Mary Ann Nichols was described as the 'Wife of William Nichols, Printing Machinist'. Annie Chapman was identified as the 'Widow of John Chapman, a coachman'. Elizabeth Stride was recorded as the 'Widow of John Thomas Stride, carpenter', and Catherine Eddowes, as a 'Supposed single woman'. Only Mary Jane Kelly, who admitted openly to working in the sex trade, was described as a 'Prostitute'.[6] These official pronouncements must be taken as the final word on whether or not we are justified in claiming that 'Jack the Ripper was a killer of prostitutes'. To insist otherwise is to fall back on arbitrary supposition informed by Victorian prejudice.

Today, there is only one reason why we would continue to embrace the belief that Jack the Ripper was a killer of prostitutes: because it supports an industry that has grown in part out of this mythology. There's no doubt that the story of Jack the Ripper is a good yarn. It's a Gothic tale of a monster on the loose, stalking the dark streets of fog-clouded London. It contains suspense and horror, and an element of sexual titillation. Unfortunately, this is also a one-sided story, and the hunt for the killer has taken centre stage. Over the centuries, the villain has metamorphosed into the protagonist: an evil, psychotic, mysterious player who is so clever that he has managed to evade detection even today. In order to gawp at and examine this miracle of malevolence we have figuratively stepped over the bodies of those he murdered, and in some cases, stopped to kick them as we walked past. The larger his profile grows, the more those of his victims seems to fade. With the advance of time, both the murderer and those he murdered have become detached from reality; their experiences and names have become entwined with folklore and conspiracy theories. To some merchandisers, they are no longer human beings, but cartoon figures whose bloody images can be printed onto T-shirts, whose deaths can be laughed about on postcards and whose entrails decorate stickers. Is it any wonder that there has been no public appetite to examine the lives of the canonical five, when they have never seemed real or of any consequence to us before?

Insisting that Jack the Ripper killed prostitutes also makes the story of a vicious series of murders slightly more palatable. Just as it did in the nineteenth century, the notion that the victims were 'only prostitutes' seeks to perpetuate the belief that there are good women and bad women; madonnas and whores. It suggests that there is an acceptable standard of female behaviour and those who deviate from it are fit to be punished. Equally, it assists in reasserting the double standard, exonerating men from wrongs committed against such women. These attitudes may not feel as prevalent as they were in 1888, but they persist – not proffered in general conversation as they would have been in Edward Fairfield's day but, rather, integrated subtly into the fabric of our cultural norms. The threads become apparent in court cases and in politics; they are found interwoven in the statements of the powerful. They can be spotted in instances like *People v. Turner* (2015), which saw Brock Turner, a Stanford University student charged with the rape and sexual assault of a heavily intoxicated woman, receive a reduced prison sentence of six months, which his father complained 'was a steep price to pay for 20 minutes of action'.[7] They are manifest when it becomes necessary for the judge in the trial of the Suffolk serial killer, Steve Wright, to instruct the jury to lay aside their prejudices against the five victims, four of whom were sex workers, before making their decision about the guilt of the defendant. In a statement that is chillingly resonant with echoes of 1888, he reminds the jurors: '. . . You may view with some distaste the lifestyles of those involved . . . whatever drugs they took, whatever the work they did, no-one is entitled to do these women any harm, let alone kill them.'

When a woman steps out of line and contravenes the feminine norm, whether on social media or on the Victorian street, there is a tacit understanding that someone must put her back in her place. Labelling the victims as 'just prostitutes' permits those writing about Polly, Annie, Elizabeth, Kate and Mary Jane even today to continue to disparage, sexualize and dehumanize them; to continue to reinforce the values of madonna/whore. It allows authors to rank the women's level of attractiveness based on images of their murdered bodies and to declare 'pulchritude was, it appears, of no interest to the Whitechapel Murderer', before concluding, 'Mary Jane Kelly was pretty, Stride, lively and . . . at least attractive . . . Otherwise, his victims were gin-soaked drabs.'[8] This attitude gives such authors free rein to speculate pruriently on how frequently these women had sex before they were murdered. It makes it acceptable to dismiss these daughters, wives and mothers as 'a few moribund, drunken trug-moldies', which 'all [Jack] did was execute, [and] then gralloch'.[9] It elevates the status of the murderer to that of celebrity and confers favour on his victims because they 'got intimate with one of the most famous men on earth'.[10] At its very core, the story of Jack the Ripper is a narrative of a killer's deep, abiding hatred of women, and our cultural obsession with the mythology only serves to normalize its particular brand of misogyny.

We have grown so comfortable with the notion of 'Jack the Ripper', the unfathomable, invincible male killer, that we have failed to recognize that he continues to walk among us. In his top hat and cape, wielding his blood-drenched knife, he can be spotted regularly in London on posters, in ads, on the sides of buses. Bartenders have named drinks after him, shops use his moniker on their signs, tourists from around the world make pilgrimages to Whitechapel to walk in his footsteps and to visit a museum dedicated to his violence. The world has learned to dress up in his costume at Halloween, to imagine being him, to honour his genius, to laugh at a murderer of women. By embracing him, we embrace the set of values that surrounded him in 1888 which teaches women that they are of a lesser value and can expect to be dishonoured and abused. We enforce the notion that 'bad women' deserve punishment and that 'prostitutes' are a sub-species of female.

In order to keep him alive, we have had to forget his victims. We have become complicit in their diminishment. When we repeat the accepted Ripper legend in newspapers, in television documentaries and on the internet, when we teach it to school children without questioning the origins of the story and its sources, without considering the reliability of the evidence or the assumptions that contributed to forming it, we not only assist in perpetuating the injustices committed against Polly, Annie, Elizabeth, Kate and Mary Jane but we also condone the basest forms of violence.

It is only by bringing these women back to life that we can silence the Ripper and what he represents. By permitting them to speak, by attempting to understand their experiences and see their humanity, we can restore to them the respect and compassion to which they are entitled. The victims of Jack the Ripper were never 'just prostitutes'; they were daughters, wives, mothers, sisters and lovers. They were women. They were human beings, and surely that, in itself, is enough.

A Life in Objects

FOLLOWING THEIR DISCOVERY, POLLY, Annie, Elizabeth, Kate and Mary Jane's bodies were removed by the police from the scenes of the crime. Their bodies were then stripped of their clothing and whatever small artefacts they had stowed on themselves for safe-keeping. As the first four victims had been found outdoors, inventories were made of their possessions. A similar list of personal effects was not made for Mary Jane Kelly, who had been killed in her bed, wearing only a chemise.

These objects offer a final imprint of a life, a humble snapshot of what each woman valued and what they felt they could use to assist them through their uncertain days.

POLLY

Black straw bonnet trimmed with black velvet
Brown ulster with seven large buttons bearing the pattern of
    a man standing beside a horse
Linsey frock
White flannel chest cloth
Blue ribbed wool stockings
Two petticoats, one grey wool, one flannel. Both stencilled
    on bands 'Lambeth Workhouse'
Brown stays (short)
Flannel drawers

Men's elastic- (spring-) sided boots with the uppers cut and
    steel tips on the heels
A comb
A white pocket handkerchief
A piece of a looking glass

ANNIE

Long black figured coat that came down to her knees
Black skirt
Brown bodice
Another bodice
2 petticoats
A large pocket worn under the skirt and tied about the waist
    with strings (empty when found)
Lace-up boots
Red and white striped woollen stockings
Neckerchief, white with a wide red border
A scrap of muslin
A small-toothed comb
A comb in a paper case
Scrap of envelope containing two pills, bearing the seal of the
    Sussex Regiment, postal stamped 'London, 28 Aug. 1888'

ELIZABETH

Long black cloth jacket, fur-trimmed around the bottom,
    with a red rose and white maidenhair fern pinned to it
Black skirt
Black crepe bonnet (the back stuffed with newspaper)
Checked neck scarf knotted on left side
Dark brown velveteen bodice
2 light serge petticoats
1 white chemise

White stockings
Spring-sided boots
2 handkerchiefs
A thimble
A piece of wool wound around a card
A key to a padlock
A small piece of lead pencil
1 small and 6 large buttons
A comb
A broken piece of comb
A metal spoon
A hook (as from a dress)
A piece of muslin
1 or 2 small pieces of paper

KATE

Black straw bonnet trimmed in green and black velvet with
   black beads. Black strings, worn tied to the head
Black cloth jacket trimmed around the collar and cuffs with
   imitation fur and around the pockets in black silk braid
   and fur. Large metal buttons
Dark green chintz skirt, 3 flounces, brown button on
   waistband. The skirt is patterned with Michaelmas daisies
   and golden lilies
Man's white vest, matching buttons down front
Brown linsey bodice, black velvet collar with brown buttons
   down front
Grey stuff petticoat with white waistband
Very old green alpaca skirt (worn as undergarment)
Very old ragged blue skirt with red flounces, light twill lining
   (worn as undergarment)
White calico chemise

No drawers or stays

Pair of men's lace-up boots, mohair laces. Right boot repaired with red thread

A piece of red gauze silk worn as a neckerchief

1 large white pocket handkerchief

1 large white cotton handkerchief with red and white bird's-eye border

2 unbleached calico pockets, tape strings

1 blue striped bed-ticking pocket

Brown ribbed knee stockings, darned at the feet with white cotton

2 small blue bags made of bed ticking

2 short black clay pipes

1 tin box containing tea

1 tin box containing sugar

1 tin matchbox, empty

12 pieces of white rag, some slightly bloodstained (menstrual rags)

1 piece of white coarse linen

1 piece of blue and white shirting, 3-cornered

1 piece of red flannel with pins and needles

6 pieces of soap

1 small-toothed comb

1 white-handled table knife

1 metal teaspoon

1 red leather cigarette case with white metal fittings

1 ball of hemp

1 piece of old white apron with repair

Several buttons and a thimble

A mustard tin containing 2 pawn tickets

Portion of a pair of spectacles

1 red mitten

Notes

Introduction: *A Tale of Two Cities*

1 Howard Goldsmid, *A Midnight Prowl Through Victorian London* (London, 1887).
2 *Sheffield Daily Telegraph*, 20 July 1887.
3 PRO: Metropolitan Police Files: file 3/141, ff. 158–9.
4 Ibid.
5 Joseph O'Neill, *The Secret World of the Victorian Lodging House* (Barnsley, 2014), p. 117. Women were believed to make up under half of the total lodging-house population in London.

1. *The Blacksmith's Daughter*

1 Max Schlesinger, *Saunterings In and About London* (London, 1853), p. 89.
2 The printing trade relied heavily on the skills of blacksmiths for its machinery and typeface, and it is likely that Walker moved the family to the area for this reason.
3 By 1861, Walker was describing himself as a blacksmith and engineer – one involved in the creation of much larger machinery. Possibly, given the family's location, equipment used in printing.
4 John Hollingshead, *Ragged London* (London, 1861), p. 39, p. 282.

5 *First Report of the Commissioners for Inquiring into the State of Large Towns and Populous Districts*, vol. 1 (London, 1844), pp. 111–13.

6 George R. Sims, *How the Poor Live* (London, 1883), p. 12.

7 *First Report*, vol. 1, pp. 111–13.

8 Following Caroline's death, a Mary, along with Edward, is cited in Frederick's baptismal record as being his 'parent'. It is also possible that Edward, as a widower, may have formed a temporary relationship with another woman of this name, though he was not known to have any further children, nor is there any record to indicate that he lived with another woman.

9 *Coventry Standard*, 27 June 1845.

10 LMA: London Parish Register: P69/BRI/A/01/MS6541/5. I am indebted to Neal and Jenni Shelden for this discovery.

2. *The Peabody Worthies*

1 Franklin Parker, *George Peabody: A Biography* (Nashville, 1995), p. 126.

2 *Daily News*, 29 January 1876.

3 'New Peabody Buildings in Lambeth', *The Circle*, 11 April 1874.

4 Ibid.

5 Phebe Ann Hanaford, *The Life of George Peabody* (Boston, 1870), p. 133.

6 *London Daily News*, 29 January 1876.

7 Hanaford, *Life*, p. 137.

8 *Daily Telegraph*, 24 December 1878.

9 LMA: Stamford Street Registers Acc/3445/PT/07/066.

10 Ibid.

11 Ancestry.com: *Glasgow, Scotland, Crew Lists, 1863–1901*.

12 Henry Alfred would be her fifth child to survive.

13 It has been suggested that Eliza Sarah was born in 3 J block, but this is a misreading of the faded handwritten script on her birth certificate which reads 3 D block.

3. An Irregular Life

1   LMA: Board of Guardian Records, 1834–1906; Church of England Parish Registers, 1754–1906, P 73/MRK2/001.
2   Polly's statement is part of a settlement examination: LMA: Holborn Union Workhouse records: HOBG 510/18 (Examinations). NB: Records for Renfrew Road for the period in which Polly claims to have entered the workhouse in Lambeth are missing; however, her name does not appear in the 1880 records of the Union's other workhouse on Princes Road.
3   G. Haw, *From Workhouse to Westminster: The Life Story of Will Crooks M.P.* (London, 1907), p. 109.
4   Report HMSO *Royal Commission on Divorce and Matrimonial Causes*, 1912 (b and c), p. 291 and p. 318.
5   John Ruskin, 'Of Queens' Gardens', *Sesame and Lilies* (London, 1865).
6   George C. T. Bartley, *A Handy Book for Guardians of the Poor* (London, 1876), pp. 152–3.
7   Ibid., p. 59.
8   LMA: Holborn Union Workhouse records: HOBG 510/18 (Examinations).
9   Charles Booth, *Life and Labour of the People in London: The Trades of East London* (London, 1893), p. 295.
10 C. Black, *Married Women's Work* (London, 1983), p. 35.
11 Ancestry.com: New South Wales, Australia, Unassisted Immigrant Passenger Lists, 1826–1922. Woolls emigrated to Australia on board the P&O steamer *Barrabool*.

12 Although she is cited as being four years older than her actual age (such age discrepancies are common on census returns), her place of birth in the Finsbury Ward of London would accord with someone who had claimed they were born near to Shoe Lane.

13 *East London Observer*, 8 September 1888.

14 It is possible this strike-through was made after Nichols's private affairs were made public during the course of the inquest into his wife's death.

15 *Daily Telegraph*, 3 September 1888.

16 Ibid.

17 Charles Booth, *Life and Labour of the People in London: Religious Influences*, series 3, vol. 1 (London, 1902), pp. 55–6.

4. 'Houseless Creature'

1 *Pall Mall Gazette*, 5 August 1887.

2 *Evening Standard*, 26 October 1887.

3 Ibid.

4 *Daily News*, 26 October 1887.

5 Ibid.

6 *Evening Standard*, 26 October 1887.

7 LMA: Lambeth Board of Guardians Creed Registers, X113/011.

8 The etymology of the word 'spike' in reference to the casual ward is debatable. Peter Higginbotham offers a number of possibilities, including a reference to the spiked implement that was used for oakum picking, the spike on which one's admission ticket to the workhouse was placed upon entry, or as a derivation of the word 'spiniken', another tramp's name for the workhouse. See Peter Higginbotham, *The Workhouse Encyclopedia* (London, 2012), p. 254.

9 Peter Higginbotham, http://www.workhouses.org.uk/Stallard (retrieved 16 January 2018).

10 George Augustus Sala, *Gaslight and Daylight* (London, 1859), p. 2.

11 William Booth, *In Darkest England and the Way Out* (London, 1890), p. 30.

12 Numbers are all taken from Margaret Harkness, *Out of Work* (London, 1888), p. 171; Rodney Mace, *Trafalgar Square: Emblem of Empire* (London, 2005), p. 171; Booth, *Darkest England*, p. 30.

13 Booth, *Darkest England*, pp. 26–7.

14 Peter Higginbotham, http://www.workhouses.org.uk/Higgs/ TrampAmongTramps.shtml, from Mary Higgs, *Five Days and Nights as a Tramp* (London, 1904).

15 Higginbotham, http://www.workhouses.org.uk/Stallard from J. H. Stallard, *The Female Casual and Her Lodging* (London, 1866).

16 J. Thomson and Adolphe Smith, 'The Crawlers', *Street Life in London* (London, 1877), pp. 116–8.

17 George R. Sims, *Horrible London* (London, 1889), pp. 145–8.

18 *Evening Standard*, 26 October 1887.

19 Archway Infirmary is now London's Whittington Hospital.

20 LMA: Holborn Union Workhouse records: HOBG 510/18 (Settlement Examinations).

21 Neal Stubbings Shelden, *The Victims of Jack the Ripper* (Knoxville, TN, 2007), p. 8.

22 Before entering casual wards, it was a well-known trick among tramps to hide or bury their belongings and cash in secret locations and to return for them upon release. This was so they didn't risk losing valuables or having them confiscated.

23 *East London Observer*, 8 September 1888; *Morning Advertiser*, 4 September 1888; *Exmouth Journal*, 8 September 1888. Holland is said to have claimed she knew Polly for both six weeks and three weeks. This could be down to inconsistencies in reporting, or it is possible that Polly may have taken up residence at Wilmott's shortly after leaving the Cowdrys.

24 *East London Observer*, 8 September 1888.

25 *Western Daily Press*, 4 September 1888.

26 *The Star*, 1 September 1888.

27 *East London Observer*, 8 September 1888.

28 Ibid.

29 *Evening Standard*, 4 September 1888. More recently, many books on Jack the Ripper have deliberately rewritten this quote to read 'a house where men and women were allowed to sleep together'.

30 *East London Observer*, 8 September 1888.

31 Ibid.

32 *Manchester Guardian*, 8 September 1888.

33 *Morning Advertiser*, 3 September, 1888; *Evening Standard*, 3 September, 1888; *Illustrated Police News*, 8 September, 1888.

34 *Daily News*, 3 September 1888.

35 *East London Observer*, 8 September 1888.

36 *London Times, Daily Telegraph, St James's Gazette*, 1 September 1888.

37 Ibid.

38 Ellen Holland was variously named as Emily Holland, Jane Oram or Jane Oran, and Jane Hodden.

39 *The Times*, 3 September 1888.

5. Soldiers and Servants

1 *Morning Chronicle*, 11 February 1840.

2 Henry Mayhew, 'Prostitution in London: "Soldiers' Women"', *London Labour and The London Poor*, (London, 1862).

3 Ibid.

4 Cavalry soldiers were marginally better paid than ordinary foot soldiers and at mid-century earned 1s. 3d. per day. (Peter Burroughs, 'An Unreformed Army? 1815–1868', in David Chandler and Ian Beckett (eds.), *The Oxford History of the British Army* (Oxford, 1994), p. 173.

5 With the arrival of a second child and the solemnizing of their union in 1842, Ruth and George also decided to have Annie baptized on 23 April, at Christ Church, St Pancras.

6 Myrna Trustram, *Women of the Regiment and the Victorian Army* (Cambridge, 1984), p. 106.

7 *Windsor and Eton Express*, 24 April 1830.

8 Henry George Davis, *The Memorials of the Hamlet of Knightsbridge* (London, 1859), pp. 103, 144.

9 Servants and the working classes consumed low-alcohol beer rather than water, the supply of which was considered potentially hazardous in London. Servants in some urban households were also expected to buy their own refreshments from the local pubs and shops.

10 'A Member of the Aristocracy', *The Duties of Servants: A Practical Guide to the Routine of Domestic Service* (London, 1894), pp. 49–50.

11 Isabella Beeton, *Mrs Beeton's Book of Household Management* (London, 1861), pp. 416–7.

12 *Chester Chronicle*, 20 June 1863.

13 Ibid.

14 Ibid.

15 GRO: Death certificate for George Smith, 13 June 1863, Wrexham.

16 29 Montpelier Place had the added benefit of being around the corner from Thomas Smith and his wife, at 36 Montpelier Row. (George and Ruth do not appear on the 1851 census, but the birth certificate of Miriam in 1851 gives their address as 29 Montpelier Place.)

6. Mrs Chapman

1 Neal Stubbings Shelden, *Victims*, p. 15.

2 William Lee, *Classes of the Capital: A Sketch Book of London Life* (Oxford, 1841), p. 43.

3 The Chapmans lived for at least three years at 17 South Bruton Mews, off Berkeley Square (near to Bond Street), as well as at 69 Onslow Mews, behind Onslow Square in Belgravia, and at 4 Wells Street, off Jermyn Street. Neither the Chapmans nor 17 South Bruton Mews appear on the rate books for the period they lived there, which suggests that the property may have belonged to part of a larger holding that paid rates separately. This would support the theory that John was employed by a nobleman – as of yet unidentified.

4 Berkshire Record Office: St Leonard's Hill Estate Sale Catalogue, D/EX 888/1, Illustrated Sales Catalogue with plan of the St Leonard's Hill Estate, D/EX 1915/5/11/1–2.

5 *Evening Standard*, 11 September 1888.

6 *The Court*, 18 June 1881.

7 *Penny Illustrated Paper*, 18 June 1881.

7. Demon Drink

1 *Pall Mall Gazette*, 1 May 1889.

2 I am indebted to Neal and Jenni Shelden for this information.

3 Miriam Smith's letter asserts that Annie gave birth eight times, though to date it has only been possible to identify seven of the children she bore. The other child may not have been carried to full term or was perhaps a stillbirth, which didn't require registration.

4 'Inebriety and Infant Mortality', *Journal of Inebriety*, vol. 2 (March 1878), p. 124.

5 Caroline Elsbury is cited on the death certificate as having witnessed the death.

6 In 1884, after the death of 'Miss Antrobus', Spelthorne was taken over by the order of St Mary the Virgin in Wantage, an Anglican

convent. Interestingly, this order also had links with the Anglican Sisters of Mercy in Clewer, an organization who concerned themselves with the rehabilitation of fallen and troubled women. The order had a very large presence in Clewer during Annie's residence at St Leonard's Hill and it is possible they offered some assistance or advice in dealing with her behaviour.

7 'Visitor's Day at Spelthorne', *Woman's Gazette*, December 1879.

8 *Windsor and Eton Gazette*, 15 September 1888.

8. Dark Annie

1 https://booth.lse.ac.uk: Charles H. Duckworth's Notebook, Police District 23, Booth/B/359, p. 143.

2 'The Female Criminal', *Female's Friend*, 1846.

3 *Daily News*, 11 September 1888.

4 https://booth.lse.ac.uk: Interview with Sub-division Inspector W. Miller . . . Booth/B/355, pp. 166–85.

5 'The Worst Street in London', *Daily Mail*, 16 July 1901.

6 Amelia Palmer was not always very reliable in recalling details about Annie's family and it's likely that her in-laws did not live on or near Oxford Street in Whitechapel, but rather on or near New Oxford Street in Holborn. John Chapman's brother Alfred and his wife Hannah were the only members of his family to have lived in London and, according to the 1871 and 1881 censuses, they seemed to be settled at addresses in Holborn. When the police made inquiries on and near Oxford Street in Whitechapel, they were unable to find anyone who knew or was related to John Chapman.

7 Some casual wards loosely applied the two-night rule and the facility at Colnbrook was believed to be one of them.

8 This is now St Leonard's Road, New Windsor.

9 *Evening Standard*, 11 September 1888.

10 Neal Stubbings Shelden, *Victims*, p. 18.

11 While John did drink, it is questionable whether his condition was on account of his habits or due to other factors such as hepatitis or genetic causes. If he did drink excessively it did not seem to impair his ability to work, and his extremely vigilant sister-in-law failed to spot any hint of dependency.

12 *Daily News*, 11 September 1888.

13 Ibid.

14 Phillips was brief about the nature of Annie's illness because it played no role in her death. His entire (paraphrased) statement was that she displayed a 'disease of the lungs [which] was long standing, and there was disease of the membranes of the brain'. Recently, a number of authors have, without any evidence, stated that Annie suffered from syphilis, because of the mention of damage to the brain. The type of damage that Phillips reported is known to occur in cases of tuberculosis, where the bacteria spread to other parts of the body. If Annie had been exposed to syphilis, signs of the brain degeneration or neurosyphilis that occurs in the tertiary phase of the illness would not have appeared for at least ten to thirty years after the initial exposure. There is no evidence whatsoever to support the suggestion that Annie engaged in prostitution as a teen or through her married years, or that she was ever exposed to syphilis.

15 The Brompton Hospital in Chelsea was a hospital for respiratory illnesses, and specifically for those suffering from tuberculosis. It catered to people of all classes, from the rich to the very poor. It's possible that Annie went there for treatment and Amelia recalled this association.

16 *Penny Illustrated Paper*, 22 September 1888.

17 *The Star*, 10 September 1888; *The Times*, 20 September 1888. In other versions of this interview the engagement ring is described as 'an oval'.

18 PRO: Home Office Papers: HO 45/9964/x15663 (Police Correspondence: Charles Warren).

19 PRO: Home Office Papers: HO 144/221/A49301C, f 136, ff. 137–45 (Police investigation: Elizabeth Stride).

20 In the past, notwithstanding the wealth of contradictory newspaper summaries of Amelia's statements, those who have written about the murder of Annie Chapman have always selected the version of her testimony that supports the presumption that all the victims were prostitutes. In the absence of a definitive set of inquest transcripts, it is impossible to determine the truth from journalistic sources alone.

21 *The Times*, 20 September 1888. Again, to confuse matters further, there are several versions of this statement. *The People* claimed Cooper said 'bring men *into* the lodging house', while various other papers, such as the *Freeman's Journal* on the same date, claimed she said that Annie 'used to bring them to the public house', which holds different implications altogether.

22 *Daily Telegraph*, 11 September 1888.

23 *The Star*, 27 September 1888.

24 'Worst Street', *Daily Mail*.

25 *Manchester Courier*, 11 September 1888. The many varying newspaper reports of this conversation claim that Annie either went to the infirmary or the casual ward.

26 M. A. Crowther, *The Workhouse System, 1834–1929: The History of an English Social Institution* (Athens, GA, 1982).

27 Howard Goldsmid, *Dottings of a Dosser* (London, 1886), ch. 7.

28 PRO: Metropolitan Police Files 3/140, ff. 9–11. Donovan was accused by some of the newspapers of having a hand in Annie's death because he turned her out on to the street rather than extending her credit for a bed.

29 Shortly after Annie's death, a man was found sleeping rough in the very place she was killed.

9. The Girl From Torslanda

1 Orvar Lofgren, 'Family and Household: Images and Realities: Cultural Change in Swedish Society', *Households: Comparative and Historical Studies of the Domestic Group*, ed. Robert McC. Netting et al. (1984), p. 456.

2 Göteborg Lansarkivet: SE/GLA/13186/E I/1, Picture 17; SE/GLA/13566/B/2 (1835–1860).

3 Göteborg Lansarkivet: SE/GLA/13566/B/2 (1835–1860); SE/GLA/13186/A I/30 (1858–1864), p. 141.

4 The antiquated term *månadskarl* has two distinct meanings: literally it means 'a worker who is hired on a monthly basis', but in Western Sweden it was also used to describe a caretaker or manager.

5 Therese Nordlund Edvinsson and Johan Söderberg, 'Servants and Bourgeois Life in Urban Sweden in the Early 20th Century', *Scandinavian Journal of History*, 35, no. 4 (2010), pp. 428–9.

6 Christer Lundh, 'Life-cycle Servants in Nineteenth-Century Sweden: Norms and Practice', *Domestic Service and the Formation of European Identity* (Bern, 2004), p. 73.

7 Göteborg Lansarkivet: SE/GLA/13186/B I/3.

10. Allmän Kvinna 97

1 Françoise Barret-Ducrocq, *Love in the Time of Victoria* (London, 1991), p. 60.

2 Yvonne Svanström, *Policing Public Women: The Regulation of Prostitution in Stockholm, 1812–1880* (Stockholm, 2000), pp. 146–7.

3 Göteborg Lansarkivet: SE/GLA/12703 D XIV a.

4 It is likely that the person transcribing her answers confused her response with the age she was when she had come to Gothenburg.

5 Göteborg Lansarkivet: SE/GLA/12703 D XIV a.

6 Göteborg Lansarkivet: SE/GLA/13566/F/H0004.

7 Göteborg Lansarkivet: SE/GLA/12703 D XIV a.

8 *Göteborgs-Posten*, 25 September 1888; also: SE/0258G/GSA 1384-1/ D1. Elizabeth's miscarriage may have been a result of either the treatment she received or the disease itself.

9 Göteborg Lansarkivet: SE/GLA/12703 D XIV a.

10 Ibid.

11 At this time in Sweden, the traditional surname for women, which took their father's first name and the suffix '-dotter' or daughter, was being gradually replaced with a single version of the family name, with a '-son' suffix. Gustafsdotter became Gustafsson. SE/GLA/13187/P/10.

12 Göteborg Lansarkivet: SE/GLA – Holtermanska (Kurhuset records, uncatalogued papers – original document has been lost).

13 I am indebted to Stefan Rantzow for this information.

14 Göteborgs Domkyrkoförsamling (O) – B:7 (1861–1879) and Emigranten Populär 2006/Gustafsdotter/Elisabet (Emibas).

11. *The Immigrant*

1 *Maidstone Telegraph*, 2 March 1861. Daniel Elisha Stride eventually married and became a chemist, though he ended his life in an asylum in 1900.

2 George Dodds, *The Food of London* (London, 1856), pp. 514–5.

3 Elisabeth's name became anglicized to Elizabeth when she moved to London and appears in English records as such from the time of her relocation.

4 Ulrika Elenora Församling (UT) HII: 1 Picture 2110. I am indebted to Daniel Olsson for the discovery of this document in the Gothenburg Archives.

5 Walter Dew, *I Caught Crippen* (London, 1938).

6 *The Times*, 4 October 1888; *Daily Telegraph*, 4 October 1888.

7 An ad for Goffrie's lessons at 67 Gower Street appears in the *Daily Telegraph*, 19 January 1869.

8 Jerome K. Jerome, *My Life and Times* (London, 1927), p. 38.

9 Charles Dickens, 'London Coffee Houses', *Household Words* (London, 1852).

10 Alfred Fournier, *Syphilis and Marriage* (London, 1881), p. 157.

11 *Sheerness Times and General Advertiser*, 13 September 1873.

12 Probate Wills: William Stride the Elder of Stride's Row, Mile Town, Sheerness, proven 30 September 1873.

12. *Long Liz*

1 LMA: Stepney Union; Bromley and Hackney Union Workhouse records: Admissions and Discharge Registers: SH BG/139/003, STBG/L/133/01.

2 *Evening Standard*, 31 December 1878.

3 *Reynolds' Newspaper*, 29 September 1878.

4 Goldsmid, *Dottings* (Kindle loc. 1250).

5 *Birmingham Daily Post*, 2 October 1888.

6 'Nooks and Corners of Character, The Charwoman', *Punch Magazine*, Jan–Jun 1850.

7 Daniel Olsson, 'Elizabeth Stride: The Jewish Connection', *Ripperologist*, no. 96 (October 2008).

8 Elizabeth Watts had been married to a wine merchant in Bath, but it appears his family disapproved of the union and set about trying to get rid of her. She was placed in an asylum and her children were taken away from her. He then eventually moved to the United States, though she seems to have been under the impression that he had died.

9 *Evening Standard*, 3 October 1888.

10 LMA: Thames Police Court Ledgers PS/TH/A/01/005.

11 G. P. Merrick, *Work Among the Fallen as Seen in the Prison Cell* (London, 1890), p. 29.

12 LMA: PS/TH/A01/008.

13 *The Times*, 4 October 1888.

14 *Daily Telegraph*, 2 October 1888.

15 *Bath Chronicle and Weekly Gazette*, 4 October 1888.

16 *Evening Standard*, 3 October 1888.

17 Ibid.

18 *Lloyd's Weekly Newspaper*, 7 October 1888.

19 'Baby-farming', as it was called in the nineteenth century, was the practice of accepting the care of an infant or infants while its mother worked. Parents, who paid a small fee for the child to be looked after, often never returned to reclaim it, thereby making this a convenient way of disposing of an unwanted baby. As the care of the abandoned child eventually outstripped the fee that was originally offered, it was more expedient to allow the infant to die from neglect or to sell the child onto someone else. The practice of baby-farming continued into the twentieth century.

20 After Mary Malcolm gave her testimony, the real Elizabeth Watts, the sister from whom she'd been estranged, appeared. It turned out that she had been living with a new husband (her

third), a Mr Stokes, a labourer at a brick works in Tottenham, north London. She confirmed that she had not seen Mrs Malcolm in years, and that Elizabeth Stride must have been impersonating her during that time. In the course of the inquest it also emerged that her first husband, who she thought was dead, was actually alive and well in the United States and that she was now married bigamously.

21 *Londonderry Sentinel*, 2 October 1888.

22 *Evening Standard*, 6 October 1888.

23 *The Times*, 9 October 1888.

24 *Illustrated Police News*, 13 October 1888.

25 *North London News*, 6 October 1888.

26 In 1896 the wrongful conviction of Alfred Beck by witnesses who all incorrectly identified him as being a notorious fraudster called John Smith assisted in demonstrating the fallibility of witness-identification procedures in use by the police during this period.

27 The question as to whether Elizabeth Stride was murdered by the Ripper or someone else has long been a subject of debate among experts.

13. Seven Sisters

1 *Wolverhampton Chronicle and Staffordshire Advertiser*, 4 March 1840.

2 Ibid., 15 February 1843.

3 W. H. Jones, *Japan, Tin-Plate Working, and Bicycle and Galvanising Trades in Wolverhampton* (London, 1900), p. 15.

4 *W. C. & S. A.*, 25 January 1843.

5 Ibid., 29 March 1843.

6 Ibid.

7 This is roughly £1 7s. 5d.–£2 2s. in circa 1820. The figure above accords with the full-time wages Edward Perry was paying in 1842.

8 George Eddowes was the third of twelve children.

9 Margaret Llewelyn Davies (ed.), *Maternity: Letters from Working Women* (London, 1915), p. 5.

10 Both John and William died within a few months of their births. While the cause of an infant's demise is often cited on nineteenth-century death certificates as 'convulsions', a term that seems to have described what a parent might have observed in the last moments of their child's life, another explanation appears on John's documentation: 'cyanosis', a condition caused by abnormalities of the heart, the lungs or the blood. In the case of the young child, the cyanosis may have been congenital or brought on by external conditions. The sulphur-laden, coal-smoked air of urban industrial districts and damp, closely inhabited quarters sucked the vitality from many adults and children, leaving their weakened lungs the perfect hosts for respiratory disease.

11 Birth records, workhouse examinations and the 1851 census have the family living at 35 West Street from 1849 until at least 1851, 7 Winter's Square in July 1854 and 22 King's Place from roughly April until 2 December 1857.

12 According to census-taking practice in that year, children were to be designated as 'scholars' if they were 'above five years of age and daily attending school, or receiving regular tuition under a master or governess at home'.

13 National Illiteracy Rates, circa 1841; see Pamela Horn, *The Victorian Town Child* (Stroud, Gloucestershire, 1997), p. 73.

14 LMA: Bridge, Candlewick and Dowgate Schools, Minutes: CLC/215/MS31.165.

15 *Manchester Weekly Times*, 6 October 1888.

16 *Gloucestershire Echo*, 5 October 1888.

17 LMA: Bridge, Candlewick and Dowgate Schools, Minutes: CLC/215/MS31.165.

18 Clement King Shorter (ed.), *The Brontës Life and Letters*, vol. 2 (Cambridge, 2014).

19 *Morning Advertiser*, 27 June 1851.

20 That George Eddowes contracted tuberculosis from his wife is suggested by Neal Shelden in *The Victims of Jack the Ripper* (2007).

21 *Manchester Weekly Times*, 6 October 1888.

22 LMA: Bermondsey Board of Guardians, Settlement Examinations: Indexed, 1857–1859; Reference Number: BBG/523: Workhouse examination for the Eddowes children, Alfred, George, Thomas, Sarah Ann and Mary, on 16 December 1857.

14. *The Ballad of Kate and Tom*

1 Nearly three quarters of women under the age of twenty in the industrial regions of the Midlands were employed as servants rather than in factory work, so Kate herself may have been surprised at where circumstance had landed her. See George J. Barnsby, *Social Conditions in the Black Country, 1800–1900* (Wolverhampton, 1980), pp. 14–5.

2 Charles Dickens, *The Old Curiosity Shop* (London, 1840–1), p. 73.

3 *Shields Daily Gazette and Shipping Telegraph*, 4 October 1888.

4 Mrs Croote's version of events is recounted in the *Shields Daily Gazette and Shipping Telegraph*, 4 October 1888.

5 *Bell's Life in London, and Sporting Chronicle*, 18 September 1866.

6 Pierce Egan, *Boxiana; Or, Sketches of Ancient and Modern Pugilism* (London, 1824), p. 285, p. 293.

7 There is some dispute about the actual date and place of Conway/Quinn's birth. I'm using the information cited by Anthony

J. Randall in *Jack the Ripper, Blood Lines* (Gloucester, 2013). Conway's army medical records suggest he was twenty-four in 1861 and born in Kilgeever, near Louisburgh, Co. Mayo.

8 PRO: WO97/1450/058 (Discharge papers for Thomas Quinn); WO118/33 (Royal Hospital Kilmahain: Pensioner Register).

9 It is possible that Conway was asthmatic, a medical condition that was not properly recognized until the 1960s. It is also likely, as the medical officer's notes seem to imply, that he had contracted rheumatic fever while in India, which had weakened his heart.

10 PRO: WO22/180, Monthly ledger for Kilkerry District, Ireland, 1861; WO23/57 Yearly ledger 1855–64 for Royal Chelsea Hospital; WO23/57 Yearly ledger 1864–74 for Royal Chelsea Hospital.

11 See PRO: WO22/23 for Thomas Quinn's pension records.

12 It is also believed that when Kate returned to Wolverhampton, Elizabeth and William banned her from the house and sent her to live for a short while with her recently widowed grandfather, around the corner.

13 https://www.attackingthedevil.co.uk/; Andrew Mearns, *The Bitter Cry of Outcast London: An Inquiry into the Condition of the Abject Poor* (London, 1883).

14 According to *The Times*, 5 October 1888, Kate was noted for singing. Singing and music were also taught to all pupils at the Dowgate School.

15 Unfortunately, most ballads and chapbooks were written anonymously and so, with a rare exception, it is virtually impossible to trace their authors.

16 *Sheffield Independent*, 10 January 1866.

17 Jarett Kobek, the author of 'May My End a Warning Be: Catherine Eddowes and Gallows Literature in the Black Country' (https://www.casebook.org/dissertations/dst-kobek.html) builds a case for attributing the ballad to Kate Eddowes and Thomas Conway.

18 *Black Country Bugle*, January 1995.

15. Her Sister's Keeper

1 Montague Williams, *Round London: Down East and Up West* (London, 1894), ch. 5; 'Down East: Griddlers or Street Singers'.

2 Frederick William Eddowes was born at Greenwich Union Workhouse infirmary on 3 February 1877. Kate, who had been claiming she did not have a husband or male partner to support her from the time she first started accepting relief from Greenwich Union, had to continue with this charade by not disclosing the identity of Frederick's father. If she had given the name of the child's father, the parish would have pursued Thomas Conway for support (which he was unable to provide) and inevitably discovered Kate's ongoing deception.

3 http://www.workhouses.org.uk/WHR/.

4 Sarah Ann was not so fortunate. She appears to have developed a mental disorder and was removed to an asylum.

5 Nancy Tomes, 'A Torrent of Abuse', *Journal of Social History*, vol. 2, issue 3 (March 1978), pp. 328–45.

6 Ibid.

7 Kate also appears in the prison records for August 1878 on the same charge of drunk and disorderly behaviour. In 1877 she had Frederick, her infant, with her. PRO: Wandsworth Prison, Surrey: Register of Prisoners Series PCOM2 Piece number 284; Wandsworth Prison, Surrey: Register of Prisoners Series PCOM2 Piece number 288. I am indebted to Debra Arif for this information.

8 *Daily News*, 4 October 1888.

9 Workhouse admission records also indicate that Kate was pregnant during the summer and autumn of 1877 for the sixth time. There is no indication that the pregnancy was brought to term or resulted in a live birth.

10 *Daily News*, 4 October 1888.

11 It's worth noting that there were in fact two Mill Lanes relatively near to one another: Mill Lane in Woolwich, which ran alongside the army barracks, and Old Mill Lane in Deptford, known as one of the area's worst slums. On 17 October 1877, Kate was brought into the local workhouse and an unusual note was written next to her entry on the admissions ledger: 'pesters Mill Lane'. This is likely to refer to Mill Lane near to the barracks, where a military maternity hospital was located. Kate had recently given birth to Frederick and he is recorded as being with her when she was admitted on the 17th. In addition to hawking and begging along that road, it is possible that Kate made a nuisance of herself outside the maternity hospital, in hope of receiving charity.

12 LMA: GBG/250/12 Greenwich Workhouse Admissions and Discharge Registers.

13 *Manchester Courier and Lancashire General Advertiser*, 6 October 1888.

14 Eliza bore three children, two of whom died before maturity.

15 *Hull Daily Mail*, 4 October 1888.

16 Goldsmid, *Dottings*, ch. 3.

17 It's also possible that Kelly and Kate met each other through Charles Frost. Both men claim to have worked transporting and selling fruit in some capacity. *Worcestershire Chronicle*, 6 October 1888.

18 *Manchester Weekly Times*, 6 October 1888; *MC & LGA*, 6 October 1888.

19 *MC & LGA*, 6 Oct.

20 Although John Kelly claims he was not a heavy drinker, a statement echoed by Frederick Wilkinson, the deputy lodging-house-keeper, Kelly's answers at Kate's inquest indicate that when he had money he drank to excess.

21 *Lloyd's Weekly Newspaper*, 7 October 1888. Although these women were able to identify Kate, they were not asked to testify

at the inquest, nor did the police, who were searching for a murderer of prostitutes, seem to consider their statements to be of importance to the case.

22 *MC & LGA*, 6 October 1888.

23 LMA: CLA/041/IQ/3/65/135: John Kelly statement (Catherine Eddowes Inquest Records); *The Times*, 5 October 1888; *Evening News*, 5 October 1888.

24 Ibid.

25 The autopsy performed on Kate demonstrated that she was suffering from Bright's Disease. Today this is referred to as acute nephritis, and subdivided into three distinct forms, all of which result in significant damage to the kidneys. The disease's causes are not entirely known and may be hereditary or brought on by other diseases such as lupus, strep or bacterial infections. Symptoms can include exhaustion, blood or protein in the urine, and water retention. In the nineteenth century, the disease was erroneously linked to alcoholism.

16. 'Nothing'

1 *The Echo*, 5 September 1888.

2 Ibid.

3 *W. C.*, 6 October 1888.

4 Sidney and Beatrice Webb (eds.), *The Break-Up of the Poor Law* (London, 1909).

5 Unlike the inquests for Polly Nichols, Annie Chapman and Elizabeth Stride, some of the official reports from the coroner's inquest into Catherine Eddowes's death have survived.

6 In the course of their wanderings in Kent, Kate had met a woman calling herself Emily Burrell, who had given her a pawn ticket for a man's flannel shirt. Both the tickets for the boots

and the shirt were kept at Joseph Jones's shop at 31 Church Street.

7 *Daily Telegraph*, 5 October 1888.

8 *The Times*, 5 October 1888.

9 Kelly's response to being questioned about the anomaly of Kate's early release from Mile End is reported variously in a number of newspapers. In the account in *The Times* of 5 October, it is said that he didn't know what the rules were at Mile End and if she could have discharged herself when she liked. It was also suggested that her early discharge was down to 'there being some bother at the casual ward'. In truth, Kelly, as a habitué of London casual wards, would have known very well what the routine was at Mile End for discharge. It is almost certain that he was covering for his own negligence in allowing her to sleep on the streets.

10 LMA: CLA/041/IQ/3/65/135: Frederick William Wilkinson statement.

11 Ibid.; *Daily Telegraph*, 5 October 1888.

12 *Morning Post*, 5 October 1888; *The Times*, 5 October 1888. Like so many statements made in the course of the inquests, this one too had been transcribed in a variety of ways. John's statement has also been written as, 'I mean that if we had no money to pay for our lodgings we would have to walk about all night.'

13 Goldsmid, *Dottings*, ch. 7.

14 *Daily Telegraph*, 3 October 1888.

15 LMA: CLA/041/IQ/3/65/135: George Henry Hutt.

16 LMA: CLA/041/IQ/3/65/135: James Byfield.

17 LMA: CLA/041/IQ/3/65/135: Hutt.

18 In fact, John Kelly was at Cooney's. He had managed to procure fourpence for his bed since parting with Kate and when someone told him that Kate had been arrested, he asked Wilkinson for a single bed.

19 *Hull Daily Mail*, 4 October 1888.

17. Marie Janette

1 'Walter', *My Secret Life*, vol. 10 (London, 1888).

2 LMA: MJ/SPC NE 1888 Box 3, case paper 19, Inquest statement of Joseph Barnett, 12 November 1888.

3 *The Echo*, 12 November 1888.

4 *Evening News*, 12 November 1888; *The Star*, 10 November 1888.

5 *Morning Advertiser*, 12 November 1888; *Eddowes Journal and General Advertiser for Shropshire and the Principality of Wales*, 14 November 1888.

6 In contrast to these comments, some have questioned whether Mary Jane was even literate. Numerous newspapers paraphrased and misquoted Joseph Barnett's inquest statement about 'reading newspapers to her'. The definitive version of his statement as it appears in the official coroner's inquest document reads: 'She had on several occasions asked me to read about the murders.'

7 *Evening News*, 12 November 1888.

8 In mapping areas of wealth, deprivation and crime in the 1890s, Arthur Baxter, one of Charles Booth's inspectors, mentions that Beauchamp Place, located across the Brompton Road from the square, was noted for its 'respectable knocking shops'. Many of the buildings were inhabited by prostitutes who worked in Piccadilly and brought their clients home. Nearby Pelham Place was also noted for its 'colony of foreign prostitutes'. On the whole, Baxter comments that the prostitutes in the area were of a higher calibre and mostly solicited in the West End. See http://booth.lse.ac.uk, Booth/B/362, Arthur L. Baxter's notebook: Police District 27 (Brompton).

9 'Walter', *My Secret Life*, vol. 2.

10 Despite extensive research into the names of those in the Scots Guards, no one has been able to turn up a Henry or John or

Johnto Kelly among the enlisted privates. In spite of inquiries, no one from the Scots Guards came forward in response to the description of Mary Jane Kelly in 1888 either. If Mary Jane's story as told to Joseph Barnett is to be believed, the likelihood of a poor, working-class boy based in rural Wales joining a London-based Scottish regiment is remote. The 2nd Scots Guards was based at Westminster Barracks during the second half of the 1880s, with periods spent abroad in Egypt, the Sudan and in Dublin. Mary Jane is more likely to have met an officer from the regiment through her professional connections, who may have acquired a fondness for her. Referring to former lovers with whom one still maintained contact as 'brothers' or 'cousins' in order to disguise an intimate history from a new lover was common among women in the sex trade.

11 Daniel Joseph Kirwan, *Palace and Hovel: Phases of London Life* (London, 1878), p. 466.

12 Ibid., pp. 467–8.

13 Ibid., p. 474.

14 'Walter', *My Secret Life*, vol. 10.

15 Julia Laite, *Common Prostitutes and Ordinary Citizens: Commercial Sex in London, 1885–1960* (London, 2012), Kindle loc. 1656.

16 W. T. Stead, 'The Maiden Tribute of Modern Babylon IV: the Report of our Secret Commission', *Pall Mall Gazette*, 10 July 1885.

17 Sallecartes was the source interviewed in part IV of Stead's 'Maiden Tribute'.

18 Bridget O'Donnell, *Inspector Minahan Makes a Stand* (London, 2012), p. 71.

19 Stead, 'Maiden Tribute'.

20 Ibid.

21 Ibid.

22 Ibid.

18. *The Gay Life*

1 Neal Shelden, *The Victims of Jack the Ripper: The 125th Anniversary* (n.p., 2013). Adrianus's daughter Wilhelmina claimed that she grew up in a brothel in Poplar between 1884 and 1891.

2 Edward W. Thomas, *Twenty-Five Years' Labour Among the Friendless and Fallen* (London, 1879), p. 36.

3 Ibid.

4 Ibid., p. 37.

5 Madeleine Blair, *Madeleine: An Autobiography* (London, 1919), Kindle loc. 912.

6 The *Morning Advertiser*, 12 November 1888.

7 The *Echo*, 12 November 1888.

8 The census enumerator in 1891 accidentally indicated that the three female boarders at 1 Breezer's Hill in their twenties were 'unfortunates', or prostitutes, before crossing out his indiscretion.

9 *Evening Standard*, 10 May 1891; see also Neal Shelden, *The Victims of Jack the Ripper: The 125th Anniversary* (n.p., 2013).

10 *Daily Telegraph*, 12 November 1888.

11 LMA: MJ/SPC NE 1888 Box 3, case paper 19, Inquest Witness statement of Julia Venturney, 9 November 1888.

12 In his testimony, Joe Barnett states that Mary Jane lived with a man called Morgenstern (a reference to Mrs Boekü's husband Johannes) and also Joe Fleming. His statement is a very confused one. At one point he mentions that Kelly lived near Stepney Gas Works, or a gas works with one of these two men. As Pennington Street is not near a gas works and there is no evidence that she lived with Adrianus Morgenstern, it is more likely he was referring to Fleming. The eastern part of Old Bethnal Green Road faces on to what would have been Bethnal Green Gas Works.

13 LMA: MJ/SPC NE 1888 Box 3, case paper 19, Julia Venturney.

14 *Evening Star*, 12 November 1888; *The Echo*, 12 November 1888.

15 Walter Dew, *I Caught Crippen* (Blackie & Son, London, 1938).

16 *Pall Mall Gazette*, 12 November 1888.

17 Paul Begg, *Jack the Ripper: Just the Facts* (London, 2004), Kindle loc. 5156.

18 LMA: MJ/SPC NE 1888 Box 3, case paper 19, Inquest statement of Joseph Barnett, 12 November 1888.

19 Begg, *Jack the Ripper*, Kindle loc. 5188.

20 Ibid. The term 'bully' might be read in two ways here – the conventional definition, or in reference to the sex trade. A bully was also another name for a pimp.

21 LMA: MJ/SPC NE 1888 Box 3, case paper 19, Julia Venturney.

22 Begg, *Jack the Ripper*, Kindle loc. 5156.

23 LMA: MJ/SPC NE 1888 Box 3, case paper 19, Julia Venturney.

24 The identity of this first woman is unknown. The name Julia appears in *Lloyd's Weekly Newspaper* on 11 November, but the journalist may have mistakenly inserted the name of Julia Venturney, who appeared before Maria Harvey at the inquest for that of the actual woman concerned.

25 LMA: MJ/SPC NE 1888 Box 3, case paper 19, Inquest statement of Joseph Barnett, 12 November 1888.

26 LMA: MJ/SPC NE 1888 Box 3, case paper 19, Inquest statement of Mary Ann Cox, 9 November 1888.

Conclusion: Just Prostitutes

1 *The Times*, 1 October 1888.

2 John Holland Rose (ed.), *The Cambridge History of the British Empire*, vol. 1 (Cambridge, 1940), p. 745.

3 Nina Attwood, *The Prostitute's Body: Rewriting Prostitution in Victorian Britain* (London, 2010), pp. 51–4.

Notes

4 PRO: Home Office Papers: HO 45/9964/x15663.

5 PRO: Metropolitan Police Files: file 3/141, ff. 158–9.

6 GRO: Death Certificates for Mary Ann Nichols: 1888, J-S Whitechapel 1c/219; Annie Chapman: 1888, J-S Whitechapel 1c/175; Elizabeth Stride: 1888 O-D St George in the East, 1c/268; Catherine Eddowes: 1888 O-D London City 1c/37; Mary Jane 'Marie Janette' Kelly: 1888 O-D Whitechapel 1c/211.

7 *Washington Post*, 6 June 2016; *Huffington Post*, 7 June 2016.

8 Maxim Jakubowski and Nathan Braund (eds), *The Mammoth Book of Jack the Ripper* (London, 2008), p. 470.

9 Mickey Mayhew, 'Not So Pretty Polly', *Journal of the Whitechapel Society* (April 2009); Mark Daniel, 'How Jack the Ripper Saved Whitechapel' in Jakubowski and Braund, *Mammoth Book*, p. 140.

10 Mayhew, 'Not So Pretty Polly'.

Acknowledgements

Writing this book has taken me on an incredible journey, both intellectually and emotionally, and I am indebted to a number of people who have assisted me at various stages along the way. From the outset, Claire McArdle and Julia Laite have been two invaluable sounding boards and have not only contributed to my knowledge but helped me to consolidate my ideas. The same can be said of both Daniel Olsson and Stefan Rantzow, who have each offered their invaluable insights into Elizabeth Stride's world as well as their assistance in helping me acquire and understand much of the material in Sweden. Helena Berlin and Arne and Olaf Jacobson in Gothenburg are also deserving of my thanks.

It was a great pleasure to be able to meet and exchange thoughts and research with Neal and Jennifer Shelden, who first ventured into the archives many years ago and began piecing together the basic information about the lives of the five women. Anyone who has had an interest in Polly, Annie, Elizabeth, Kate and Mary Jane will be indebted to their efforts. I'm grateful to Melanie Clegg for facilitating this connection, as well as to Adam Wood and to Frogg Moody who helped me make contact with people within the Ripperology community.

My research schedule has been intense and the volume of material I have had to cover in the preparation of this book enormous. The assistance offered by Lucy Santos, Phoebe Cousins and Wendy Toole has been of great value to the project, as have the eagle-eyed contributions of Sarah Murden and Joanne Major. I owe Hannah Greig and the University of York a debt for sending me the diligent and skilled historian Sarah Murphy as an intern. I am also grateful for the expertise offered by Anthony Rhys, Lindsey Fitzharris, Anthony Martin and Drew Grey, while Christine Wagg at Peabody, Mark and Wendy at the LMA, and Sister Elizabeth Jane at the Community of St Mary the Virgin were especially generous with their time. It would be negligent of me if I did not also thank the London Library for providing such a reliable resource and a perfect place to work.

Finally, there have been those cheering me on from the inception of this book whose support cannot go unmentioned: my agents, Sarah Ballard and her assistant, Eli Keren, as well as Yasmin McDonald at United Agents and Eleanor Jackson at Dunow, Carlson & Lerner, have been a dream team. Similarly, this book would not have come into being without the vision and tireless enthusiasm of the editorial teams in the UK and in the US. Jane Lawson, my editor at Transworld, has been an absolute star (as usual), as has Nicole Angeloro at Houghton Mifflin Harcourt. Sophie Christopher, Emma Burton, Kate Samano, Josh Benn, Richenda Todd and many others at Transworld and HMH have had a hand in bringing this book into being, and for that I am truly grateful.

Authors, who lead most of their lives in their heads, would be nothing without those who pull them forcefully back into reality. My husband has endured my temporary transformation into an obsessive Ripperologist and I am certain I have bored my family and friends with lengthy discourses on my latest research. To you, my most beloved and cherished, I not only offer my heartfelt gratitude but, equally, my sincerest apologies.

Picture Acknowledgements

Every effort has been made to trace copyright holders; any who have been overlooked are invited to get in touch with the publishers.

Page 1: (*top*) Alamy Image Library; (*bottom*) Peabody Trust.
Page 2: Andy and Sue Parlour.
Page 3: (*top*) author's photo; (*bottom*) private collection.
Page 4: (*top left*) private collection; (*top right*) private collection; (*bottom*) public domain photo, black and white parliamentary album, 1895.
Page 5: (*top*) author's collection; (*bottom*) Alamy Image Library.
Page 6: (*top*) Stefan Rantzow; (*bottom*) Alamy Image Library.
Page 7: (*top*) Wolverhampton Archives and Local Studies; (*bottom*) Getty Picture Library.
Page 8: (*top*) Bridgeman Art Library; (*bottom*) Mary Evans Picture Library.

Bibliography

PRIMARY SOURCES

Abbreviations

HO: Home Office
MEPO: Metropolitan Police
PCOM: Home Office and Prison Commission
WO: War Office

Public Records Office (PRO), Kew

HO45/9964/x15663 (Police correspondence: Charles Warren)
HO144/221/A49301C (Police investigation: Elizabeth Stride)
MEPO3/140 (Police investigation: Polly Nichols, Annie Chapman, Mary Jane Kelly)
MEPO3/141 (MacNaghten Report into the murders)
PCOM2/284, 288 (Wandsworth Prison, Surrey: Register of Prisoners)
WO22/23 (Thomas Quinn pension records)
WO22/180 (Monthly ledger for Kilkerry District, Ireland, 1861)
WO23/57 (Yearly ledgers 1855–64, 1864–74 for Royal Chelsea Hospital)
WO97/1274/160, 166 (Discharge papers for Thomas Smith and George Smith)
WO97/1450/058 (Discharge papers for Thomas Quinn)

WO118/33 (Royal Hospital Kilmahain: Pensioner Register)

WO400/81/523 (Soldiers' documents, Household Cavalry, 2nd Life Guards: George Smith)

London Metropolitan Archives (LMA)

ACC/3445/PT/07/066 (Peabody Trust: Stamford Street)

BBG/523 (St Mary Magdalen Bermondsey Settlement Records)

CLC/215–11, CLC/215/MS31.165 (Sir John Cass Foundation: Bridge, Candlewick and Dowgate Schools, meetings and minutes)

GBG/250/008–013 (Greenwich Woolwich Road Workhouse Admissions and Discharge)

HABG/308/001 (Hackney Workhouse Admissions and Discharge)

HOBG/510/18, HOBG/535/21 (Holborn Union Workhouse Settlement Examinations)

HOBG/535/020–023 (Holborn Union Workhouse Admissions and Discharge)

LABG/044, 047; LABG/056/001 (Lambeth Board of Guardians, minutes)

LABG/162/008–014 (Lambeth Princes Road Workhouse Admissions and Discharge)

POBG/169/05–12 (Poplar Workhouse Creed Registers and Admissions and Discharge)

PS/TH/A/01/005, 008, 007, 011, 003 (Thames Magistrate Court Registers)

SOBG/100/013–019 (Southwark Workhouse Admissions and Discharge)

STBG/SG/118/025–043 (Stepney Workhouses Admissions and Discharge)

WEBG/ST/135/001 (Edmonton Workhouse/Strand Union/Westminster Admissions and Discharge)

Bibliography

X020/413; X100/072, 073, 070 (Brighton Road School and South Metropolitan District School, microfilm)

LONDON METROPOLITAN ARCHIVES INQUEST DOCUMENTS
CLA/041/IQ/3/65/135 (Catherine Eddowes Inquest Records)
MJ/SPC/NE/376/1–11 (Mary Jane Kelly Inquest Records)

LONDON METROPOLITAN ARCHIVES,
ACCESSED VIA ANCESTRY.COM
London Church of England Parish Registers, 1754–1906
London Church of England Marriages and Banns, 1754–1921
London Church of England Deaths and Burials, 1813–1980
London Church of England Births and Baptisms, 1813–1917
London Poor Law and Board of Guardian Records, 1834–1906
London Workhouse Admissions and Discharge Records, 1659–1930
United Kingdom Census Records, 1841–1911
Glasgow, Scotland, Crew Lists, 1863–1901
New South Wales, Australia, Unassisted Immigrant Passenger Lists, 1826–1922

Berkshire Record Office

D/P39/28/9, 11 (National School Admission Registers and Log Books, 1870–1914)
D/EX 888/1 (St Leonard's Hill Estate Sale Catalogue, 1869)
D/EX 1915/5/11/1–2 (Illustrated Sales Catalogue with plan of the St Leonard's Hill Estate, 1923)

Göteborg Lansarkivet, Gothenburg, Sweden

SE/GLA/12703 D XIV (Police Registers of 'Public Women')
SE/GLA/13186/A I/30 (1835–60 Employment Records)

Bibliography

SE/GLA/13186/E I/1 (Marriage Records)
SE/GLA/13187/P/10 (Uncatalogued Parish Records)
SE/GLA/13566/B/2 (1835–60 Gothenburg Censuses)
SE/GLA/13566/F/H0004 (Kurhuset Records)

(Available as Digitized Records through Göteborg Lansarkivet)

Emigration Records: Emigranten Populär 2006; Göteborgs Domkyrkoförsamling (O) – B:7 (1861–79)
Swedish Church in London Records: Ulrika Eleonora församling (UT) H II

Library and Archive of the Convent of St Mary the Virgin, Wantage

Spelthorne Sanatorium, Log Books

City of Westminster Archive Centre

St Margaret and St John, Westminster, Rate Books (Knightsbridge)

London Guildhall Library and Archive

Kelly's Directories, 1861–78

General Register Office (GRO)

Birth records
Death certificates

Wills and Probate (www.gov.uk)

Probate Wills: William Stride the Elder of Stride's Row, Mile Town, Sheerness, proven 30 September 1873

SECONDARY SOURCES

Books

Ackroyd, Peter, *London: The Biography* (London, 2000)

Acton, William, *Prostitution Considered in Its Moral, Social, and Sanitary Aspects, in London and Other Large Cities and Garrison Towns: With Proposals for the Control and Prevention of Its Attendant Evils* (London, 1870)

Alford, Stephen, *Habitual Drunkards' Act of 1879* (London, 1880)

Arthur, Sir George, *The Story of the Household Cavalry*, vol. 2 (London, 1909)

Ashton, John R., *A Short History of the English Church in Gothenburg, 1747–1997* (Gothenburg, 1997)

Ashton, John R., *Lives and Livelihoods in Little London: The Story of the British in Gothenburg, 1621–2001* (Gothenburg, 2003)

Atkinson, David and Roud, Steve (eds.), *Street Ballads in Nineteenth-Century Britain, Ireland, and North America* (Farnham, 2014)

Attwood, Nina, *The Prostitute's Body: Rewriting Prostitution in Victorian Britain* (London, 2010)

Bakker, Nienke and Pludermacher, Isolde (eds.), *Splendeurs & Misères: Images de la Prostitution, 1850–1910* (Paris, 2015)

Barnsby, George J., *Social Conditions in the Black Country, 1800–1900* (Wolverhampton, 1980)

Barret-Ducrocq, Françoise, *Love in the Time of Victoria* (London, 1991)

Bartley, George C. T., *A Handy Book for Guardians of the Poor* (London, 1876)

Bartley, George C. T., *The Parish Net: How It's Dragged, and what it Catches* (London, 1875)

Bartley, Paula, *Prostitution: Prevention and Reform in England, 1860–1914* (London, 1999)

Bateman, John, *The Great Landowners of Great Britain and Ireland* (Cambridge, 2014)

Bates, Barbara, *Bargaining for Life: A Social History of Tuberculosis, 1876–1938* (Philadephia, 1992)

Beaumont, Matthew, *Nightwalking: A Nocturnal History of London* (London, 2015)

Beeton, Isabella, *Mrs Beeton's Book of Household Management* (London, 1861)

Begg, Paul, *Jack the Ripper: Just the Facts* (London, 2004)

Begg, Paul and Bennett, John, *The Complete and Essential Jack the Ripper* (London, 2013)

Begg, Paul, Fido, Martin and Skinner, Keith (eds.), *The Complete Jack the Ripper A to Z* (London, 2015)

Benjamin, Walter, *A Short History of Photography* (London, 1972)

Berg, William, *Contributions to the History of Music in Gothenburg, 1754–1892* (Gothenburg, 1914)

Black, C., *Married Women's Work* (London, 1983)

Blaine, Delabere Pritchett, *An Encyclopaedia of Rural Sports; Or, A Complete Account, Historical, Practical, and Descriptive, of Hunting, Shooting, Fishing, Racing, and Other Field Sports and Athletic Amusements of the Present Day*, vol. 1 (London, 1840)

Blair, Madeleine, *Madeleine: An Autobiography* (New York, 1919)

Booth, Charles, *Life and Labour of the People in London: Religious Influences* (London, 1902)

Booth, Charles, *Life and Labour of the People in London: The Trades of East London* (London, 1893)

Booth, William, *In Darkest England and the Way Out* (London, 1890)

Bowley, A. L., *Wages in the United Kingdom in the Nineteenth Century* (Cambridge, 1900)

Bumstead, Freeman J., *The Pathology and Treatment of Venereal Diseases* (Philadelphia, 1861)

Burnett, John, *Plenty and Want: A Social History of Food in England from 1815 to the Present Day* (Abingdon, 2013)

Butler, Josephine Elizabeth, *Rebecca Jarrett* (London, 1886)

Bynam, Helen, *Spitting Blood: The History of Tuberculosis* (Oxford, 1999)

Carlsson, A., *Göteborgs Orkesters Repertoar* (Gothenburg, 1996)

Chandler, David and Beckett, Ian (eds.), *The Oxford History of the British Army* (Oxford, 1994)

Chisholm, Alexander, DiGrazia, Christopher-Michael and Yost, Dave (eds.), *The News From Whitechapel: Jack the Ripper in the Daily Telegraph* (Jefferson, NC, 2002)

Clark, Anna, *The Struggle for the Breeches: Gender and the Making of the British Working Class* (Berkeley, CA, 1997)

Clarke, Edward T., *Bermondsey: Its Historic Memories and Associations* (London, 1901)

Clayton, Antony, *London's Coffee Houses* (Whitstable, 2003)

Clowes, W. B., *Family Business 1803–1953* (London, 1969)

Cohen, Deborah, *Family Secrets: Living with Shame from the Victorians to the Present Day* (London, 2013)

Covell, Mike, *Annie Chapman: Wife, Mother, Victim* (2014)

Crompton, Frank, *Workhouse Children* (Stroud, 1997)

Crowther, M. A., *The Workhouse System, 1834–1929: The History of an English Social Institution* (Athens, GA, 1982)

Cunnington, Phillis and Lucas, Catherine, *Charity Costumes* (London, 1978)

Curtis, L. Perry, Jr, *Jack the Ripper and the London Press* (New Haven, CT, 2002)

Curtis & Henson, *Royal Windsor: Illustrated Particulars of the St. Leon-ards Hill Estate Originally Part of Windsor Forest . . . For Sale by Private Treaty* (London, 1915)

Davidson, Roger and Hall, Lesley A. (eds.), *Sex, Sin and Suffering: Venereal Disease and European Society Since 1870* (London, 2003)

Davies, Margaret Llewelyn (ed.), *Maternity: Letters from Working Women* (London, 1915)

Davin, Anna, *Growing Up Poor: Home, School and the Street, 1870–1914* (London, 1996)

Davis, George Henry (ed.), *The Memorials of the Hamlet of Knights-bridge* (London, 1859)

Dew, Walter, *I Caught Crippen* (London, 1938)

Dickens, Charles, *Dombey and Son* (London, 1846–8)

Dickens, Charles, *The Old Curiosity Shop* (London, 1840–1)

Dickens, Charles, Jr, *Dickens's Dictionary of London* (London, 1879)

Dodds, George, *The Food of London* (London, 1856)

Egan, Pierce, *Boxiana; Or, Sketches of Ancient and Modern Pugilism* (London, 1824)

English Heritage, *Kent Historic Towns' Survey: Sheerness – Kent Archaeological Assessment Document* (London, 2004)

Evans, Stewart P. and Skinner, Keith, *The Ultimate Jack the Ripper Sourcebook* (London, 2001)

Fauve-Chamoux, Antoinette (ed.), *Domestic Service and the Formation of European Identity* (Bern, 2004)

First Report of the Commissioners for Inquiring into the State of Large Towns and Populous Districts, vol. 1 (London, 1844)

Fournier, Alfred, *Syphilis and Marriage* (London, 1881)

Frost, Ginger, *Living in Sin: Cohabiting as Husband and Wife in Nine-teenth-Century England* (Manchester, 2008)

Frost, Ginger, *Promises Broken: Courtship, Class, and Gender in Victor-ian England* (Charlottesville, VA, 1995)

Frost, Rebecca, *The Ripper's Victims in Print: The Rhetoric of Portrayals Since 1929* (Jefferson, MO, 2018)

Fryer, Peter (ed.), *The Man of Pleasure's Companion: A Nineteenth Century Anthology of Amorous Entertainment* (London, 1968)

Gavin, Hector, *Unhealthiness of London: The Habitations of Industrial Classes* (London, 1847)

Gay, Peter, *The Cultivation of Hatred: The Bourgeois Experience: Victoria to Freud* (London, 1993)

Gibson, Clare, *Army Childhood: British Army Children's Lives and Times* (London, 2012)

Gibson, Colin S., *Dissolving Wedlock* (Abingdon, 1994)

Goldsmid, Howard, *Dottings of a Dosser* (London, 1886)

Goldsmid, Howard, *A Midnight Prowl Through Victorian London*, edited by Peter Stubley (London, 2012)

Gordon, Mary Louisa, *Penal Discipline* (London, 1922)

Gorham, Deborah, *The Victorian Girl and the Feminine Ideal* (Abingdon, 2012)

Gray, Drew D., *London's Shadows: The Dark Side of the Victorian City* (London, 2010)

Greenwood, James, *The Seven Curses of London* (London, 1869)

Gretton, George Le Mesurier, *The Campaigns and History of the Royal Irish Regiment from 1684 to 1902* (Edinburgh, 1911)

Hadfield, Charles, *Canals of the West Midlands* (London, 1966)

Hanaford, Phebe Ann, *The Life of George Peabody* (Boston, 1870)

Harkness, Margaret, *A City Girl* (London, 1887)

Harkness, Margaret, *Out of Work* (London, 1888)

Harkness, Margaret, *Toilers in London; Or, Inquiries Concerning Female Labour in the Metropolis* (London, 1889)

Hart, H. G., *Hart's Annual Army List, Special Reserve List, and Territorial Force List* (1857)

Hartley, Jenny, *Charles Dickens and the House of Fallen Women* (2012)

Haw, G., *From Workhouse to Westminster: The Life Story of Will Crooks, M.P.* (London, 1907)

Heise, Ulla, *Coffee and Coffee Houses* (West Chester, 1999)

Higginbotham, Peter, *The Workhouse Encyclopedia* (London, 2012)

Higgs, Mary, *Five Days and Nights as a Tramp* (London, 1904)

Hiley, Michael, *Victorian Working Women: Portraits from Life* (London, 1979)

HMSO, Report HMSO *Royal Commission on Divorce and Matrimonial Causes* (London, 1912)

Hollingshead, John, *Ragged London* (London, 1861)

Horn, Pamela, *The Rise and Fall of the Victorian Servant* (Stroud, 1975)

Horn, Pamela, *The Victorian Town Child* (Stroud, 1997)

Howarth-Loomes, B. E. C., *Victorian Photography: A Collector's Guide* (London, 1974)

Hughes, Kathryn, *The Victorian Governess* (London, 2001)

Jakubowski, Maxim and Braund, Nathan (eds.), *The Mammoth Book of Jack the Ripper* (London, 2008)

Jerome, Jerome K., *My Life and Times* (London, 1927)

Jesse, John Heneage, *London: Its Celebrated Characters and Remarkable Places* (London, 1871)

Jones, W. H., *The Story of Japan, Tin-Plate Working and Bicycle and Galvanising Trades in Wolverhampton* (Wolverhampton, 1900)

Kelly's Directory of Berkshire (London, 1883)

Kirwan, Daniel Joseph, *Palace and Hovel: Phases of London Life* (London, 1878)

Knight, Charles, *London* (1841)

Knowlton, Charles, *Fruits of Philosophy*, edited by Charles Bradlaugh and Annie Besant (London, 1891)

Koven, Seth, *Slumming: Sexual and Social Politics in Victorian London* (Oxford, 2004)

Laite, Julia, *Common Prostitutes and Ordinary Citizens: Commercial Sex in London, 1885–1960* (Basingstoke, 2012)

Larkin, Tom, *Black Country Chronicles* (Eastbourne, 2009)

Lee, William, *Classes of the Capital: A Sketch Book of London Life* (London, 1841)

Lindahl, Carl Fredrik, *Svenska Millionärer, Minnenoch Anteckningar* (Stockholm, 1897–1905)

Lindmark, Daniel, *Reading, Writing and Schooling: Swedish Practices of Education and Literacy 1650–1880* (Umeå, 2004)

Lloyd's Insurance, *Lloyd's Register of British and Foreign Shipping* (London, 1874)

Lock, Joan, *The Princess Alice Disaster* (London, 2014)

London, Jack, *People of the Abyss* (New York, 1903)

Longmate, Norman, *The Workhouse; A Social History* (London, 2003)

Lundberg, Anna, *Care and Coercion: Medical Knowledge, Social Policy and Patients with Venereal Disease in Sweden 1785–1903* Umeå, 1999)

Mace, Rodney, *Trafalgar Square: Emblem of Empire* (London, 2005)

Macnaghten, Melville L., *Days of My Years* (New York, 1914)

Mason, Frank, *The Book of Wolverhampton: The Story of an Industrial Town* (Buckingham, 1979)

Mason, Michael, *The Making of Victorian Sexuality* (Oxford, 1995)

Mayhew, Henry, *London Labour and the London Poor* (London, 1862)

McNetting, Robert, Wilk, Richard R. and Arnold, Eric J. (eds.), *Households: Comparative and Historical Studies of the Domestic Groups* (Berkeley, 1984)

Mearns, Rev. Andrew, *The Bitter Cry of Outcast London: An Inquiry into the Condition of the Abject Poor* (London, 1883)

'A Member of the Aristocracy', *The Duties of Servants: A Practical Guide to the Routine of Domestic Service* (London, 1894)

Merrick, G. P., *Work Among the Fallen as Seen in the Prison Cell* (London, 1890)

Metropolitan Board of Works, *Minutes of Proceedings of the Metropolitan Board of Works* (London, 1880)

Miles, Henry Downes, *Pugilistica: The History of English Boxing* (Edinburgh, 1966)

Miltoun, Francis, *Dickens' London* (London, 1908)

Mirbeau, Octave, *A Chambermaid's Diary*, translated by B. R. Tucker (New York, 1900)

Morrison, Arthur, *Tales of Mean Streets* (London, 1895)

Nicholls, James, *The Politics of Alcohol: A History of the Drink Question in England* (Manchester, 2013)

Nokes, Harriet, *Twenty-Three Years in a House of Mercy* (London, 1886)

O'Donnell, Bridget, *Inspector Minahan Makes a Stand* (London, 2012)

O'Neill, Joseph, *The Secret World of the Victorian Lodging House* (Barnsley, 2014)

Parker, Franklin, *George Peabody: A Biography* (Nashville, 1995)

Parochial Council, Parish of St Paul, Knightsbridge, *Report Upon the Poor of the Parish of St. Paul's Knightsbridge, Receiving Legal and Charitable Relief, by a Sub-Committee Appointed by the Parochial Council* (London, 1872)

Pearsall, Ronald, *The Worm in the Bud: The World of Victorian Sexuality* (Stroud, 2003)

Pickard, Sarah (ed.), *Anti-Social Behaviour in Britain* (Basingstoke, 2014)

Prynne, G. R. *Thirty-Five Years of Mission Work in a Garrison and Seaport Town* (Plymouth, 1883)

Randall, Anthony J., *Jack the Ripper Blood Lines* (Gloucester, 2013)

Reynardson Birch, C. T. S., *Down the Road; Or, Reminiscences of a Gentleman Coachman* (London, 1875)

Ribton-Turner, C. J., *A History of Vagrants and Vagrancy* (London, 1887)

Richter, Donald C., *Riotous Victorians* (Athens, 1981)

Roberts, Henry, *The Dwellings of the Labouring Classes, Their Arrangement and Construction, with the Essentials of a Healthy Dwelling* (London, 1867)

Robinson, Bruce, *They All Love Jack: Busting the Ripper* (London, 2015)

Robinson, Sydney W., *Muckraker: The Scandalous Life and Times of W. T. Stead, Britain's First Investigative Journalist*(London, 2012)

Rodríguez García, Magaly, Heerma van Voss, Lex and van Nederveen Meerkerk, Elise (eds.), *Selling Sex in the City: A Global History of Prostitution, 1600s–2000* (2017)

Rose, John Holland (ed.), *The Cambridge History of the British Empire* (Cambridge, 1940)

Rose, Lionel, *Rogues and Vagabonds: Vagrant Underworld in Britain, 1815–1985* (Abingdon, 1988)

Royal Commission on the Ancient and Historical Monuments of Scotland, *The Sir Francis Tress Barry Collection* (Edinburgh, 1998)

The Royal Windsor Guide, with a brief account of Eton and Virginia Water, (1838)

Rule, Fiona, *Streets of Sin: A Dark Biography of Notting Hill* (Stroud, 2015)

Rule, Fiona, *The Worst Street in London* (Stroud, 2010)

Rumbelow, Donald, *The Complete Jack the Ripper* (London, 2004)

Ruskin, John, 'Of Queens' Gardens', *Sesame and Lilies* (London, 1865)

Russell, William Howard, *My Diary in India, in the Year 1858–9* (London, 1960)

Rutherford, Adam, *A Brief History of Everyone Who Ever Lived* (New York, 2016)

St Leonard's Hill Estate Sales Catalogue (London, 1907)

Sala, George Augustus, *Gaslight and Daylight* (London, 1859)

Schlesinger, Max, *Saunterings In and About London* (London, 1853)

Schlör, Joachim, *Nights in the Big City: Paris, Berlin, London 1840–1930* (London, 1998)

Scott, Christopher, *Jack the Ripper: A Cast of Thousands* (n.p., 2004)

Scott, Franklin D., *Sweden: The Nation's History* (Carbondale, 1978)

Shelden, Neal, *Annie Chapman, Jack the Ripper Victim: A Short Biography* (n.p., 2001)

Shelden, Neal, *Catherine Eddowes; Jack the Ripper Victim* (n.p., 2003)

Shelden, Neal Stubbings, *Kate Eddowes: 2007 Conference Tribute* (n.p., 2007)

Shelden, Neal, *Mary Jane Kelly and the Victims of Jack the Ripper: The 125th Anniversary* (n.p., 2013)

Shelden, Neal, *The Victims of Jack the Ripper: The 125th Anniversary* (n.p., 2013)

Shelden, Neal Stubbings, *The Victims of Jack the Ripper* (Knoxville, TN, 2007)

Sherwood, M., *The Endowed Charities of the City of London* (London, 1829)

A Short History of the Royal Irish Regiment (London, 1921)

Simonton, Deborah, *A History of European Women's Work: 1700 to the Present* (London, 1998)

Sims, George R., *How the Poor Live* (London, 1883)

Sims, George R., *Horrible London* (London, 1889)

Smith, Charles Manby, *The Working Man's Way in the World: Being an Autobiography of a Journey Man Printer* (London, 1854)

Souter, John, *The Book of English Trades and Library of the Useful Arts,* (London, 1825)

Stallard, J. H., *The Female Casual and Her Lodging* (London, 1866)

Stanley, Peter, *White Mutiny: British Military Culture in India* (London, 1998)

Stead, W. T., *The Maiden Tribute of Modern Babylon* (London, 1885)

Sugden, Philip, *The Complete History of Jack the Ripper* (New York, 2006)

Svanström, Yvonne, *Policing Public Women: The Regulation of Prostitution in Stockholm, 1812–1880* (Stockholm, 2000)

Swift, Roger, *Crime and Society in Wolverhampton: 1815–1860* (Wolverhampton, 1987)

Thomas, Edward W., *Twenty-Five Years' Labour Among the Friendless and Fallen* (London, 1879)

Thompson, F. M. L., *The Rise of Respectable Society: A Social History of Victorian Britain, 1830–1900* (London, 1988)

Thomson, J. and Smith, Adolphe, *Street Life in London* (London, 1877)

Townsend, S. and Adams, H. J., *History of the English Congregation and its Association with the British Factory in Gothenburg* (Gothenburg, 1946)

Tristan, Flora, *Flora Tristan's London Journal 1840: A Survey of London Life in the 1830s,* translated by Dennis Palmer and Giselle Pincetl (London, 1980)

Trustram, Myrna, *Women of the Regiment and the Victorian Army* (Cambridge, 1984)

Tweedie, William, *The Temperance Movement: Its Rise, Progress and Results* (London, 1853)

Valverde, Mariana, *Diseases of the Will: Alcoholism and the Dilemmas of Freedom* (Cambridge, 1998)

Vicinus, Martha (ed.), *Suffer and Be Still: Women in the Victorian Age* (London, 1973)

Victoria County History, *A History of the County of Berkshire,* vol. 3 (London, 1923)

Victoria County History, *A History of the County of Warwick,* vol. 7 (London, 1964)

Vincent, Davia, *Literacy and Popular Culture: England, 1750–1914* (Cambridge, 1993)

Walkowitz, Judith R., *City of Dreadful Delight: Narratives of Sexual Danger in Late-Victorian London* (Chicago, 2013)

Walkowitz, Judith R., *Prostitution and Victorian Society: Women, Class, and the State* (Cambridge, 1983)

Walsh, J. H., *A Manual of Domestic Economy: Suited to Families Spending from £150 to £1500* (n.p., 1874)

'Walter', *My Secret Life* (London, 1888)

Warne, Frederick, *Warne's Model Housekeeper* (London, 1879)

Warne, Frederick, *The Servant's Practical Guide* (London, 1880)

Warwick, Alexandra and Willis, Martin (eds.), *Jack the Ripper: Media, Culture, History* (Manchester, 2013)

Watson, J. N. P., *Through the Reigns: A Complete History of the Household Cavalry* (Staplehurst, 1997)

Webb, Sidney and Beatrice (eds.), *The Break-Up of the Poor Law* (London, 1909)

Werner, Alex, *Jack the Ripper and the East End* (London, 2012)

Westcott, Tom, *Ripper Confidential: New Research on the Whitechapel Murders*, vols 1–2 (n.p., 2017)

Weston-Davies, Wynne, *Jack the Ripper: A True Love Story* (London, 2015)

White, Jerry, *London in the Nineteenth Century* (London, 2007)

Whitechapel Society (eds.), *The Little Book of Jack the Ripper* (Stroud, 2014)

White-Spunner, Barney, *Horse Guards* (London, 2006)

Whittington-Egan, Richard, *Jack the Ripper: The Definitive Casebook* (Stroud, 2013)

Wikeley, N., *Child Support: Law and Policy* (Oxford, 2006)

Williams, Lucy, *Wayward Women: Female Offending in Victorian England* (Barnsley, 2016)

Williams, Montagu, *Round London: Down East and Up West* (London, 1894)

Wise, Sarah, *The Blackest Streets: The Life and Death of a Victorian Slum* (London, 2008)

Wohl, Anthony S., *The Eternal Slum: Housing and Social Policy in Victorian London* (London, 2001)

Wyndham, Horace, *The Queen's Service* (London, 1899)

Yates, Edmund, *His Recollections and Experiences* (London, 1885)

Yost, Dave, *Elizabeth Stride and Jack the Ripper: The Life and Death of the Reputed Third Victim* (Jefferson, 2008)

Journals

'Inebriety and Infant Mortality', *Journal of Inebriety*, vol. 2 (March 1878), p. 124

'Nooks and Corners of Character, The Charwoman', *Punch Magazine* (Jan–Jun 1850)

'Spelthorne Sanatorium', *Medical Temperance Journal*, vols 12–13 (1881), p. 7

Arif, Debra, 'Goodnight, Old Dear', *Ripperologist*, no. 148 (February 2016), pp. 2–8

Blom, Ida, 'Fighting Venereal Diseases: Scandinavian Legislation *c.* 1800 to *c.* 1950', *Medical History 50* (2006), pp. 209–34

Edvinsson, Therese Nordlund and Söderberg, Johan, 'Servants and Bourgeois Life in Urban Sweden in the Early 20th Century', *Scandinavian Journal of History*, 35, no. 4 (2010), pp. 427–50

Edwards, C., 'Tottenham Court Road: the changing fortunes of London's furniture street 1850–1950', *The London Journal*, 36(2) (2011), pp. 140–60

Lofgren, Orvar, 'Family and Household: Images and Realities: Cultural Change in Swedish Society', *Households: Comparative and Historical Studies of the Domestic Group*, ed. Robert McC. Netting, et al. (1984), pp. 446-69

Lundberg, Anna, 'The Return to Society, Marriage and Family Formation after Hospital Treatment for Venereal Disease in Sundsvall 1844–1892', *Annales de Demographie Historique*, 2 (1998), pp. 55–75

Lundh, Christopher, 'The Social Mobility of Servants in Rural Sweden, 1740–1894', *Continuity and Change*, 14, no. 1 (1999), pp. 57–89

McLaughlin, Robert, 'Mary Kelly's Rent', *Ripperana*, no. 41 (July 2002), pp. 19–22

Mayhew, Mickey, 'Not So Pretty Polly', *Journal of the Whitechapel Society* (April 2009)

Mumm, Susan, 'Not Worse Than Other Girls: The Convent-Based Rehabilitation of Fallen Women in Victorian Britain', *Journal of Social History*, vol. 29, issue 3 (Spring 1996), pp. 527–47

Oddy, Derek J., 'Gone for a Soldier: The Anatomy of a Nineteenth-Century Army Family', *Journal of Family History*, 25, no. 1 (January 2000), pp. 39–62

Olsson, Daniel, 'Elizabeth's Story: A Documentary Narrative of Long Liz Stride's Early Life in Sweden', *Ripperologist*, no. 52 (March 2004)

Olsson, Daniel, 'Elizabeth Stride: The Jewish Connection', *Ripperologist*, no. 96 (October 2008)

Olsson, Daniel, 'The Ultimate Ripperologist's Tour of Gothenburg', *The Casebook Examiner*, issue 11 (April 2011)

Parlour, Andy, 'The Life and Death of William Nichols', *Journal of the Whitechapel Society* (April 2009), pp. 10–12

Pollock, Ernest M. and Latter, A. M., 'Women and Habitual Drunkenness', *Journal of the Society of Comparative Legislation*, new ser., vol. 2, no. 2. (1900), pp. 289–93

Rantzow, Stefan, 'In Memory of Elizabeth Stride', *East London History Society Newsletter*, vol. 3, issue 17 (winter 2013/14), pp. 7–12

Skelly, Julia, 'When Seeing is Believing: Women, Alcohol and Photography in Victorian Britain', *Queen's Journal of Visual & Material Culture*, vol. 1 (2008), pp. 1–17

Tarn, John Nelson, 'The Peabody Donation Fund: The Role of a Housing Society in the Nineteenth Century', *Victorian Studies* (September 1966), pp. 7–38

Tomes, Nancy, 'A Torrent of Abuse', *Journal of Social History*, vol. 11, issue 3 (March 1978), pp. 328–45

Weld, C. R., 'On the Condition of the Working Classes in the Inner Ward of St. George's Parish, Hanover Square', *Journal of the Statistical Society of London*, vol. 6, no. 1 (April 1843), pp. 17–23

Wilcox, Penelope, 'Marriage, mobility and domestic service', *Annales de Démographie Historique* (1981), pp. 195–206

Online Sources

BRITISH-HISTORY.AC.UK (BRITISH HISTORY ONLINE)

Ditchfield, P. H. and Page, William (eds.), 'Parishes: Clewer', in *A History of the County of Berkshire: Volume 3* (1923)

Greenacombe, John (ed.), 'Knightsbridge Barracks: The First Barracks, 1792–1877', in *Survey of London: Volume 45, Knightsbridge* (2000)

Greenacombe, John (ed.), 'Knightsbridge Green Area: Raphael Street', in *Survey of London: Volume 45, Knightsbridge* (2000)

Greenacombe, John (ed.), 'Montpelier Square Area: Other Streets', in *Survey of London: Volume 45, Knightsbridge* (2000)

Malden, H. E. (ed.), 'Parishes: Bermondsey', in *A History of the County of Surrey: Volume 4* (1912)

Sheppard, F. H. W. (ed.), 'Brompton Road: Introduction', in *Survey of London: Volume 41, Brompton* (1983)

CASEBOOK.ORG/DISSERTATIONS

DiGrazia, Christopher-Michael, 'Another Look at the Lusk Kidney'

Kobek, Jarett, 'May My End a Warning Be: Catherine Eddowes and Gallows Literature in the Black Country'

Marsh, James, 'The Funeral of Mary Jane Kelly'

Rantzow, Stefan, 'Elisabeth Gustafsdotter's last Stride: In the memory of Elizabeth Stride – Jack the Ripper's third victim'

Sironi, Antonio and Coram, Jane, 'Anything But Your Prayers: Victims and Witnesses on the Night of the Double Event'

Wescott, Tom, 'Exonerating Michael Kidney: A Fresh Look At Some Old Myths'

CHARLES BOOTH'S LONDON

https://booth.lse.ac.uk/

Maps Descriptive of London Poverty

Inquiry into Life and Labour in London (Notebooks)

VICTORIANWEB.ORG

Diniejko, Dr Andrzej, 'Arthur Morrison's Slum Fiction: The Voice of New Realism'

McDonald, Deborah, 'Clara Collet and Jack the Ripper'

Skipper, James and Landow, George P., 'Wages and Cost of Living in the Victorian Era'

Zieger, Dr Susan, 'The Medical "Discovery" of Addiction in the Nineteenth Century'

W. T. STEAD RESOURCE SITE

https://attackingthedevil.co.uk

'Rebecca Jarrett's Narrative' (*c.* 1928), Salvation Army Heritage Centre

WOLVERHAMPTON HISTORY AND HERITAGE WEBSITE

http://www.wolverhamptonhistory.org.uk/work/industry/

http://www.historywebsite.co.uk/Museum/OtherTrades/TinPlate

http://www.historywebsite.co.uk/articles/OldHall/Excavation.htm

http://www.historywebsite.co.uk/Museum/metalware/general/perry.htm

Contemporary Newspapers and Periodicals

Bath Chronicle and Weekly Gazette

Bell's Life in London and Sporting Chronicle

Bilston Herald

Birmingham Daily Post

Black Country Bugle

Chester Chronicle

The Circle

Coventry Standard

Daily Mail

Daily News

Daily Telegraph

East London Observer

The Echo

Eddowes Journal and General Advertiser for Shropshire and the Principality of Wales

Evening News

Evening Standard

Evening Star

Exmouth Journal

Female's Friend

Freeman's Journal

Göteborgs-Posten

Hull Daily Mail

Illustrated Police News

Lloyd's Weekly Newspaper

Londonderry Sentinel

Maidstone Journal and Kentish Advertiser

Maidstone Telegraph

Manchester Courier and Lancashire General Advertiser

Manchester Guardian

Manchester Weekly Times

Manitoba Daily Free Press

Morning Advertiser

North London News

Pall Mall Gazette

Penny Illustrated Paper

The People

Reading Mercury

Reynolds' Newspaper

St James's Gazette

Bibliography

Sheerness Guardian and East Kent Advertiser
Sheerness Times and General Advertiser
Sheffield Independent
Shields Daily Gazette and Shipping Telegraph
The Star
The Sun
The Times
Woman's Gazette
Western Daily Press
Windsor and Eton Express
Windsor and Eton Gazette
Wolverhampton Chronicle and Staffordshire Advertiser
Wolverhampton Evening Express and Star

Index

Index

Index

Index

Index

Index

Index

Index